RETHINKING THE
BELOVED COMMUNITY

Ecclesiology, Hermeneutics, Social Theory

Lewis S. Mudge

WCC Publications, Geneva
and
University Press of America,® Inc.
Lanham · New York · Oxford

Copyright © 2001 by
University Press of America,® Inc.
4720 Boston Way
Lanham, Maryland 20706

12 Hid's Copse Rd.
Cumnor Hill, Oxford OX2 9JJ

Library of Congress Cataloging-in-Publication Data

ISBN 0-7618-1866-9 (pbk. : alk. paper)

⊖™ The paper used in this publication meets the minimum
requirements of American National Standard for Information
Sciences—Permanence of Paper for Printed Library Materials,
ANSI Z39.48—1984

Table of Contents

Part IV: Civil Society

Part V: Householding

Acknowledgements

The author is grateful to the following sources for permission to publish copyrighted material.

"Searching for Faith's Social Reality" is reprinted by permission from the September 22, 1976, issue of *The Christian Century,* copyright 1976 Christian Century Foundation.

"Jesus and the Struggle for the Real," appeared in the *Journal of Religion*, Vol 51, No 4, (October, 1971), copyright 1971 by the University of Chicago. All rights reserved. Reprinted by permission of the University of Chicago Press.

"Ecclesia as Counter-Consciousness" appeared in the *Journal of Ecumenical Studies*, Vol 8, No 1, copyright 1971 Temple University. It is reproduced by permission.

"The Servant Lord and His Servant People" is reprinted by permission from *The Scottish Journal of Theology*, May, 1959, copyright 1959 T. and T. Clark Ltd.

"Paul Ricoeur on Biblical Interpretation" is reprinted by permission (in abridged form) from *Biblical Research*, XXIV-XXV (1979-1980), copyright 1980 The Chicago Society of Biblical Research.

"Church and Human Salvation: The Contemporary Dialogue" appeared in *Chicago Studies* for November, 1983, copyright 1983 The Civitas Dei Foundation. It is used by permission.

"Thinking in the Community of Faith: Toward an Ecclesial Hermeneutic" is reprinted from *Formation and Reflection: The Promise of Practical Theology*, edited by Lewis S. Mudge and James N. Poling, copyright 1987 Fortress Press. Used by permission of Augsburg Fortress.

"Toward a Hermeneutic for Ecclesiogenesis" is adapted from chapter 3 of *The Sense of a People: Toward a Church for the Human Future,* copyright 1992 by Lewis S. Mudge, reproduced by permission of Trinity Press International, Harrisburg, Pennsylvania.

"Faith, Ethics and Civil Society" previously appeared in *Loccumer Protokolle* 23/95, published by the Evangelische Academie, Loccum, Germany. The rights are held by the author.

"Traditioned Communities and the Good Society: The Search for a Public Philosophy" appeared as Protocol 3 (new series), 1995, of the Center for Hermeneutical Studies of the University of California, Berkeley, and the Graduate Theological Union, copyright 1995 The Center for Hermeneutical Studies. It is reproduced by permission.

"Remodeling the Household: Ecclesiology and Ethics After Harare" appeared (as "Towards a Hermeneutic of the Household") in the *Ecumenical Review*, Vol. 51, No. 3 (July 1999), copyright 1999 The World Council of Churches. It is used by permission.

"Moral Hospitality for Public Reasoners" was contributed to the Fourth Visser 't Hooft Memorial Consultation at the WCC Ecumenical Institute at Bossey, near Geneva, in June 1999. It is used by permission.

Foreword

It is a pleasure and an honor for me to respond to the suggestion by Lewis Mudge that I might write a Foreword to this book, which collects a selection of his shorter writings during a distinguished career of more than forty years as a creative theological teacher and ecumenist. I am happy to count myself among the many of his students and colleagues who have been challenged and inspired by him to "think new thoughts."

Through his most recent books--*The Sense of a People* (1992) and *The Church as Moral Community* (1998)--Lewis Mudge has confirmed his reputation as one of the most insightful interpreters of what it means to be church today. He has stimulated ecumenical discussion both in his own country, the United States of America, and internationally in ways that are quite exceptional within the academic community. For this he deserves recognition and gratitude from ecumenical friends at a time when the ecumenical endeavor does not attract much attention and support in academic circles.

While his basic theses and the particular approach of his theological reflection are known already from his recent books, this volume is of special interest because the essays collected here show an experimental theology in the process of production. They introduce the reader to a fascinating dialogue between theological reflection and evolving forms of social analysis and philosophical interpretation of the human reality. They manifest an ongoing struggle and search for the adequate instruments to understand the human condition in society in the light of God's promise of the fullness of life for all.

The essays reflect three distinct periods in the theological explorations of the author. There is first the period of the 1960's, with its revolutionary ferment and the struggle for new forms of social and political organization challenging the traditional church institutions.

Then follows the period from the mid-1970's through the 1980's, with a growing suspicion of universal claims and heightened sensitivity to the hermeneutical problem of understanding the dynamics of social cohesion in everyday life. In the third period, the 1990's, the quest for the foundations of a moral order in human community moves into the foreground.

While the language and the categories for investigation change from one period to the next, the essays are held together by the common conviction that the Christian faith is relational at its core and must therefore find expression in tangible communal forms. Throughout his lifelong involvement in theological reflection Lewis Mudge has been exploring new ways of thinking and conceptualizing the church as a body in the wider human community, searching for models and metaphors that could restore to the church its character of a sign and sacrament of what the human community is meant to be in the eyes of God.

There is something prophetic about these explorations of Lewis Mudge. He anticipates in his writings the challenges which the churches and the ecumenical movement will be facing in the 21st century. Most churches respond to the uncertainties of the present social and cultural condition by trying to consolidate their inherited institutional identity. He is concerned with the emerging forms of being church, with discovering the space within which the "beloved community" can become again a social reality, believing firmly with Dietrich Bonhoeffer that the church should be "Jesus Christ existing in the form of a community." He is confident that the Holy Spirit provides the capacity to discern the places and the forms in which the church today can become salt of the earth and light of the world, giving sense and new meaning to human life in community and thus becoming a sign of God's salvation.

Few theologians have taken the church as the communal embodiment of faith as seriously as Lewis Mudge. One can only hope that his penetrating insights will find an echo in the ongoing ecumenical dialogue about the church, its unity, and its mission.

Konrad Raiser
General Secretary of the World Council of Churches
Geneva, February, 2000

Introduction

I am reminded of an episode in my own ecumenical life. It is January, 1984. I am seated at a conference table in Rome with some fifteen colleagues gathered for the opening session of the second series of meetings of the International Reformed-Roman Catholic Dialogue Commission.[1] Two papers are being presented. The first is by a young Catholic brother: something genuinely erudite about Church and Trinity in medieval theology. The second is my own attempt to frame the coming dialogue in the manner of the great German philosopher of ecclesial social reality, Ernst Troeltsch. At the close, the young Roman Catholic comes around the table with a genial smile: "I think, Professor Mudge, that you and I are about eight centuries apart!" Yes, I agree. But I am thinking: perhaps these were papers representing not only different centuries but different worlds of discourse co-existing in present time.

My Troeltschian point was that churches need to be aware of their nature as concrete social realities in the midst of larger ones, and of what messages are conveyed by the character of such gatherings. "Social teachings" need to arise from self-understandings that are both theologically and sociologically informed. My hope was to divert the dialogue from being simply an exercise in comparative dogmatics. I hoped we could engage one another more effectively by comparing forms of actual ecclesial reality in a commonly shared social world.

Neither paper, as I recall, made much impression on the Commission. We went on, nevertheless, to do good historical and theological work in which I gladly took part. But the theologians assembled at that opening session certainly had difficulty with the initial point I was trying to make. Still, I reflected, my paper would probably not have been any more acceptable at a meeting of the American Sociological Association! Its theological intent would have made it difficult even for scholars specializing in sociology of religion. I was then, and still am today, at work along the borders of two (and perhaps other) disciplines. The divide between constructive theologians on the one hand and sociologists of religious reality on the other remains, even if there is more mutual understanding and respect than there used to be. But now, I argue in this book, the need for sociologically informed theology--*ecclesiology* in the most concrete, realistic, sense--has become acute. As one of the anthologized articles affirms, "Churches...need to think new thoughts about how they do their thinking." So, in their own diverse ways, say all the other pieces too. But what new thinking can lead us toward insights we need concerning the concrete reality of "church" in the midst of a radically pluralistic society?

These essays follow a variety of conceptual paths. But, taken together, they are on the trail of a theologically articulated understanding of the community of faith as social reality. They see congregations as acted-out interpretations of the societies around them designed to make God's purposes by the power of the Spirit, visible. They seek to describe a kind of ecclesiology that begins with the gritty, situated "community called church" (Segundo) in all its variety and interprets the work of the Spirit in that setting. Ecclesiology then becomes, in its own right, a kind of social theory. It becomes a conceptual perspective concerned with the ways congregations can be spaces in which environing human communities can discover--perhaps in actual Christian faith and practice, perhaps by associating themselves with "secular parables of the truth" (Karl Barth)--their own origins and ends in the providence of God.

Notes on the Contemporary Situation

Why such an emphasis now on situated, social actuality? Why the stress on what churches *do*? The essays in this book, in their original contexts, addressed questions of ecclesial concreteness like these. Gathered here, I believe they offer historical perspectives for tackling very similar issues in the present day. I can think of at least three reasons for making such a claim.

First, we live at a time in which many doubt the capacity of language alone to capture reality. "Deconstruction" has attacked the integrity of the language-worlds, both humanistic and scientific, of actors and thinkers in the Western tradition. If language "speaks us" rather than the other way around, we wonder if it can be a medium for a theology of the Word. A "cultural-linguistic" (George Lindbeck) understanding of doctrine identifies theology as the grammar or syntax of actual communal life, with the clear implication that social and liturgical practices are prior to normative verbal descriptions of them.

Second, novel manifestations of Christian faith and practice, tending to bypass traditional ecclesiological categories, proliferate across the globe. This is true particularly in the southern hemisphere, but the phenomenon is by no means unknown in the north. Witness the language about "post-denominational Christianity" in China and elsewhere. These manifestations need to be studied in participatory, not merely prescriptive or categorizing ways. Before calling them to any sort of conceptual or confessional conformity, we need to see what they are in the concrete. We need to ask what sorts of situated enactments of faith they produce.

And, finally, the first two points together lead us to a third. The subordination of theological language to communal practice and the multiplication of new church forms combine to raise questions about existing ways of expressing the catholicity or universality of Christian faith. If there *is* one gospel for the whole world, have we words or communal structures for articulating it? Most of us acknowledge that no historic confession or communion alone is adequate to express the wholeness of Christ's people on earth. But attempts so far to build fragile conceptual bridges between these worlds have not produced spans on whose strength many are prepared to stake their lives. Theologians produce hard-won bilateral and multilateral agreements. But little happens to turn these agreements into continuing forms of common life. We meet, we write reports (some of them quite commendable), and then we retreat once more to the seemingly firmer ground of long-established communions and confessions.

All this is disorienting. Global communions and ecumenical bodies alike struggle to redefine their particular vocations. The ecumenical world becomes increasingly decentered. Initiatives become disorganized and dispersed. The southern hemisphere rightly begins to assert itself as the home of the majority of Christians now alive on earth. When we

say, as some bilateral conversations do, and as ecumenical
organizations seek to express in action, that certain doctrinal issues no
longer need to be seen as "church dividing" we imply that we are held
together by something else, some concrete actuality of life for which
doctrine itself is regulative but not constitutive.

But how do we get at such concreteness in ecumenical discussion?
We have sought to catch it and act it out in the very reality of conciliar
programs and activities, only in recent times to experience debilitating
internal conflict and diminishing support by member churches. If the
reality of "church" exists in the world, it may lie precisely in concrete
initiatives to *be* the Una Sancta in very specific places and situations.
Hence my long-term effort, of which these essays are evidence, to
articulate a theological interpretation of sociologically self-aware
ecclesial actuality in its many contemporary forms.

What Sort of Sociology?

But what sort of theologically motivated sociological awareness do
I have in mind? Are there precedents for this sort of thing? A notable
(and far more ramified) earlier attempt to link theology and sociology
in search of ecclesial concreteness is found in Dietrich Bonhoeffer's
1927 dissertation *Sanctorum Communio* (the "Communion of Saints").
Bonhoeffer wished, he wrote, "To understand the structure, from the
standpoint of social philosophy and sociology, of the reality of the
Church of Christ which is given in the revelation of Christ."[2] Later
he noted that for him "The church is the pragmatic world understood
in its true depth, as it is truly meant to be."[3] Bonhoeffer argued that
analysis of social reality should precede idealistic theological
constructions or claims by churches about their own foundations. I
associate myself with this view, including the insistence that the reality
sought is the one "given in the revelation of Christ." Whether such a
graft is any more acceptable today than it was in 1927 remains to be
seen. The year Bonhoeffer's book appeared his cousin Christoph von
Hase wrote: "There will not be many who really understand it; the
Barthians won't because of the sociology, and the sociologists won't
because of the Barth."[4]

How well I know! My essays are neither as long, as dense, or for
that matter as profound, as Bonhoeffer's chapters. I am less wedded to

Barth, and times have changed. But my basic intent is the same: to use human-science methods, now hermeneutically understood, in the interest of understanding how the church given in the revelation of Jesus Christ takes actual form in the kind of world we know.

In 1990 a book appeared which gives me further opportunity to clarify what I am, and am not, trying to do. In *Theology and Social Theory*, John Milbank takes on "political theologians" who in his opinion have sold out to a form of secular humanism. Sociologically inclined theologians should also take note! Milbank writes,

> Contemporary "political theologians" tend to fasten upon a particular social theory, or else put together their own eclectic-theoretical mix, and then work out what residual place is left for Christianity and theology within the reality that is supposed to be authoritatively described by such a theory. ...the faith of humanism has become a substitute for a transcendent faith now only half-subscribed to.[5]

I plead not guilty. But I take these words as a warning. What Milbank is against here is old-fashioned reductionism: so easy and so dangerous. Theologians who find their reality sense in the social realm, rather than in the gospel, for him are only halfway believers. But now comes the paradox. While "political" theologians have sought reality in sociality, at least some sociologists, passing critically beyond Nietzsche, have begun to recognize "the necessity and yet the ungrounded character of some sort of metanarrative, some privileged transcendent factor, even when it comes disguised as the constant element in an immanent process."[6] In sum,

> Theology accepts secularization and the autonomy of secular reason; social theory increasingly finds secularization paradoxical, and implies that the mythic-religious can never be left behind. Political theology is intellectually atheistic; post-Nietzschian social theory suggests the practical inescapability of worship.[7]

This is suggestive indeed. But one wonders what social theory Milbank has in mind. Who are these sociologists who find secularization paradoxical? Where I come from most academic social theory is still positivistic to the core. Milbank at one point wants to lay this mantle on the whole brood, including the likes of Max Weber.

Milbank's argument from this point seems to gain comfort from the idea of a "social theory [that] increasingly finds secularization paradoxical." But instead of exploring these unnamed writers he produces such a theory himself, sketching in the end "a theology aware of itself as culturally constructed, yet able to elaborate its own self-understanding in terms of a substantive and critical theory of society in general..." "If truth is social," he continues,

> it can only be through a claim to offer the ultimate "social science" that theology can establish itself and give any content to the notion of God. And, in practice, providing such a content means making a historical difference in the world.[8]

I have long thought something like this. Several essays in this collection imply it. The point is that ecclesiology is itself a kind of social theory: not merely a theory of church, but a theory of *society*. Ecclesiology does not abdicate its own sense of social reality to that of some other discipline. It is a sociological discipline with its own, biblical, understanding of reality. But, to realize such an identity, it does *not* need to swallow up or nullify other perspectives, as Milbank seems to do in his lengthy "genetic" investigations which display "scientific" social theories as "theologies or anti-theologies in disguise." For Milbank, "The social knowledge advocated is but the continuation of ecclesiastical practice," seemingly in communication with no one else. What results is a closed community that seems to have no truck with the social analysis of communities beyond it, a "radical orthodoxy" whose nature would seem to differ little from a rather aggressive form of Wittgensteinian fideism.

The key requisite is to make the connection with *this world*. Let sociology be sociology and yet take it up into the task of envisioning and living the beloved community. Otherwise one risks a kind of institutional docetism. I fear as well that Milbankian communities are going to be unable to communicate with Christian communities of other persuasions, but only with other Milbankian communities, a prospect which looks very much like the birth of some new communion. I want churches to share many of the common preoccupations of a world that human science is helping to make one. We may well find affinities between ecclesiological social science and social theories of other kinds, owing, it may be, to common origins or common aims. But, whether or not this happens, we want ecclesiological social theory to hold other viewpoints in respect: to be in conversation with them. They can help keep us honest.

What should ecclesiology *as* social theory look like methodologically? I depart to a degree from both Bonhoeffer and Milbank in arguing that hermeneutical method is the appropriate one. A case can be made for saying that most social philosophies are implicitly hermeneutical in any case. They read the expressive "texts" of common life and draw systematic conclusions. They say that our lived texts have this meaning or that. Thus social theories are based on stories and tell stories. Ecclesiology understood as social theory does the same thing. It is a social theory based upon the biblical story which reads and interprets the stories told by congregations of God's people in their concrete social existence. It explores the various "signs" by which churches express themselves in the midst of their social environments. It considers the ways in which congregations "read" their surroundings and appropriate meanings from them that eventually become part and parcel of their own self-understandings. Ecclesiology tries to judge the appropriateness and faithfulness of this ongoing hermeneutical process.[9]

Clearly ecclesiology as social theory must make use of many assisting disciplines, philosophical and otherwise, which show what it means to think of social organization as if it were a "text" to be read (Paul Ricoeur), which argue that what we do together is inherently expressive (Hegel, as interpreted by Charles Taylor). Related and highly useful perspectives can be borrowed from political philosophy (John Rawls and Jürgen Habermas) the field of semiotics or theory of signs (Thomas Sebeok and others as interpreted by Robert Schreiter), the phenomenology of the social world (Alfred Schutz). Above all, it is important to understand that, so understood, ecclesiology is not merely a theory of the church as social institution. It is also a theory *of human society as such*. It is a theory of society *as* pregnant with the possibility of being ecclesia. It is a theory of society *as* a place in which ecclesia, as society's true fulfillment, is, by God's grace, coming to be. The church as visible institution lives by acting so as continually to make space for that communal *parousia*.

What Sort of Ecclesiology?

But isn't the ecclesiology just portrayed pretty much confined to analysis of what tradition has called the "visible church"? Does it not leave out a whole dimension of the church's being: all that has been meant by "communion of saints," "the elect," "invisible church," "mystical body," and other such expressions? All these terms imply that the visible reality of the church is not properly understood apart from the conviction that there exists a community truly called by God by being incorporated into the body of Jesus Christ, a reality somehow present in the visible church but not identical with it? Isn't the "visible church" inevitably a *corpus permixtum*, an amalgam of saints and sinners, as Augustine said? Is it not unintelligible apart from its relationship to a "city of God" understood as the *telos* of our social being here on earth?

I agree with the need to say something like this. In my book *The Sense of a People*[10], indeed, I speak, with Joseph Haroutunian, of "the people of God and their institutions." This would seem to imply some form of unseen "communion of saints" existing both logically and temporally *prior* to the visible ecclesiastical institutions we know so well. There is need to clarify what is going on here. Obviously, if all I am trying to construct is a "sociology of religion," the problem of transcendence evaporates. But I have already affirmed, with Bonhoeffer, that the reality sought is that "given in the revelation of Christ." How can ecclesiology as hermeneutical social theory accommodate such an expectation? Is there an invisible communion behind, or "in, with and under," the visible one?

Formulations of the visible/invisible problematic have tended to depend on the metaphysical conventions of the times and places concerned. Augustine's notion of a "city of God" in relation to the mixed ecclesial body living for now in the "city of man" owes something to Platonic idealism. The medieval identification of the "mystical body" with the established church of the West owes something to Aristotle. Luther's nominalism shows through in his tendency to make the "invisible church" the name of a critical principle at work in the church visible. For Calvin, visible and invisible seem to be two ways of seeing, or perspectives upon, the *one* church. The Westminster Confession of Faith simply declares the "catholic or universal church" to be invisible as such, and to consist of the whole number of the "elect," a company whose size and composition we cannot in principle know. Each formulation carries its own particular nuance, leading in each case to a characteristic line of argument.

The Vatican II document *Lumen Gentium* (1964) likens the relationship of the "mystical body" to the Church on earth to the relationship between the divine and human natures of Christ. It then affirms that this "mystical body" "subsists in" (*subsistit in*) the Roman Catholic Church. This Latin phrase has provoked much discussion. The Council fathers evidently wanted a softer term than the simple *est*, or "is." Cardinal Ratzinger has claimed that *subsisit* is derived from the root *substans* from which is derived the Aristotelian notion of "substance." If this is true, we have something very close to a Latin version of *homoousios*, "of one substance with," applied to the relation between the Roman Church and the "mystical body" as in the relation between the first and second persons of the Trinity.[11] Much else is said later in this Vatican II document about the larger conception of a "people of God"[12] and about relationships with other Christian communions and other religious bodies. But the fundamental Chalcedonian analogy between a communion in and with God and the earthly gathering in which this communion subsists remains central.

How does this problematic change when one replaces the philosophical reality-assumptions implied in these traditions with an ecclesiology of expressive, therefore interpretable, *social* reality? The main thing that happens is that we avoid all dualisms between the church as seen and the church as unseen--whether formulated in the manner of Augustine, Luther, Calvin, Westminster or Vatican II. As André Dumas quotes Bonhoeffer in *Act and Being*:

> The Church starts from what actually happens when Jesus Christ takes form as community. But the event of Jesus Christ is also the advent of a communal being and not simply an individual existential encounter. Revelation does not only come *to* the community; it takes place *within* the community.[13]

The underlying idea here is that *social* reality, in contrast to other kinds of reality (e.g. psychological-personal, or substantial-metaphysical) *exists* only in the form of living patterns of communicative interaction. Social reality is not the mere appearance of some other, more fundamental, reality. Its patterns of meaning *are* what they express. They are not less real because they are incomplete. The very incompleteness of these acted-out meanings raises questions about the transcendental conditions of their own possibility. In that sense, social meanings point beyond themselves to as yet unrealized completions. These completions do not constitute some other reality, distinct from the reality we know. They constitute *this* already-known reality trans-signified. Such pregnant-with-possibility and acted-out meanings may be *interpreted* with varying degrees of penetration and insight. Such interpretation is a matter of decoding actions and processes--bringing to light the narratives implied in repeated patterns of interaction, asking--in concrete social terms--what it might mean for such narratives to be intrinsically transformed while remaining fully recognizable to the social actors concerned.

Put this a little differently. By making a certain kind of *sense*, social reality simultaneously comes to *be*. "Saints" and "sinners" are both needed, and will inevitably from time to time exchange roles, in living out the story. Words are instruments of these meaning-bearing exchanges. But our actions themselves "speak" and can be "read." Much of the time such speaking and hearing in action is routinized, hence such action forms itself into "institutions." But the institutions are but instruments within the narratives through which the "beloved community" comes into being. There are not two realities here, but one. The *corpus permixtum* is the medium in which the story of God's people comes to expression, in and through whose struggles the message takes historical form.

In this view there is no behind-the-scenes world in which some persons are revealed as constituting the true church and others discovered to be there, as it were, under false pretenses. The church on earth *as a whole*--through the interacting, meaning-bearing nature of its social reality--signifies to the society around it the shape of God's calling to the human race. The entire church on earth is this signifying medium. It cannot signify, it cannot tell the story, *except* as a *corpus permixtum*, any more than a painting can communicate apart from colors both light and dark in *chiaroscuro*. The church can only signify the gospel through its handling of the dialectical ambiguities of its social location, the perennial confusions of its moral witness, the war between sincerity and hypocrisy in its prayers. In short, the church signifies not by the idealism of what it says but by the ways it steers its course among all the meaning-bearing elements of the social world, critically appropriating certain meanings and rejecting others as it goes. Without the presence of both sin and grace, there would be no message. Every member has a part to play in constituting this message in the "readable" configurations of the congregation's life.

How, then, is such sociality open to transcendence? Can it *contain* the infinite, or only point to it? My answer is that social reality so understood, with all its imperfections, can take on a shape called *ekklesia* implying narratives that in their earthly form are open to intrinsic yet unexpected fulfillments. *Ekklesia* moves through history, encountering and transforming the lived meanings (that are sociality in its essence) into configurations which demand (if only for dramatic or even aesthetic reasons) something more before mind and heart are satisfied. Sacrificial love, as Reinhold Niebuhr calls it, must rest on assurances not apparent to us and lead to equally inconceivable consequences. Otherwise it is a surd that does not belong in this world. Reconciliation happens, and when it does, as Karl Barth says, it *is* revelation. This is so, I think, because it does not make sense in terms of any finite calculus of costs and benefits, but rather opens a space of radical questioning. What, we ask, is going on here? Something more than human calculation has to be at work.

We finite human beings do not possess categories adequate for understanding these things, yet they are present to us in the interactions constituting *ekklesia* in the midst of society. Our analysis interprets social space as open to the "privileged transcendent factor" of which the church is sign, sacrament, and instrument. It thus makes good on Bonhoeffer's promise to deal with the "reality given in the revelation of Jesus Christ." An ecclesiological social theory implicitly tells the scriptural story, and thereby can name what other social theories refuse to name: the real origins and endings of the stories they tell. The biblical story is not coherent without images of creation and consummation, not understandable apart from convictions concerning God's providential care throughout. An ecclesial, hermeneutical, social theory is thus servant to the conviction that the reality of *ekklesia* is *given* through God's calling, through Jesus Christ and in the power of the Spirit, of the human race into "beloved community."

It is important to grasp the sweep of what is included in this plot. The narrative or narratives which impel ecclesial social reality dynamically forward in time are not contained *within* the church alone, or solely *about* the church. They are narratives about a larger world in which the Christian community articulates in a catalytic and expressive way. The ecclesial community is thus called to act so as to make clear that the communal shape, the trace, the gestalt of what God has done in calling the beloved community to being extends beyond visible ecclesiastical boundaries. The narrative transmitted in the medium of sociality needs explicitly to characterize the metaphorical space it requires in order to make sense. To be the church is to project an action-field adequate to the message it embodies in its sociality. In short, this very sense implies, indeed requires, a vast action-stage for its performance. That stage is the cosmos itself, in Calvin's words, the "theater of God's glory." On such a stage, the question whether particular individuals are or are not among the elect is no longer the foreground issue. To know that one's part, whatever it is, is being played out on such a stage breeds a strange combination of confidence and awe. The meaning of the play in *this* theater is larger than the meaning of what happens to us as individuals. We are called only to interpret the script in dramatic action. God takes care of members of the cast. There is a great party, the "messianic banquet," planned for the end of the run.

An Overview of the Essays

So much, then, for the theological context in which these essays are set. I have offered something more than a synthesis of what these articles, read anew today, seem to imply. I have tried very briefly to locate them on a larger topographical map: to make clear the kind of sociology and the kind of ecclesiology they work with. By no means is this whole picture laid out in each piece. Rather each essay, assuming some such background as this, attacks the immediate situation that called it forth. Had they been written in the light of this introduction rather than prior to it, the resulting picture might be more conceptually coherent. Still, an intelligible conversation emerges. These essays belong within a loose but recognizable fabric of ideas unfolding through the experiences and reflections of one human life lived in a particular historical period of time.

I think it is a good thing, in fact, that no single philosophical or methodological conceptuality dominates what follows. The reader will find   social   phenomenology,   semiotics,   historical   criticism, hermeneutical theory, political philosophy, and other perspectives. I say that this is a good thing because it permits the church as constant subject-matter to stay in focus while different conceptualities come and go. My strategy is something like Karl Barth's procedure of borrowing ideas--existential ones, for example--where they illuminate his argument without allowing any single philosophical position to dominate.

But there is something more. As Paul Ricoeur argues, when words pass into written form they take on an independent life of their own. Interpreters make of them what they will. The original "authorial intention" (if that can indeed be ascertained apart from being inferred from the work) is only part of an ongoing hermeneutical story. The essays in this anthology have enjoyed varying careers--all of them by any account modest indeed. Now the author joins his readers, with the advantage of seeing writings done over forty years for the first time together in one place. I am rediscovering not only what I think I originally meant but what my words say to me now at a later time in my life.

Why this particular set of essays? As the word "essay" indicates, these pieces are "tries"--on various occasions and from various points of view--to get at the meaning of an ecclesiology understood as theologically responsible social theory. Hence a distinct thread of intention runs through them. They are chosen from a larger body of material, and in one case adapted to fit the present format. I have arranged the material topically rather than chronologically. There are five sections, of either two or three essays each, dealing respectively with social reality, hermeneutics, ecclesiogenesis, civil society, and the ecumenical household. In sections one, three, and four, again irrespective of original chronology, I have tried to lead off with a shorter and more accessible piece, followed by another or others that underlie the shorter presentations or dig more deeply. In sections two and five the pieces are complementary. As one would expect, tone and style reflect the variety of original contexts. Where the original publications mandated no footnotes I have not supplied any here. Each grouping of essays is now introduced with brief comments on their interrelationships, followed by the argument of each piece in précis form.

Social Reality

The three articles dealing with "social reality" are mid-career pieces: from the years 1971 to 1976. They explore the nature of the reality in which God in Jesus Christ becomes present "in the form of a community." What sort of medium is this? It is symbolically maintained space. It is a world "constructed" though social processes. It is a kind of shared "consciousness." Each of these notions makes an appearance. Metaphysical implications are not drawn, yet it is plain that social interaction and discourse *is* the medium, in the sense of "felt whole," in which we make judgments *about* the "real." As the nature of social reality becomes clearer, we begin to ask how the gospel changes it.

"Searching for Faith's Social Reality" was my inaugural lecture as Dean and Professor at McCormick Theological Seminary, Chicago, published in *The Christian Century* for September 22, 1976. Speaking to students, faculty, and trustees of an institution noted for its involvement with the inner city and with industry, a rather academic new Dean needed to reach for gritty social substance, yet try to open new vistas. Quoting Troeltsch's call for thoughts "that have not yet been thought," and borrowing thoughts from Bonhoeffer, I sought to describe a social space of God-ruling as this world decentered and recentered by the word and work of Jesus Christ. "Within this space," I wrote, "men and women live by a power that is promised but not yet manifest, knowing that despite appearances, the truth of this world is grace." The *Century* called special attention typographically to a sentence reaching for larger implications: "We possess today more factual knowledge about humankind than ever before, but we have no universal symbols of the human essence."

"Jesus and the Struggle for the Real," from the May, 1971, issue of *The Journal of Religion*, discloses some of the intellectual explorations lying behind the inaugural lecture. No obvious, agreed, reality-sense underlying shared life is evident among us today. "We do not believe just as we breathe." Foundations, such as they are, cannot be taken for granted and are self-consciously pursued. We share only the seemingly stable common-sense environment given with our social existence. And even this is becoming fragmented, problematic. Fulfilled personhood presupposes precisely what we lack: a given, redeeming, gracious sociality.

The "life-world" of Jesus with his disciples offers a clue to the answer: "A socially constructed life-world in which Messiah and messianic people are dynamically interrelated." This is the world of the gospel narratives. But the same life-world is detectable behind passages having to do with the "Christ of faith:" for example, the so-called "primitive christologies" of Acts 3:12-26 and Phil 2:5-11. Alfred Schutz's notion of a "we-relation"--standing at the center of his phenomenology of the social world and drawing in part on the work of George Herbert Mead--seems to grasp the kind of "reality" found in such passages. That reality-sense is mediated by the kind of social "space" in which prevailing understandings of power are transformed in new movements of the imagination which empower human beings transformingly, differently.

Paul's notions of justification and of the body of Christ both elaborate the point. As Markus Barth explains, my neighbor's empowerment as a person rests on his or her being justified by grace through faith. *I* do not know what justification *means* unless I know what it means to receive confirmation of my own justification through my openness to him or her. Such "vivid immediacy" is the core of the redeeming sociality we seek. Yet such immediacy dissolves the minute we try to objectify it. Like the environing sociality which gives us our basic reality-sense, it can be mediated only in symbols.

"Ecclesiology as Counter-Consciousness" from the *Journal of Ecumenical Studies* for fall, 1971, develops related themes. "For whatever else may be said of our time, it is one in which humanity has come to a kind of deliberate self-consciousness about the workings of its institutions and symbols." But here there is an unmistakably "sixties" flavor, with references to Theodore Roszak's *The Making of a Counter-Culture*, and Charles Reich's largely forgotten development of "Consciousness III" in *The Greening of America*. Actual experiments, underground churches, innovative liturgies (such as those explored in the author's 1970 book *The Crumbling Walls*) have reopened the question of "church" in our culture. But such moves have not done much to clarify the conceptual problems involved, e.g. ecclesiological questions, questions of how "church" actually takes form in social reality. The word "consciousness" in the title does not signal a move into psychological categories. It rather functions in contrast to Marx's "false consciousness" to refer to a socially maintained awareness of the world. Do the inherited structures of church and their symbols constitute a kind of "false consciousness?"

Today we are reconstituting the action-world cybernetically, as different life-worlds communicate with one another. Karl W. Deutsch argues in *The Nerves of Government* that in the cybernetic model we have more than a mere analogy for grasping social process; we have a revolutionary paradigm. Society can be seen as based on constantly reproduced, yet varied, patterns of "information:" systems of symbols interconnected by communications links. Consciousness seems less than ever before the mere product of economic circumstances or means of production. We are going beyond Marx, witnessing the liberation of consciousness from economic determinism. We can begin to explore the storehouse of symbols where the human future is made.

Hermeneutics

I group here two essays written 21 years apart. These can now be seen as complementary. The first explores the relevance of a biblical theme, that of the "suffering servant," for the ecclesial "counter-consciousness" we seek. The second asks, in the manner of Paul Ricoeur, the single philosopher most influential in my work, what goes on when such content is heard as summons, appropriated as constitutive of personal and social being, and lived forth as testimony. I call this combined inquiry "hermeneutics:" that is, reflection on methods of interpretation.

"The Servant Lord and His Servant People," from *The Scottish Journal of Theology* for summer, 1959, is the earliest piece of writing in this collection. It is both a report on a dissertation then in progress[14] and an exploration of the biblical evidence supporting the theme of the 18th General Council of the World Alliance of Reformed Churches (Sao Paulo, Brazil, 1959) on whose Geneva staff I served at the time. For me this theme represented then, and still does, an approach to the very substance of incarnation. I was saying that incarnation taken as bare fact or as theological principle alone is empty. The key to its meaning lies in its narrative, and hence symbolic and metaphorical, specificity. "Servant" imagery feeds the imaginative transformation of power, and therefore conveys the immediacy of the life-world shared by Jesus with his disciples. Grace is mediated, not in some abstract transaction, but in a particular, irreplaceable, story which founds and norms a community.

What manner of scholarship is this? It is the work of a young biblical scholar testing the import of his conclusions for systematic theology, all the time writing for the delegates to an international meeting. This piece, it can now be seen, was composed toward the end of the so-called "biblical theology" movement connected with the names of Paul Minear, George Ernest Wright, Oscar Cullmann, John Bright and many others, soon to be called into serious question by the work of James Barr and Brevard Childs. In 1959 many of us still believed that consistent themes such a "covenant, "people," "justice," the "body" and other motifs could be tracked consistently through the varied works composing the Bible. For many, Kittel's *Wörterbuch* provided the key. My paper was an effort, I think still partly legitimate, to find interpretable patterns of imagination in the sociality composed by the Messiah with his People.

More than twenty years after this foray into "servant" symbolism, I find myself looking for a philosophical understanding of how biblical symbols and metaphors, appropriated into the lives of persons and communities, issue a call to faith "beyond the desert of criticism." This is the burden of my critical introduction to Ricoeur's biblical hermeneutics in *Essays on Biblical Interpretation* (Fortress, 1980). The servant motif as such is not in the foreground here. But that particular symbol-set could certainly function along with other biblical figures in the ways suggested in Ricoeur's "hermeneutic phenomenology." As James Barr effectively argued against the "biblical theologians" of the fifties and sixties, the Bible expresses itself in sentences, not single words. And metaphor, which stands at the center of Ricoeur's hermeneutic phenomenology, has precisely this quality of subject-predicate expression, however strange and unexpected the resulting figure may be.

Ricoeur sees us called, not in Bultmannian fashion by a bare *kerygma* addressing each solitary exister, but by all the imagery, symbol and metaphorical utterance of scripture understood in the "fullness" of its language. In Ricoeur's view, his German colleague does not see how the whole text of the Bible, with all its literary genres, speaks to us. In Bultmann, the individual's being is transformed in the bare existential encounter, but his or her imagination is not furnished with transformative symbolic content. For Ricoeur, in contrast, our "effort to exist and desire to be" leads us to "appropriate" the figures and meanings through which we have passed. Metaphorical language enables us to bring to reflective awareness both radical evil and grace-empowered hope.

Furthermore, biblical texts enable us to see new life-possibilities "ahead" or "in front of" them. Parables, especially, function metaphorically to transform our action-worlds. This transformation involves a "decentering" of our autonomous selves, a divestiture or *dépouillement* of self-claims as we turn toward "a life lived for others." An unspoken reference to *kenosis* or self-emptying, as expressed in Phil 2:5-11, can surely be detected here. One forfeits self-absorption to become totally implicated in the scriptural signs of hope. A total self-implication in such signs generates a life of "testimony," which in turn generates revelatory forms of lived *poesis*.[15]

How does this conceptuality link to social reality or to the community of faith *per se*? In all honesty it must be said that Ricoeur's work before about 1980 does not stress communal motifs. His chosen task "is not the exposition of the Bible within the community of faith. It is, rather, the rational clarification of human existence in the world." There is a clear parallel here to his Chicago colleague David Tracy's notion of the Bible as a "classic," in principle available to believers and unbelievers alike. Still, both scholars would agree that it is the faith community which preserves the text and interprets it. The text's existence and power, the space it makes for itself in the world, *is* a social reality from the start. Ricoeur's concept of new creation, indeed, is less centered on personal authenticity than on the achievement of social and political justice. He writes of "freedom in the light of hope," and enthuses over the work of Jürgen Moltmann. But Ricoeur is deeply suspicious of institutions, including ecclesiastical ones. As he puts it, "the true malice of man appears only in the state and in the church, as institutions of gathering together, of recapitulation, of totalization," In the end the gospel is not an action program but an "impossible demand."

It should be said that a concern for social reality, at best implicit in Ricoeur's hermeneutics up to 1980 when my essay included in this volume was first published, has since become more marked. Works such as *Hermeneutics and the Human Sciences* (1981), *From Text to Action* (1986) and above all *Oneself as Another* (1992), develop the implications of this philosopher's thinking in the interpersonal realm. An early signal is an article in the first-named volume arguing that social realities themselves may be understood "on the model of the text."[16] That is, they are text-like in that they consist of interconnected networks of signifying elements and actions. Hence, as patterns of human interactions, they can be "read." This idea finds expression in several of the essays found in part III of this anthology. It is implicit already in Ricoeur's idea of "testimony" or total personal--and now I add communal--implication in a text. This can mean that the way a community acts out its primal narratives "speaks," and therefore it can best be grasped by a hermeneutically sensitive, ecclesiologically deployed, social theory.

Ecclesiogenesis

Equipped with the modes of thought just described, the next three articles in this collection explore "ecclesiogenesis." I first encountered this term in the work of Leonardo Boff, who uses it to describe what goes on in the Latin American "base communities:" a process by which "church" takes form in a highly situated and predominantly pre-institutional sense. My essays see formation of the primary faith community in each place as a sociolinguistic process empowered by the Spirit and articulated metaphorically by the whole content of Scripture. It is possible to think in hermeneutical sociological terms *about* the formation of such ecclesial spaces. It is also possible to describe, with some of the same conceptual equipment, the internal thinking processes which generate such spaces, maintain them in being, and eventually build institutions which protect them and make them tangible.

"Church and Salvation: The Contemporary Dialogue" was a commissioned article for the November, 1983, issue of *Chicago Studies*, a Roman Catholic journal. The topic assigned concerned the church's role in addressing humanity's condition in the present epoch. The cybernetic metaphor appears: I have used it before and will use it again. By means of the computer we are close to being able to list the members of the entire human race by name, and by the transistor radio to imagine addressing all the earth's people simultaneously. But we are far from having any universal *idea* of what it mans to be human. Global theories of human nature break down before Foucault's "insurrection of subjugated knowledges." What would we say to all humankind if we could? Might the greeting be simultaneously practical and eucharistic: Have you eaten?

But the attempt even to think about such a world discloses serious differences of perspective, especially between the northern and southern hemispheres. Wolfhart Pannenberg's running argument with José Miguez-Bonino displays the issues well. Our contexts of life shape the "prisms" we use in describing reality, and therefore influence who "makes sense" to whom and how. As Edward Farley says, theological decisions within traditional "houses of authority" are less and less persuasive. We need to look, beyond the "clerical paradigm," at the question of how *ekklesia* takes form in the world. We need to consult the experiences people have had of "being church" in circumstances of immediate human need. The actual thinking of congregations needs to be critically honored and studied. Doing so discloses theology in its primary, embodied, mode.

Such an inquiry, for example, could turn on discerning how the church functions as "sign" in the midst of the world. The "sign-ature" of Jesus Christ can be sought in the congregation's comportment in relation to surrounding structures of power. It can be shown how congregants find their imaginations energized by the figure of Jesus to see what is actualizable in the world: visioning possibilities "in front of" the communally enacted "text" (Ricoeur). Such possibilities extend beyond the ones established structures of society let us see. And such visioning is not only social and political. Imagination-crippling power also stands over against us--as well as beyond us and within us--as we confront the natural boundaries and limits to life itself. The church should be seen as a parabolic community, or lens, or prism, through which human beings are able to discern the factors around them that have to do with both personal and communal salvation.

"Thinking in the Community of Faith: Toward an Ecclesial Hermeneutic," an essay from the anthology *Formation and Reflection*, edited by James Poling and myself, (Fortress, 1987) takes this conception of ecclesiogenetic thinking one step further. The essay asks, "What is the nature of the thinking that underlies, accompanies and sustains faithful life-together?" What accounts for what makes sense in the church? Do such questions get at what Edward Farley means by theology as *habitus*? We ask such questions in the midst of a triple epistemological crisis: of authority (sources), of context (radical pluralism) and of conceptualization (the nature of theological argument). Traditional answers in all three of these realms have become unglued. Yet new and innovative forms of Christian community thrive. Such communities can be seen as living christocentric exegeses of the worldly signs around them. Hence the need for a "humble hermeneutic" or "hermeneutic of recognition" as we learn from these lived interpretations of gospel and world. These communities of discipleship carry on a deconstruction and reconstruction of what the world sees as "common wisdom" or "common sense."

Over the course of Western history since Constantine, however, churches typically have not deconstructed the power images around them but have rather absorbed them and reasserted them. Sociologist Guy Swanson has dramatized this fact in his book *Religion and Regime* by examining the relationship between political structures and ecclesiastical patterns in Europe during the period of the seventeenth-century "Reformation settlements." These agreements determined the confessional allegiances that would obtain in each nation, principality or territory on the principle *cuius regio, eius religio.* Consistent "immanental" (e.g. Roman Catholic, Anglican, Lutheran) or "heterarchic" (e.g. Reformed, Anabaptist) patterns, with a range of possibilities in between, generally emerge for *both* state *and* church in each political entity.

Now, I argue, it is time to break this lockstep. Churches need to put in play subversive sets of significations which deal with the interplay of power and imagination. What significations? Those, for example, connected with the biblical "suffering servant" as model for both Messiah and people. My essay recalls details from "The Servant Lord and His Servant People" (chapter 4 in this book). We are urged to *think* in a self-emptying way: *Touto phroneite*, as Paul says in Phil. 2:5. In such thinking, the faith community trans-signifies the social and cultural materials of which it is composed, much as the Eucharist does with bread and wine. Churches may thus "offer the world a language for grasping its own present truths and future possibilities." As expressions of "real presence," churches should "seek to add something to humankind's capacity to envision itself whole."

Finally, the essay "Toward a Hermeneutic for Ecclesiogenesis" from my book *The Sense of a People* (Trinity, 1992), unpacks many of the linguistic, metaphorical, and social elements of the trans-significatory process. By their relation to Jesus Christ, Christian communities of faith are lived decipherments and expressive embodiments of the people-configuring work of the Holy Spirit in the social and cultural worlds in which the churches live. Congregations discern Spirit-formed social realities in the world and bring them into a christological frame of reference which makes them visible. Congregations thereby articulate the human communities around them *as* spaces in which the Spirit's people-gathering power is active. By proclaiming the gospel, by celebrating the liturgy, by acting prophetically, they signify that God is continually forming communities of people to be agents of justice, peace and freedom.

In order to do this, congregations bring together myriad elements of shared human life. Church members bring with them specific genetic inheritances, cultural idiosyncracies, traits of character, educational backgrounds, habits of language, economic involvements, family ties, occupational perspectives, and so on. Through their networks of relationship with others they represent still wider ranges of human experience. All these things are ingredients for the church community's construal or metaphorical construction of the world. A faith community cannot be adequately understood solely by consulting its formal polity. It can only be understood as a gathering of persons who bring with them all the kinds of life-substance mentioned and more: a community which aims at configuring all this so as to represent the identity of Jesus Christ and thereby to articulate the shapes of God's presence in the world through the work of the Holy Spirit.

Out of these insights, the essay seeks "a coherently thought-through understanding of what is going on when believers form a community which interprets the world as the space of God's reign." The understanding offered involves a kind of "phenomenology of spirit"-- not Hegel's, but owing something to his example--which traces the formation of meaning as the Spirit does its shaping, configuring, work in human life (Peter Hodgson). We experience the Spirit at work in us through the signs generated by our "effort to exist and desire to be." Meanings take form in an ascending progression: from gesture and the emerging social self (G. H. Mead), to primal signification and the emergence of language (Peirce, Barthes), to grammar, syntax and logic (Wittgenstein), to metaphor, symbol and concept (Ricoeur, Lakoff and Johnson), to synthesis and making sense (Geertz and Habermas), to societies interpretable *as* texts in themselves (Ricoeur again). Churches take form in this world of social meanings.

This trans-signification of social reality brings a sense of "real presence" to the ever continuing dialectic of power and imagination: something perhaps analogous to Bellah's notion of the "felt whole" within which all other meanings unfold. We cannot stand apart and *see* this because we are in it and of it. We can deal with it only symbolically. Here the Spirit is at work, preparing earth's inhabitants to be the Holy City, God's dwelling place in the universe (Rev. 21:3).

Civil Society

How do faith communities so described bear witness to the societies around them? Is the relationship primarily one of moral example, or may congregations somehow help instigate and model what has come to be called "civil society"? What happens when a theological perspective of the sort set forth here encounters the work of secular political and social theorists? I argue that the visible church is only one product among others of the articulating work of the Spirit in the public world. The entire constituting of human sociality is a work of the Spirit. In this perspective, ecclesiology is a specialized kind of social theory which shows how the *telos* of society as a whole becomes provisionally visible in the life of congregations. Ecclesiology is not merely a theory of church organization and practice. It follows that questions of political philosophy are intrinsic to ecclesiology in its fully realized sense.

"Faith, Ethics, and Civil Society" was a paper given at the Evangelical Academy at Loccum, Germany, in June, 1995. The context was a conference co-sponsored by the World Council of Churches to take account of the revival of "civil society" dialogue among political philosophers following the fall of the Berlin Wall, the election of Nelson Mandela, and other events raising the question of cultural and other *conditions* for democracy. The former East Germany and post-apartheid South Africa were the obvious laboratories.

How useful a concept is this? It turns out to be urgently needed. The window of opportunity for democratization may prove to be short-lived. Meanwhile the "civil society" debate focuses a variety of social issues, offers common ground for theologians and political philosophers, has clear cross-cultural relevance, and offers us a mode of discourse beyond confrontation and fragmentation. Especially under such conditions, a continuing dialogue with political philosophy is indispensable for ecclesiology as the latter should be conceived.

The Loccum paper tests this hypothesis by sketching the diverse social roles churches might play, and hence might conceive of themselves ecclesiologically, in the light of five current types of social theory: reasonable political liberalism (John Rawls), communitarian particularism (Alasdair MacIntyre), communicative action (Jürgen Habermas and Seyla Benhabib), modest pragmatism (Richard Rorty and Jeffrey Stout), and resourced authenticity (Charles Taylor). In conclusion I argue that the Church functions above all as *place-holder* in the world, what Bonhoeffer called *Stellvertreter*, for the possibility that human society can overcome its violent origins, its continuing resentment and mistrust, and come to realize its true calling to become the beloved community envisioned in the biblical narrative.

The churches exist to *hold open* a social space in which society's existing structures and practices can be seen for what they are and in which human community can be articulated in a new way, a space in which the metaphors of our common life can be exposed to their transcendental ground. The community of faith can thereby declare a critical solidarity with social movements and visions which pragmatically accord with the gospel, refusing to credit underlying ideological assumptions which do not so accord.[17]

Back of the Loccum paper lay a monograph written two years earlier for the Center for Hermeneutical Studies of the Graduate Theological Union and the University of California, Berkeley. "Traditioned Communities and the Good Society: The Search for a Public Philosophy" is offered here in abridged form. I also omit for lack of space responses by Robert Bellah, Judith Berling, John Coleman, S.J., and Robert Holub. The core question here is whether civil society can be maintained in the West on the basis of a now-weakened memory of Enlightenment rationality. Might traditioned communities such as churches sufficiently shake off their addiction to self-concern to make a contribution?

"Public Philosophy" in the old sense practiced by the likes of John Dewey, Walter Lippmann, John Courtney Murray and Reinhold Niebuhr has suffered an eclipse. No longer are there coherent, widely accepted, philosophical foundations for democracy. Jürgen Habermas's theory of "communicative action" offers at least a frame of reference in which to explore the possible roles of religious traditions. What is it about language, Habermas and Gadamer both ask, which enables us to understand what seems alien or strange sufficiently to participate in a pluralistic public world? Can diverse religious communities join in a culture of communicative reason embracing many communities and cultures, especially in the mode of practical reasoning or *phronesis*?

I argue that such dialogical reasoning *must* have a transcendental basis, and hence that religious communities hold, in forms often disguised even from themselves, the secret of peaceful human communication. There is moral force behind the demand that we recognize other communicators as persons whose integrity lies beyond our human power to bestow. Trust is a gift of grace, not something we originate ourselves. Communicative action discloses a moral substance of humanity coming to expression in the social nexus. The intersubjective world is expressive. It is, at any given moment, something like what Hegel called "objective spirit." It ramifies through time to generate what can only be described as a "phenomenology" of spirit.

It follows that each tradition of life needs social philosophers to bring out what that tradition's interpretative responsibility for society requires in practical moral terms. The whole Habermasian argument about the presuppositions of communicative action reminds one of Jeremiah's "new covenant" whose principles are intrinsic to the consciousness of the Israelite people, i.e. written "within them," and "upon their hearts." Can such a covenantal tradition be offered to the larger society in broadly sharable terms? In its essence, communicative action has to do with promise-keeping and truth-telling. But such virtues cannot be articulated and maintained by the sheer logic of discourse alone. They must be rooted in an integrity of personhood formed within communities of faith which interpret the social world as a space open to transcendence.

Householding

For this generation to abandon the ecumenical vision, having once been given it by extraordinary acts of providence and inspired leadership, would amount to apostasy. So intrinsic to the church's nature is a sense of the whole household of God on earth, and so vital are our attempts to give it visible expression, that any failure now to go on seeking realization of this dimension of the churches' being would mean denial of the faith itself. The word *oikoumene* in Greek in fact *means* "household." We must not confuse the present financial and administrative difficulties of ecumenical *institutions* such as the World and National Councils of Churches, not to speak of councils in many other parts of the world, with a discrediting of the *vision* as such, or a collapse of the *movement*. But new kinds of ecumenical relationships are needed, embodying new understandings of what this "household" can mean to us. The two essays in this final section of the book press toward such new relationships and understandings.

"Remodeling the Household"[18] was published in *The Ecumenical*

Review for summer, 1999. A commissioned piece, this article seeks to analyze currents that ran through the World Council's Eighth Assembly at Harare, Zimbabwe, in December, 1998. The presenting task was to track interventions and discussions linking ecclesiology with ethics, a topic discussed at length in my book *The Church as Moral Community* (1998). It dawned on me in writing that this was not so much one topic among others to be identified as such, but rather a way of experiencing the "household" first-hand and exploring conceptually what it might mean on the present world scene. The "Padare" or town meeting format brought reports from all over the globe of Christians and others, as they struggle with concrete *local* issues reflecting *global* human concerns: human rights, the environment, the situation of women, democratization, economic justice among others. The nature of these reports, the desire to connect with others, gave credence to Robert Schreiter's notion of "global theological flows"[19] linking similar efforts in many places. These "flows" do not embody universally valid conceptualizations. But people can nonetheless understand one another across cultural barriers as engaged in mutually recognizable projects.

I call in this article for remodeling the ecumenical household according to a "ground floor strategy" that engages this new local/global dialectic. This means studying how the church comes to be and maintains its identity in specific situations, while those in such situations also have their heads up to intercept global flows of information and reflection which constitute an *oikoumene*. I argue that ecumenical theological work, especially of the "Faith and Order" kind, should now seriously pursue hermeneutical analyses of the kinds of information that flow back and forth among these loci of concrete involvement, as well as attending to the sorts of *koinonia*, including eucharistic sharing, achieved in many such situations.

"Moral Hospitality for Public Reasoners" gives the householding strategy a new application. This piece was a contribution to the Fourth Visser 't Hooft Memorial Consultation at the WCC Ecumenical Institute at Bossey, near Geneva, in June, 1999. It moves forward from reflection on the ecumenical household as such to ask what insight may flow from the notions of giving and receiving "hospitality." Those of the household live out their traditions of faith, but they may also make space for others who, without desiring to become members or profess formal "belief," seek whatever wisdom the tradition of faith may have to offer. Such moves could be described as temporary visits by perhaps "prodigal" children to their original parental households. Guests in such households would be in effect following Durkheim's steps in reverse: from the secular back to the sacred. And they might be impacting the sacred in the process. Parents, too, could have much to learn.

There may in fact be persons ready to receive this sort of hospitality, especially if offered on reciprocal terms. Certain social and political philosophers today indicate they feel a need for something like this, among them John Rawls, Michael Sandel, Ronald Dworkin, and even the eminent deconstructionist Jacques Derrida. All of which raises a fascinating question. What difference is there between "believing" and "unbelieving" versions of the same moral convictions? Is the difference that between the "intrinsic" and the "functional"? What might a body politic look like if its principles were derived from an "overlap" of moral convictions from various sources rather than from some secular theory (such as Rawls's) repristinating Enlightenment reason? And if, as some argue, all this is in fact happening, how might churches make offering "moral hospitality" to seekers a self-conscious strategy?

The Beloved Community

So where does this bring us? I have been searching for terminology which both comprehends and goes beyond all that these essays express, yet remaining faithful to my core intent. For much of a lifetime I have been arguing that we need to understand the visible church as an instrument of something much larger: a promised communal fulfillment of human life itself. There are many ways to name such a fulfillment. One that has much to commend it is Josiah Royce's term "the beloved community." As Royce puts it in *The Problem of Christianity*,

> Let your Christology be the practical acknowledgment of the Spirit of the Universal and Beloved Community. This is the sufficient and practical faith.... This is the one truth which has always been grasped, in a concrete and practical form, whenever the religion of loyalty has found on earth its own. *The name of Christ has always been for the Christian believers the symbol for the Spirit in whom the faithful--that is to say the loyal--always are and have been one.* [20]

This formulation is not exactly what I would have written, or precisely that of any organized Christian communion. But these days the expression "beloved community" speaks with power beyond all such particularities. The words suggest, not a smug gathering of the "good," but the communion of sinners whom *God* loves. "Beloved community" is the communal creation of the One "who loves in freedom." Potentially, it involves everyone. Royce's intention is to call us to loyalty, "in a concrete and practical form," to a communion of saints both within and beyond ecclesiastical boundaries. His intent can be taken as a challenge to all Christian churches and no doubt to other faiths as well. The goal of our respective communal attachments is loyalty to the Spirit of something reaching much further: be it called the reign of God, the people of God, the household of life, or the beloved community. And since we cannot discern that beloved community of humankind except in occasional fragments of itself, we must conceive of it, *think* it, allow it to be what Kant called a "regulative idea" presiding over thought and action. That, whatever the language employed, is what this book is about.

Notes

1. The writer served, with Fr. Bernard Sesboüé, S.J., of Paris, as co-moderator of this Commission from 1984 to 1991.

2. Bonhoeffer, *The Communion of Saints*, 20, as quoted in André Dumas, *Dietrich Bonhoeffer: Theologian of Reality*, tr. Robert MacAfee Brown, (New York: Macmillan, 1971), 88.

3. Dumas, Ibid., 84.

4. Eberhard Bethge, *Dietrich Bonhoeffer*, 58ff, quoted in Dumas, Bonhoeffer, 89.

5. John Milbank, *Theology and Social Theory* (Cambridge, MA: Blackwell Publishers, 1993), 2.

6. Ibid., 2.

7. Ibid., 3

8. Ibid., 6.

9. One needs to include the messages sent and received by the physical spaces the people inhabit, as well as the furnishings they use, in pursuing the calling of *being* a people of God. That, after all, is what outsiders see first: what they think of at once when they hear the word "church." It may not be as simplistic as it seems for the *Oxford English Dictionary* to define "ecclesiology" in the first instance as "the science of church building and

decoration."

10. Philadelphia, Trinity Press International, 1992.

11. I conclude, however, that *subsisit in* can mean whatever the relationships between the Roman Catholic Church and other Christian bodies at any given time permit it to mean. Someone has mischievously pointed out that in English, "subsist" can mean to "survive minimally," as in "subsistence diet."

12. On this significance of "people of God" as ecclesiological conception see *The Sense of a People*, 21-53, *et passim*.

13. Dumas, *Bonhoeffer*, 108

14. *The Servant Christology in the New Testament*, written under the supervision of Professors W.D. Davies and Franklin Young, Princeton University, 1961. University Microfilms, Ann Arbor, 1961.

15. In his "Reply to Lewis S. Mudge" in *Essays on Biblical Interpretation* Ricoeur comments on my use of the category of testimony as organizing principle. He writes, "It is at that point that I meet Lewis Mudge's reorganization of the whole field no longer in terms of the succession of my works, but in terms of their inner structure as a whole. For that purpose Mudge brings to the forefront the category of *testimony*, which seems at first sight somewhat marginal in my writings. I found this interpretation very illuminating for my own self-understanding" (42).

16. See Ricoeur, "The Model of the Text: Meaningful Action Considered as a Text," in John B. Thompson, ed., *Paul Ricoeur: Hermeneutics and the Human Sciences* (Cambridge: Cambridge University Press, 1981), 197ff.

17. I am indebted to a paper by John de Gruchy, "Dietrich Bonhoeffer and the Transition to Democracy in the German Democratic Republic and South Africa," presented at the Chicago meeting of the American Academy of Religion in November, 1994.

18. I have changed the title of this piece from "Toward a Hermeneutic of the Household" to "Remodeling the Household." References to "hermeneutics" in this book are numerous enough already.

19. See Schreiter, *The New Catholicity* (Maryknoll, NY: Orbis Books, 1997), 15ff.

20. Josiah Royce, *The Problem of Christianity* (Chicago: Henry Regnery, 1968), Vol 2, 426. Italics in the original.

I

Social Reality

1

Searching for Faith's Social Reality

In the year 1911, as he penned the final pages of his famous *Social Teachings of the Christian Churches*, Ernst Troeltsch was certain that Christianity as he knew it could not "master" modernity. The key to understanding Christian faith in general, Troeltsch thought, lay in understanding its practical social expressions. And in all the history of Christendom, only two such expressions had been truly potent: the medieval social-cultural ideal, and the form of Calvinist asceticism we know today as the "Protestant ethic." Despite continuing achievements, both these syntheses, said Troeltsch, had "exhausted themselves." If there were to be a new and culturally fruitful expression of Christianity in the modern world, new thoughts would be needed that had "not yet been thought."

I do not think that the situation has changed very much. If the key to the vitality and creativity of Christian thought lies in the vitality and creativity of Christian praxis, then--despite all that has happened since Troeltsch's time--we have little new to say. We have not worked out a vision of the social embodiment of Christian faith adequate to a post-Enlightenment world.

Meanwhile, one of Troeltsch's predictions has proved quite accurate. What was left of Christian vitality, he thought, would emerge as privatistic individualism. We see this trend today not only in a resurgence of conservative pietism but also in the syncretistic search for personal meanings, especially on college and university campuses, where interest in religious questions as such has little to do with the building of faith communities. But religious individualism seldom generates potent social practice. It tends to be parasitic on the achievements of past generations. It is not the answer we seek, but rather an evasion that could deflect us, fatally, from facing the issue.

The Question of Human Identity

We will not find the theological breakthrough we need until we have wrestled with Troeltsch's problem. But with what resources and under what conditions? Most theologians since Troeltsch have had, for reasons of their own, other agendas. Even H. Richard Niebuhr, who saw his *Christ and Culture* as linked to Troeltsch's work, was in fact pursuing something different. Niebuhr gives us a brilliant typology of theological visions, but he does not wrestle in Troeltsch's way with "the social question." And in his reluctantly written final chapter Niebuhr tries to graft the social dimension onto a fundamentally Kierkegaardian, and hence individually focused, understanding of faith. This effort does not meet either his problem or ours.

The exception, of course, is the early Bonhoeffer. In *Communio Sanctorum* Bonhoeffer is determined to go beyond idealism's stress on the individual and to come at theology by way of sociology. Indeed, he shows that Troeltsch's understanding of Christianity is itself too personalistic. The church, said Bonhoeffer, is the world as it is meant to be in Jesus Christ, the space where the world is structured according to its true center. Thus we meet the reality of God in the reality of the world. How tragic that Bonhoeffer did not live to develop these hints further. Or did the war and the Holocaust, as Bonhoeffer himself may have thought, make them invalid?

Today, at least, we have new conceptual possibilities. The theologian has colleagues in the human sciences that make available a vast array of dialogical resources. The philosophy of the human sciences in particular is becoming very important to us. But at the same time, the position of Christian thought and institutions in Western culture may have deteriorated. Troeltsch knew that Christendom had to face the problems of pluralism and historical relativism. But he also thought that European culture as such was intact, and he seemed to believe that this culture sufficiently defined what human nature is or could be. If Christianity could not "master" the social ferment of the day, at least the Western individual knew who he or she was. But today we live in the midst of a worldwide human identity crisis.

Ironically, we possess today more factual knowledge about humankind than ever before, but we have no universal symbols of the human essence. Our knowledge of the human is arranged in hundreds of conceptual systems--psychological, sociological, anthropological, theological--which cannot communicate with each other because they employ incompatible symbolic languages. The question of human identity is now a hermeneutical conundrum. We need some universal theory of symbolic communication merely to interpret to one another our different ways of knowing.

Power and Imagination

What I have to offer is no such theory. But I think it may still be helpful. I suggest that we have lost our hold on who the human being is in part because we are suffering a disruption of the relations between power and imagination in our personal and corporate lives. I mean by this that our sheer capacity to do things overwhelms and distorts our awareness of the meaning of what we are doing. And at the same time our imaginative lives, fed by media bent on exploiting us, are less and less relevant to the tasks we must perform as human beings and citizens. When, then, the need arises to put power and imagination together, we are at a loss. Soon we will have to make decisions about the uses to be made of our capacity for genetic engineering. But no available image of what it is to be human seems adequate to guide us.

The energy and know-how at our disposal today are obviously consequences of the imaginative acts of previous generations. Our forebears dreamed their dreams and channeled their capacities in ways that affect us today. But technology, once it gets going, seems to have an internal logic of its own. If we can do it, we will. Electronic information storage and retrieval, combined with the capacity of computers to talk to each other, make it inevitable that we will eventually have a data systems involving every man, woman and child on earth. The logic of computer technology will let us stop at no less. The same seems to be true of military technology. But the data-bank operator does not experience the impact of his or her mistakes in violated lives, any more than the bombardier sees the napalm-disfigured faces of children. Power tends to generate an obsessive, imaginative life of its own, far from the point of its impact on actuality.

At their best, of course, our imaginative resources are still able to expose power for what it is. But increasingly the imagination of the Western individual is exploited for profit. Mass-produced entertainment succeeds, ironically, because it makes us feel powerful vicariously. We are fed a diet of derring-do and violent conquest which arouses our fantasies, however disempowered we may be in real life. We identify with middle linebackers, dashing police officers, omnisapient and omnipotent physicians. Yet all these are action models that divert us from understanding the capacities for self-determination and action we really have.

The most striking consequence of the disordered relations of power and imagination in our civilization is surely the distortion of sexuality in pornography. Sexuality by its very nature involves physiology and fantasy in mutual support. The physical energy of sex is summoned and released by fantasy. And the art, music and literature of every civilization are informed by sexual symbols. But today sex itself has been turned into technique. Aided by the pill, and by technical manuals of every description, sex is torn away from images of fidelity, devotion and responsibility and comes to depend on pornography. The pornographic imagination, in return, turns sexual energy in the direction of selfishness, violence and exploitation.

We long today for a humanizing reintegration of power and imagination, but we find it impossible to recreate any of the great syntheses of the past, or to invent new ones. Instead, we live in a vacuum, vulnerable to totalitarian ideologies that would integrate our civilization by force. Demonic, dehumanizing syntheses seem to come alive and gain momentum in such vacuums. George Steiner, for example, has suggested that the Nazi death camps were no new invention. They were an acting out--with all the power of an industrial society--of imaginative archetypes which, for a thousand years of European history, have clustered around the idea of hell.

Diabolical junctures of power and imagination readily master our incoherence. Divinely inspired ones do not. Humanizing and regenerating images remain locked up in traditional belief-systems unavailable to society at large. Troeltsch was right, and the consequences are worse than he knew. Men and women who are bearers of the Christian tradition have something to give the world but do not know how.

Toward a Sacramental Sociology

Can Christian faith be rethought in a way that will help us break out of this box? Troeltsch believed that there were only two alternatives. Christians could provide symbolic legitimation for the prevailing society and culture, thus generating the "church type" of interaction between the tradition and the world. Or they could protest the prevailing situation and set up a countersociety, thus generating the "sect type." For us, neither is an attractive possibility. Much less so is our current, impotent religious privatism.

I want to suggest a different way of thinking. We need to formulate what I would call a "sociology of the Word of God," or, in other language, a kind of sacramental sociology. This sociology would try to understand what it might mean to speak of a social space of God-ruling as this world decentered and recentered by the word and work of Jesus Christ. The manifest structures of society would be the appearance while the social space of God-ruling would be the reality of humanity coming-to-be by his grace.

Christ's destructuring and restructuring of this world opens up a social space which is the faith-reality of this world in the midst of the world. Obviously I am using the word "space" metaphorically. Our religious traditions have been concerned with the relation of faith to space, in a variety of senses. The ancestors of some of us moved to Massachusetts Bay Colony to find in it the sense of new land for a holy commonwealth. Others sought room for the evangelical experience on the frontier. Still other traditions have understood faith-space as the religious enclave or ghetto. And some have thought of faith-space as space within the self, private and inviolate.

My notion of faith-space corresponds to none of these. There is a difference between space for faith--an opening of whatever kind where faith can grow if it will--and the space of faith, which is existing society seen as, restructured as, reconstituted by the power of grace as, the realm of God-ruling. Indeed, space for faith in the old sense is hardly available now. Certainly there is little physical room on earth for the founding of new religious commonwealths. But more important, neither the cognitive ghetto nor the sovereign self easily resists the constant implosion of normlessness and otherness which is the mark of our times.

The faith-space of this world is at the same time the true reality of this world which is what we mean by God-ruling. Clearly this use of the term "reality" threatens to become philosophical. For the moment, I want to resist such a step. We know Berger and Luckmann's book *The Social Construction of Reality*, as, well as Jurgen Habermas's *Knowledge and Human Interests*, and realize the implications for some kind of sociological ontology. But for the moment, I want to stress the experimental: what we can get hold of, grapple with, suffer through, exult over, weep over, encountered as interpersonal. This is the reality in which we encounter God-ruling.

The relation of these thoughts to the Bible should be transparent. In the Hebrew Scriptures the sense of Promised Land, of the place the Lord shall choose, involves geography but transcends it. The land becomes truly the Lord's space when it is the realm of justice and righteousness.

Jesus creates a faith-space which radically rearranges the power-images of his hearers. He does this by both word and deed. The parables re-present the social world with normal expectations overturned. And Jesus' life, death and resurrection, considered as a parable, force a re-vision of the world which reveals the meaning of the rule of God. As Mary says in the Magnificat, "He has scattered the proud in the imagination of their hearts." What can this mean but that the power elite no longer have their place? They have been displaced by the humble and the meek, whose empowerment in Christ reveals the power to come.

Paul, too, is grasped by the reality of grace as the truth of a social space in this case the nexus of centuries-long tension between Jews and gentiles. The setting is Antioch; the issue, table fellowship. Paul's doctrine of justification by grace alone is his reflection on a social experience in which the ancient barriers are overcome. The social world responsible for his reality sense is radically recentered.

The structure of the New Testament message as a whole, the line of argument which appears again and again in the preaching of the primitive church, supports this vision. Jesus is the one with power to see through, to see beyond, the styles of social imagination "in power" in this world. He is the one with imagination to subject himself to power as its victim, and power enough to engrave the subjection on the world's imagination. He is the one who makes of his disempowerment a sign of power yet to come. In all this, for those who follow him, Jesus turns this world into a space of faith. Within this space, men and women live by a power that is promised but not yet manifest, knowing that, despite appearances, the truth of tliis world is grace.

Becoming the Responsible Ones

Do these thoughts help us with Troeltsch's question? I have tried to sketch two pictures: the first, of a world spiritually incoherent and therefore vulnerable because power and imagination interact in potentially demonic configurations; the second, of this same world imaginatively reconstituted as faith-space, the space of God-ruling, by the power at work in Jesus. The result, I believe, is what H. Richard Niebuhr would have called a "transformationist" account of the relation of Christ to culture. But does this theological model help us with "the social question" as such, with the actual worldly form of this new sociality in Christ?

There will be no such new sociality unless at its center are men and women who know the biblical tradition and celebrate it. Sociologically speaking, such a company of persons is bound today to function as something of a "sect," or at least as an organized religious minority. From this status there is no escape if the tradition is taken seriously. What Bonhoeffer called his "secret discipline" his meditation upon Scripture, hymns and confessions which linked him to companions across time and beyond prison walls, was vital to him, as it must be to us.

But we are discovering that the content of this tradition demands that we see ourselves not as persons saved out of a fallen world, but rather as persons called to be that very world reconstituted as the social space, and therefore as the worldly reality of God's rule. Only if that reconstituting is possible for all humanity is it possible for us. And the essence of our being as a called community lies in the way we constitute the very notion of "humanity" at the level of awareness which forms us in both being and action. By the grace-shaped intention which brings "humankind" into being in our awareness we also become human beings under grace. Thus we beoome the responsible ones, the dependable ones, the faithful ones, the unsettling ones, the demanding ones, the free ones.

On the road to a human future there are forests, dragons and deep waters. The spiritual disorder of our culture invites adventurers. The image of the concentration camp is not descriptive of us now, but we are vulnerable. We need not adopt the eschatology either of Daniel Bell or of Robert Heilbroner to pay attention to what these men are telling us about our situation. Our rationalized, individualistic society has generated a hedonistic culture which is undermining the behavior such social rationality requires. Simultaneously we are depleting our resources, polluting our environment, and producing too many babies. Merely to survive on this planet, we are told, we will have to produce a culture oriented toward collective values. And the only way to do that may be through the technologically aided power of centralized authority combined with the sanctions of an officially sponsored religious imagination. What would that be like? Could the leaders of such a world resist the temptation of the demonic?

The Holocaust raises questions we still must confront. I hear two answers today. One, from Bruno Bettelheim, celebrates the autonomy of the individual, the integrity of the private self. The other, as presented in *The Survivor*, a new book by Terrence Des Pres, suggests that nature is our savior, that self- consciousness has gone too far, that we never should have assumed so Promethean a posture.

I can answer neither summons. I find a more authentic image in Elie Wiesel's slim but overwhelming book *Night*. What kept men and women alive in the Nazi death camps, Wiesel seems to be saying, was initiative, fidelity and concern. And none lasted longer than those who took responsibility toward others: responsibility of a son for a father, of a rabbi for his flock, responsibility for strangers. A space of faithfulness, a space of God-ruling, in the midst of hell. Something more real than power and imagination in demonic interplay. An authentic image precisely because of its brokenness, the moments of faithlessness and forgetfulness which threatened to destroy the reality but never quite did so. Deep within, Wiesel knew he wanted to be free of this responsibility. But he also knew that without it, he could have won no authentic freedom.

I envision a people for whom the space of God-ruling is the reality of this world. Might they be the ones against whose presence "the gates of hell will not prevail"? We, or our children, or our children's children, will see.

2

Jesus and the Struggle for the Real

The religious quest of our time has been called a "struggle for the real."[1] It is not that traditional systems of religious symbol have been formally invalidated or "disproved," but, rather, they have ceased to represent or inform the reality of everyday life as we experience it. The reality to which religious symbols point is not given today as an unquestioned, immediate, taken-for-granted, one-possibility perspective within which human beings can simply rest with assurance. Religious convictions come to be held, if at all, for reasons of which we are self-consciously aware. They come to be maintained in carefully defined ways which specify the kind of reality to which we think they point. We believe, knowing that it is in order to impart coherence and direction to our lives. We do not believe just as we breathe.

A Collapse of Stable Meanings

We have been brought to this crisis of the real not only by the collapse of the hegemony of Jewish and Christian symbols over our reality sense, and not only by the dissolution of religious communities as arenas of cognitive privilege. The crisis has come because the nature of "the real" is no longer self-evident to us in any area of life. Nothing has escaped to terrors, the vertigo, of history. No stable pattern of meaning seems to inform the felt quality of our life-experience. In this situation, the theologian may well find reasons both for despair and for hope. The symbolic meanings with which he or she deals will not be received by our culture on the old terms. But yet a need for meanings with which to grasp the "felt whole"[2] of our existence is very widely sensed.

If the Christian theologian is to give significant aid to contemporaries in their struggle for the real, the battle will have to be waged on some new fronts. Older versions of the struggle are, of course, still very much with us. Where the struggle was with "science" in the form of Aristotelian philosophy, it is understandable that the divine substance should have been defined as *ens realissimum*. Where the struggle had to do with God's freedom with respect to God's gifts, many came to believe that the sense of reality turned on our acknowledgment of priority of grace. Where a technocratic order began to imprison life in an iron cage, there were those for whom the quest for the real turned to the spiritual interior of the solitary exister. But the real that counts for human consciousness has always been nearest at hand in the "commonsense world," the realm of socially shared representations which make up the theater of everyday life. The character of this world has escaped analysis until the present century precisely because it has never before presented itself as so problematic, so insubstantial and ambiguous underneath its surface appearance of sanity and order.

It is beginning to be clear that the commonsense world itself is a humanly generated, symbolic reality. It is, as Peter Berger and Thomas Luckmann showed in *The Social Construction of Reality*,[3] a network of collectively generated representations which define a complex intersubjective world of significance. The commonsense world must by no means be confused with the array of abstractions which make up the corpus of "scientific" truth. The commonsense world possesses no inherent objectivity. It is in no sense just "there," but rather it depends for its "reality" on the implicit and explicit symbols which constitute the content of the collective consciousness of society.

A further insight about this commonsense world is now beginning to emerge in phenomenological investigation. Not only is its symbolic content different in basic character from the "common sense" of natural science; this content is not reducible to a more literal semantic level even on demand. Robert Bellah, in his recent essay "Christianity and Symbolic Realism,"[4] has made the case that the human life-world is full of symbolic representations which function precisely to assure the unity and coherence of the entire life-experience and which, therefore, cannot in principle be converted into propositions of other sorts. Religious symbols, above all, have this function of building bridges between the felt antinomies of the common life-world, rendering the manifold of experience into a "totality which includes subject and object and provides the context in which life and action finally have meaning." Bellah decries the "consequential reductionism" which seeks to explain religious symbols as fraudulent covers for underlying social forces (such as the "unholy alliance of priestcraft and political despotism") as well as "symbolic reductionism," which considers that religious symbols contain a certain truth, yet a truth better and more usefully expressed in the language, say, of social psychology or depth analysis. Thus, everyman's common sense is based on implicit symbolic representation and finds its ultimate, comprehensive kind of sense in some kind of religious representation. Bellah calls his position "symbolic realism", by which he means to stress that the reality of the felt whole of human existence can be grasped only in symbolic form.

But, in our present cultural situation, we can agree about very little as falling in a public, commonsense category of reality. The arena of common sense has apparently been reduced to the pragmatic, the operational, the range of sensibility needed to avoid (much of the time) running into each other in hallways and on highways. As soon as more basic considerations of the grounds for action are involved, we seem to live in a variety of sectarian universes, realms of fantasy, worlds of value.[5] Sometimes we are aware of the sectarian character of our ideologies, and sometimes we are not. Persons who consider themselves the most rational and pragmatic may, in fact, be in the grip of deep, unconscious, demonic fantasies. In general, it would seem that the more fundamental and comprehensive the issue involved, the more pluralistic our cultural situation is. We have very few symbolic resources for speaking of significant issues concerning "the real" in a way that most people can understand.

There seems little hope of inventing some new, modern or scientific vocabulary for uncovering the depth dimensions of common sense. The fates of "new religions" from Auguste Comte to the present have not been encouraging, and we must conclude that, if the rejuvenation of any established religious traditions for such a purpose is likely to be cognitively sectarian, the attempt to construct a fresh edifice of meaning for the everyday life-world is bound to be transparently synthetic. Max Weber ruefully acknowledged that no new religion was likely to be produced by intellectuals.[6] The difficulty is that, once people know, as intellectuals do, that they produce and can manipulate the symbols by which they represent the real, it is unlikely that they can adhere to those symbols with loyalty and passion. Beyond a certain point, self consciousness concerning the search for the real seems to invalidate the search, and we have returned to the starting point wiser but no more enriched.

Traditional systems of religious symbols, such as those found in Judaism and Christianity, at least have the advantage of a certain subliminal presence in our culture and, therefore, the potential of informing our felt whole if certain inherent drawbacks can be overcome. The most serious difficulty lies in the kind of truth claim such symbols appear to make. Bellah calls this claim "historical realism," by which he means the identification of religious truth with propositions of literally ascertainable fact: "Christ must have been who he said he was or he was the greatest fraud in history." For secular intellectuals, above all, this understanding of Christianity has been decisive.[7] Thus construed, as Theodore Roszak has pointed out, "a religious tradition need only prick its finger in order to bleed to death."[8] Yet historical realism has not been and need not be the only or even the central style of understanding for Judaism and Christianity. There are other possibilities. Do any of them help in our search for the real?

In our present religious situation, one may doubt that we would be much impressed even if Christian and Jewish truth claims could be substantiated on a literal basis (if one could prove that the Ten Commandments did "in fact" come in what Martin Buber has called "such optical and acoustical pomp and circumstance,"[9] for this sort of thing is quite simply not the real for us in a way that counts. Mere fact has now become supremely problematic in its relation to felt whole. It seems to have less and less to do with reality in the personal sense or the moral sense. The question today is surely that of what counts for reality at the level of shared representations of meaning which inform human action, giving it sense and coherence. The question to ask of tradition is what sort of corporate representation of conditions of human existence it embodies. This representation by definition underlies specific doctrines, specific truth claims, specific historical assertions. It is the imaginative construct with which one construes the life situation that is of interest.

This essay attempts a new look at the kind of lived reality on which the theological elaborations found in the New Testament are based. The argument seeks, first, to establish the historical and theological priority of a messianic community gathered around Jesus and persisting after his death, a community which only gradually generates explicitly theological forms of self-understanding and draws explicitly theological conclusions about the wider meaning of its existence. The line of thought then probes this primitive messianic community to determine the nature of its reality sense. Some concepts found in the thought of Alfred Schutz prove useful: the we-relation, the sense that we encounter the other in "vivid immediacy." The essay finally tries to draw some christological and social-ethical consequences. On what terms can Jesus be meaningful in the modern struggle for the real?

The Messiah With His People

What lived reality forms the basis on which the structure of New Testament thought and imagery rests? I wish to suggest that this reality is neither a set of historical facts nor a portrayal of existential faith decision in the making. It is a symbolically shared we-relation, the life-world of Jesus and his disciples, the Messiah and his people. I am led to this conclusion by two lines of argument: one based on the general nature of the New Testament evidence and the other based on examination of particularly relevant parts of the text.

First, the general nature of the evidence. Generations of scholars have tried, in vain, to distinguish with certainty in the Gospels between material based on historical fact and material reflecting the faith experience of the primitive church. Not that certain proposals, based on form-critical analysis, have lacked plausibility and usefulness. But these results are so diverse, and the arguments leading to them seemingly so subjective and intricate, that we have little confidence that the problem has been, or can be, solved in general terms. It is more to the point to recognize each Gospel as a literary whole, composed of a variety of elements, to be sure, but giving expression to a particular theological and historical consciousness. Theological commitments are presupposed by these texts, and the same commitments are also expressed in the form of details within each text, to form a fabric which cannot be unraveled without destroying the garment. We will not enter this thicket. "Event" and "interpretation," "fact" and "faith" are abstractions which prevent us from seeing the nature of the material rather than illuminating its genesis.

The Gospels appear to be multiauthored writings which represent the shared awareness, the common symbols, of religious communities. They represent neither Jesus' *ipsissima verba* nor a theological position based on later experience nor an uneasy combination of the two. They represent the way Jesus was heard and understood by a community that associated its destiny with his. They represent common symbol systems derived from shared experience. It follows that, if we accept the essential linguisticality of theological existence, and if we acknowledge that language and its literary patterns are a social product, then we are close to an understanding of the reality the Gospels permit us to see. We are permitted to see, in every line, in every summary, in every parable, whatever their ultimate verbal source, a socially constructed life-world in which Messiah and messianic people are dynamically interrelated.

This vision of the reality underlying the Gospels, moreover, is consonant with what the New Testament theologians and kerygmatists make of it. Just as proponents of the "new quest" suggest that Paul's emphasis on justification supports the view that the Gospels contain, not a history of outward events, but a history of faith decision, we may maintain that Paul's still more central theme of the church as "one body in Christ," the reconciled and reconciling community, supports the view that the Gospels represent a similar reality in more richly and diversely symbolized form. What Paul describes as one body, Jesus' disciples experience as a we-relation.[10] This shared consciousness exists not only as a network of personal feelings into which we cannot, as historians, penetrate. It exists also as a network of images and symbols cast in narrative form: the network which has come down to us in variant editions as Synoptic Gospels.[11]

We may suspect, then, that this sharing of messianic community in event-full realism, is the primary experience that leads to everything else the New Testament offers. We may even suggest that the advent of this community is seen by Christ's earliest followers as the eschatological event that has already taken place. Other interpretations of the accomplished eschatological event, centering on the themes of death and resurrection, are apparently secondary. These, at least, are among the inferences that may be drawn from a passage of central significance for our purposes, Acts 3: 12-26, as well as from the structure of the Gospel of Mark.

In his article "The Most Primitive Christology of All?"[12] J. A. T. Robinson argues that Acts 3: 12-26, an address attributed to Peter following the healing of a lame man at the "Beautiful Gate" of the temple, represents a view of Jesus' significance at sharp variance with the "Lord and Christ" theology of Acts 2: 36. For Robinson, the latter formula, part of Peter's speech at Pentecost, is presented by Luke as a kind of frontispiece to the theological achievement of the early church, while the positions of the other speeches recorded in Acts, when these are taken separately, vary considerably. The Petrine address of Acts 3: 12-26 is seen by Robinson as representing the earliest or most primitive of these christological positions. It contains such appellations for Jesus as "the holy and righteous one," "the author of life," the "servant" (or "child"), and "a prophet like Moses." The only comparable passage is Stephen's speech in Acts 7, which likewise turns on the Moses typology and stands within the Hebrew prophetic tradition. The titles just mentioned quickly drop out of use in the New Testament, to be replaced with the "Lord and Christ" language characteristic of both Luke and Paul and presupposed by most of the rest of the writers of the apostolic age.

If one discordant note is excised from Acts 3: 18, and it appears that there are good reasons for using the knife at this point,[13] the speech in Acts 3: 12-26 presents an astonishingly self-consistent and historically illuminating viewpoint. Jesus has been sent by God to Israel as "servant" and "prophet" in fulfillment of the promise of Deut. 18: 15. The purpose of this visitation was to give the Jews a last chance to repent before the dawning of the messianic age, in which the promise to Abraham would be fulfilled that in his posterity "shall all the families of the earth be blessed." Instead, the Jews have rejected and murdered God's servant-prophet. But God has not been defeated. He has exalted Jesus to heaven, where he will wait until the day of restoration the prophets foretold. Meanwhile, because the Jews acted in ignorance, the opportunity for repentance is still open. They are exhorted to seize this opportunity in order that the age of renewal may soon dawn. Jesus is the one who shall come, but he will not have the title of Messiah until he does come.

Meanwhile, those who believe that Jesus is the Messiah designate are in a very special position. This passage implies that they are a kind of protomessianic community. They are the group within Israel which has already repented, which knows that the messianic age is imminent, and which is, therefore, in a peculiar sense already the messianic people. This conclusion is suggested, not only by the logic of the situation as the speech in Acts 3 describes it, but also by the context in which the speech is set. The healing of the lame man at the Beautiful Gate of the Temple, and his subsequent entry of Solomon's Portico with Peter and John indicates not only that the Jesus community is the source of health and salvation, but that it thus holds the key to true membership in Israel, as defined by having access to the holy place. At this point, then, the redemptive act of God which Jesus' followers are proclaiming is not the Resurrection as such or the giving of the Holy Spirit but the calling of a genuinely messianic people, a people who have witnessed who the Messiah is to be, who have some idea of what his kingdom will be like, to an empowered existence on the stage of history.

Robinson argues, I think correctly, that this position is basically continuous with what must have been the self-understanding of the band of disciples who followed Jesus during his earthly career. The Crucifixion and the Resurrection are both mentioned in the passage. But it is not yet clear that they are the subject matter of the disciples' proclamation. They do not yet make a theological difference. Rather, they reaffirm what must have been the position of Jesus and his disciples, that the decisive intervention of God is yet to take place. The Crucifixion has not frustrated these hopes, because "heaven must receive" Jesus until the promised messianic denouement unfolds. Thus, the experience of the Resurrection *per se*, whatever it was, did not immediately lead the primitive church to the position, say, of Rom. 1: 4, which contains the full panoply of christological titles. On the contrary, we must trace such later theological developments, not simply to the Resurrection experience, but to this experience interpreted in the light of subsequent circumstances affecting the life of the community. At the moment represented in Acts 3: 12-26, the theology attributed to Peter is as continuous as may be with what the disciples must have shared with Jesus himself, a "story of the hanged man " in which Jesus together with his followers participated.

A striking confirmation of this supposition is at hand if Robin Scroggs is right in his view of the Gospel of Mark in his recent paper "Mark: Theologian of the Incarnation."[14] Scroggs argues that Mark, far from writing a "passion narrative with extended introduction" (Kähler), is mainly interested in what Jesus does in his ministry and therefore writes a Gospel in which narrative structure is all important. What Jesus does is precisely to make the church present at a time before the eschatological moment has begun to unfold in public, apocalyptic, fashion. This is possible because Jesus, the "obedient and righteous sufferer," has overcome Satan and is, therefore, able to perform healings and exorcisms which wrest people from demonic control. He has passed on this power to his disciples. For those who have eyes to see and are willing to join themselves to the mission, the eschatological conflict is joined, but it has not been completed. The church can begin to exist because Satan has begun to be bound.

From the confession at Caesarea Philippi onward, Mark represents Jesus, not as a divine man or savior figure, but as a model for discipleship. The church which has begun to come into existence is based on a sharing of Jesus' life and fate. Scroggs argues that the passion predictions are not used by Mark to work out a christology of death and resurrection, sin and atonement, but rather to delineate an anthropology, an ethic. The real meaning of the "messianic secret" is that only he who relates himself bodily to Jesus' mission can see who Jesus is. Official Israel as community of reconciliation is now doomed, the new community is begun, and Jesus' work is accomplished. For Mark, his death and Resurrection do not accomplish anything new, except to place Jesus in a position to come as exalted Son of Man to judge mankind. In Mark 13, indeed, the resurrected Jesus is not expected to help the church in any way. That role is given to the Holy Spirit. Jesus' followers must work out their life between the times with the powers Jesus gave them during his ministry on earth.

The similarity of this picture to that suggested by Acts 3: 13-26 is evident. One can conjecture, on the one hand, that Mark (as the Papias tradition has it) is in fact reflecting what he learned from Peter and that he thus gives us information about the primitive community's original self-understanding. On the other hand, Mark no doubt goes beyond the position of Peter in developing an understanding of Jesus' ministry on earth as the arena of an accomplished eschatological work. Mark becomes a theologian of incarnation, no doubt explicitly to counter tendencies, already at work by A.D. 70 or so, to attach the mission of Jesus to one or another variety of divine savior mythology or mythologized foundation event.

We are, then, within striking distance of an important conclusion about the kind of historical reality on which the theological elaborations of the New Testament are based. In advance of the messianic age and before the coming of the Messiah in his fully revealed dignity, a band of disciples is permitted an ecstatic anticipation of the power that is to come. Judaism is here asked to entertain the possibility of an incursion of messianic power into present time, in the form of a community of

persons who claim to know who the Messiah will be and who claim to
have shared with him an earthly experience which represents the power
struggle between this age and the age to come. This is the new
possibility within the standard prophetic framework: the possibility that
a community may exist whose story is the story of the future coming
toward the present and whose symbols and images therefore have
peculiar eschatological significance.

An Alternative to Historicization and Mythologization

But these eschatological symbols soon undergo two kinds of
distortion. We may call these distortions historicization and
mythologization. On the one hand, the "delay of the Parousia" seems
to make it necessary to establish what has happened in the events
concerning Jesus in such a way as to justify the Christian community
in its increasingly separate existence. It is no longer enough to interpret
Jesus' being "raised up" as an event to be completed and confirmed by
the fulfillment of an eschatological promise. The Resurrection becomes
a distinct event in the past, a foundation event on the analogy of those
posited by other ancient Near Eastern politico-religious communities.
But the difference between ecstatic expectation and foundation event is
vast. It is important, moreover, to see that the delay of the Parousia
alone is insufficient to account for this development in symbolism.
Rather, the institutional response of Jesus' followers to this delay is
involved. The fall of Jerusalem makes it seem necessary for the Jesus
community, the members of the proto-messianic body, to establish
themselves in a more perduring social form, and, with such a social
form, goes a view of reality different from that held by the original
"Christian" generation.

On the other hand, the same institutionalizing process gives rise to
a borrowing of Gnostic and Hellenistic mythologies which understand
the power behind human experience as essentially above man in eternity
rather than in front of him in time, and corresponding to his inward,
spiritual nature. Thus, the whole fabric of reasoning about Jesus'
preexistence and his descent into human form from a heavenly realm
is attached to the church's reasoning about the incarnation as foundation
event. The mythology is further enriched by speculation about Jesus'
preaching to the spirits imprisoned in the underworld, his bodily

resuscitation, his ascension, and his cosmic status as Lord of all the principalities and powers active both on earth and in the different celestial spheres.

It seems clear enough that these particular historicizations and mythologizations of original eschatological symbols of Jesus and his disciples do not represent the only possible theological development of the primordial community-sense they seek to represent. On the contrary, if the general outlines of the original symbol system can be recovered, we should be free today to elaborate it along quite different lines. The problem faced by the New Testament community, especially after A.D. 70, was that of ensuring both its independence from Judaism and its continuing existence in a hostile Roman environment. The ecstatic eschatological experience of Jesus and his disciples had to be given a protective structure in which it could perdure. Today, however, the ecstatic eschatological experience has jumped over the walls originally built to protect it. It is to be found scattered to the four winds, subliminally present in, with, and under many cultural forms, largely free of its original symbolic norms, but nonetheless alive. A very different theological strategy is called for now. With Bultmann, we must strip away mythology of one sort and replace it with another more appropriate to the present situation.

The idiom in which we do this, however, will not be that of Heideggerian existentialism. Heidegger's thought is too ahistorical and too individualistic to deal with the corporate nature of the primordial Christian experience, too innocent of the intricacies of symbolic interaction in a social context to be sensitive to the relevant symbols and myths in the contemporary environment. We must call today, not on existentialists, but on social philosophers: in particular, upon those associated with the phenomenological school and upon those interested in the relation between human community and power relationships.

The work of Alfred Schutz[15] may be particularly valuable for this new work of demythologization, because it deals, among other things, with the way complex social structures and symbol systems are derived from the basic unit of social reality, the we-relation. For Schutz, the we-relation is social reality at the rudimentary level, the level of the lived world of self and other. It is the fundamental intersubjectivity, which is presupposed in any account of the social world--scientific, ideological, or otherwise. The anatomy of Schutz's we-relation resembles the dialectical scheme of the emergence of self and symbol proposed by George Herbert Mead.[16] For Mead, the infant in his or her crib makes a "gesture," and begins to learn what his gesture "means" by observing the responses of others. Thus, the individual's whole sense of personal meanings, of personal being as expressed in the ability to use symbols, emerges in a primary social setting. The self is a social self, the I is derivative from the we. Schutz refines Mead's picture. The very existence of other consciousnesses constitutes a problem when intersubjectivity is seen from a scientific or philosophical point of view; but, for the everyday world as we live it, others, as centers of consciousness analogous to our own, form part of a pregiven matrix which is prior to my experience of myself. The "other" consciousness must be present to me before I can use sign, gesture, symbol, language, or myth as the mode of my own consciousness. This intersubjective world has to exist if there are to be such things as self and society at all; yet, on this primary, face-to-face level, the intersubjective world cannot be investigated as if it were an object. We must grasp this primary social reality by participation rather than through objectification.

In Schutz's theory, I cannot reflect on my own vivid, living present while I am living it. I can only make an object out of my own consciousness in retrospect. But I can objectify and grasp the vivid living presence of another as she or he lives it. I know the other's stream of consciousness in vivid simultaneity. That is how I know the other is like me. In fact, in this sense, I know more of him or her than he or she knows of him- or herself, and, likewise, he or she knows more of me. The present that is thus common to both of us is, for Schutz, the pure sphere of the we. This sphere of the we is pregiven to the sphere of the self. I actualize my own "now" as my vivid present only through the other, just as he actualizes his or hers now through my presence for him or her. It follows that we depend upon each other in the we-relation for the confirmation of our being-in-the-world. Our possibilities of actualization as self-in-the-world depends upon the intersubjective experience of self and other. This intersubjectivity in vivid presence is, for Schutz, the basis of all subsequent elaborations of self, symbol, and society: elaborations which gradually become routinized and typified in the form of layers of social sediment to constitute the complex life-worlds which we know as the multiple contexts in which we live.

Power, Imagination and Intersubjectivity

The circumstances under which the messianic we-relation comes into being in the New Testament suggest that the focal issue has to do with power. For Mark, the power of the demonic has to be bound before the church can begin to be gathered. For Paul, "principalities and powers" represent, among other things, sacral or quasi-sacral political entities which are overcome "in Christ." The binding, the circumscription, of the demonic leaves open a political realm in which the power of God can be at work. This realm takes concrete form as a social reality within which the power relationships are quite different in both structure and meaning from what they are in the world. What the Synoptic Gospels treat as a we-relation free of the power of the demonic, Paul describes as a "body" which is the tangible manifestation of the Messiah's presence in history.

In the Jesus community, empowerment in intersubjectivity is symbolized by anticipation of the kingdom. The community of Jesus and his disciples is a reconstituted, renewed Israel, but its mythohistorical foundation has yet to enter history with power. The ground of this community, therefore, is not the sedimented layering of symbol and structure, the Torah with its interpretations, which constitutes the Jewish social fabric. It borrows symbols from this source to be sure, but the new intersubjectivity is not ordered or legitimated by the entrenched system of symbols and relationships. It is ordered and legitimated by a power of God yet to be revealed. This is a community whose leader "has scattered the proud in the imagination of their hearts." He has, in other words, broken down the system of legitimations which has, up to now, dominated the self-image of the establishment! Thus, it is perfectly understandable to find the gospel records full of sayings that put the first last and the last first, which speak of the opening of the eyes of the blind, the liberation of prisoners, the feeding of the poor. The Beatitudes speak of a reversal of social roles, and the parables repeatedly challenge routine social typifications. Where James and John try to conceive of the new social order after the analogy of the old (they wish to sit on thrones at Jesus' right and left), they are told that in the kingdom men do not lord it over each other as the Gentiles do and that the Son of Man came "not to be served but to serve." And, at the end, Jesus, faithful to Isaiah's vision, is "reckoned among the transgressors." The temptations which beset Jesus, from the wilderness to Gethsemane, are all temptations to express the power of the future in terms of recognizable royal symbols, to turn the coming of the kingdom into the all-too-familiar form of holy war. To do so would not only have been to invite bloodshed, defeat, and repression for the Jewish people; it would have been to destroy the liberating basis of the new we-relation which Jesus sought to implant in the world as a seed of humanity's future. God's act, the saving event, if one can speak this way, is the coming into being of a community, a social reality capable of representing to an unwilling world the order to come.[17]

One can, with the help of Paul's interpretation of the nature of this new social reality, describe the kind of intersubjectivity which was its root. Paul's doctrine of justification, as Markus Barth has shown,[18] is coordinate with his symbolization of the Body of Christ as a social reality which breaks through the barriers between Jew and Gentile, man and woman, slave and free. The justifying grace of God received in faith overcomes the power of the law, *nomos,* not only in the life of individuals; it overcomes the power of the many *nomoi* which have ordered tribalized gatherings of human beings. The power represented by *nomos* is the power of the principalities, those mythohistorical entities which symbolically legitimated the humanly limited and partial social structures of both temple and empire. Life in grace, lived in faith, is a life of intersubjectivity which is not ordered and limited by pregiven powers and symbols. In the body of Christ, no person has his or her relationship to another typified by primordially or politically given symbols. Intersubjectivity is not controlled by the past. Rather, it looks toward the future. As Markus Barth explains, my neighbor's empowerment as person rests in his or her being justified by grace through faith, and I do not know what justification means unless I know what it means to receive the confirmation of my own justification by my openness to that other. Here, then, is an intersubjectivity which does not permit its structures to form dead sediments. This is an intersubjectivity in which I find the confirmation of my being-in-the world always anew in the power by which my neighbor is justified and, therefore, in which I am justified. This, for Paul, is how *nomos* is overcome in the Body of Christ. This, surely, is what he means by being "in Christ." To be in Christ is to participate in the intersubjectivity which characterized the we-relation of the Jesus community. Christ is the new Torah, the new Temple, because he is the new social reality in which people are called to live. But he is new Torah and new Temple in a way which looks to the future rather than to the past for its manifest, historical foundation. Its public legitimation is not yet.

Power Structures and the "We-Relation"

Can Schutzian terminology help us resymbolize these forms of the New Testament we-relation so as to produce an expression of it for today? The Schutzian standpoint is hospitable to the biblical analysis of social reality in terms of power. If my own being-in-the-world is confirmed, or undermined, by my immediate relation to significant others, then I am partly dependent on them for my subjective sense of power in the situation. At this worldly level, my power could be defined as my capacity to command a response to my gestures and projects on the part of significant others. This power factor is obviously present in such evanescent social realities as the cocktail party in which people size each other up with respect to relative "clout" and, in any given culture, reveal the rankings that apply to the situation by such subtle signs as eye movements and body gestures. And the power structure that emerges will be influenced by whatever symbols, whatever preexisting crystallizations of meaning, are operative in the context. Whose "turf" is the party on? What occupational "pecking order" do most of these people have in common? What qualities of appearance, dress, posture, and demeanor are interpreted in what ways by this culture?

As the primordial we-relation becomes elaborated, predefinitions of power relationships become built into the society's accumulated symbols. *Nomoi*,[19] legitimations of shared activity, accumulate in the form of social sediments. Usually the result is not only pronounced inequality of power (Reinhold Niebuhr thought that inequalities of power were the inevitable price of social stability)[20] but also the alienation of human beings from creative interaction at every level. The quality of possible we-relations, in other words, is profoundly affected by the legitimating symbol systems or *nomoi* characteristic of the society as a whole. And societies which are organized on a large scale for maximum economic output, political stability, and military security seem to suffer profoundly alienating human by-products. Great power in the hands of society as a whole produces serious disempowerment at the level of personal intersubjectivity.

But, surely, the New Testament understanding of power overturns the assumptions on which society operates. If worldly power is the extent to which I can command the response of others, power in the New Testament is an affirmation of my being that I receive from others and that I give in return. Power originates, not in the impersonal dimension, but in the personal realm of the we. How, concretely, can this empowering we-relation take form in a society which symbolizes and exercises power so differently?

The Schutzian model of the we-relation requires that the relation be one of "vivid immediacy." The Jesus of history, of course, is a predecessor with whom (Kierkegaard notwithstanding) we can have no such relationship. We, therefore, must construct a Christology in which contemporary persons represent Jesus to each other and to the world in the required immediacy. The reality with which the Christian we-relation has to do, then, is a network of relationships whose vivid immediacy conveys personal empowerment and therefore the negation of the demonic. In this kind of "collective representation" (using here Durkheim's pregnant phrase), symbol and reality are one. The personal reality encountered in the we-relation is symbolic in the sense that it re-presents, stands for, the reality of the original we-relation. It is real in the sense that it itself consists of that which is unmediated, present beyond any conceivable question in living personal confrontation.

Yet, like the we-relation of Jesus with his disciples, this empowering network of vivid immediacy in which Jesus is really represented rests on no public manifestation of power. It confers a personal empowerment (in which we receive, and are received by, the neighbor as justified) which enjoys no manifest historical legitimation. On the contrary, it is likely to run counter to what society at large conceives as power. Indeed, it may tend to undermine, to relativize, the power relationships of the political and economic orders. Thus, the relation of this social reality to others is an urgent question: one which has a long history, which is no doubt far from concluded. How, precisely, does one go about the task of representing before an unwilling world an order which is yet to come? Here, perhaps, Schutz's notions of "multiple realities" and "provinces of meaning" can be of use. Clearly, the empowering we-relation constitutes one province of meaning among others. Compared to them, it is, in one sense, insubstantial and perhaps evanescent. The provinces of meaning which represent society's conscious business embody a presently legitimated reality which has its own kind of immediacy, although not the vivid immediacy encountered in the we. But it is in the immediate we that we find the confirmation of our being-in-the-world. That is, we find here the empowerment of ourselves as persons on the basis of which we are able to be in other relationships. The self *is* in the world, but not all provinces of meaning in the world undergird that *is*: only those relationships in which reality is encountered as an unmediated intersubjective representation of the Christ.

Thus, the confirmation of our being-in-the-world can only be assured in a relationship which is itself grounded in a reality to which we look forward. Every symbolization of this reality must therefore be anticipatory in its implications. Such symbolization (what we call theological language) will naturally draw its metaphors from the actual social processes by which empowering we-relations continue to come to be, rather than from the deposit of past imagery which all too easily suggests that this empowerment is established as definitive historical fact. A phenomenology of the vivid immediacy by which human beings are empowered thus can strip away the layers of characterization with which the reality has been wrapped, leaving the way open for new experiments in theological language in every generation.

Notes

1. The phrase appears as the title of the last chapter in Clifford Geertz's Terry Lectures, *Islam Observed* (New Haven, Conn.: Yale University Press, 1968).

2. Herbert W. Richardson, *Toward an American Theology* (New York: Harper & Row, 1967), chap. 3, esp. p. 64.

3. New York: Doubleday & Co., 1966.

4. Delivered under this title as an address before a plenary session of the American Academy of Religion in Cambridge, Mass., October 1969. This essay is now published as the second half of chap. 15, "Between Religion and Social Science," in Bellah's *Beyond Belief* (New York: Harper & Row, 1970).

5. Cf. Peter Berger, "A Sociological View of the Secularization of Theology," *Journal of the Society for the Scientific Study of Religion*, 6 (Spring 1967): 3 ff.

6. Weber offers this opinion in *The Sociology of Religion* (Boston: Beacon Press, 1964), pp. 136-37: "Many elements conspire to render unlikely any serious possibility of a new communal religion borne by intellectuals.... No matter how much the appearance of a widespread religious interest may be

simulated, no new religion has ever resulted from the needs of intellectuals or from their chatter."

7. Bellah (n. 4 above), p. 247.

8. *The Making of a Counter-Culture* (New York: Doubleday & Co., 1969), p. 212.

9. *Moses: The Revelation and the Covenant* (New York: Harper & Bros., Harper Torchbooks, 1958), p.110.

10. The term "we-relation" plays a part in the thought of Alfred Schutz, whose position will be described more fully below.

11. This approach is similar in its implications to the method which has been worked out by the "phenomenological" school of literary critics, mainly in Switzerland and France (see Sarah N. Lawall, *Critics of Consciousness* [Cambridge, Mass.: Harvard University Press, 1968]). Speaking of the relation between a work of literature and the one whose awareness it represents, Mrs. Lawall writes, "The word 'incarnate' may seem too strong, and yet it is a key word in this theory. For these critics, the 'author' is not the man who wrote the book but the implied being who gradually assumes form as the work is created. The text itself depicts this 'author' just as a photograph would depict the historical author.... The 'author' is incarnate in the book because he does not exist outside it" (p. 266).

12. Originally published in the *Journal of Theological Studies*, n.s., 7 (1936): 177-89; reprinted in *Twelve New Testament Studies, Studies in Biblical Theology,* no. 34 (Naperville, Ill.: Alec R. Allenson, Inc., 1962), pp. 139-53.

13. The words "that his Christ should suffer" in Acts 3: 18 are regarded by Robinson as a Lucan addition to the text because (a) they introduce, as if in passing, an idea not otherwise present in the speech, that the prophets had foretold the suffering of the Messiah (not just of the righteous prophet Jesus), and (b) this idea is evidently a characteristic Lucan emphasis: it occurs only in the Lucan summaries of the meaning of Jesus' ministry and death (Luke 24:26 f., 45 f.; Acts 17:2 f., 26-22 f.), and is found in what is generally regarded as a Lucan interpolation into a block of Q material at Luke 17:25: "But first he must suffer many things and be rejected of this generation."

14. Delivered at the Society of Biblical Literature, New York, October 1970.

15. Schutz's principal works are published in his *Collected Papers,* ed. Maurice Natanson, 3 vols. (The Hague: Martinus Nijhoff, 1962). I have been helped by the exposition of Schutz in Gibson Winter's *Elements for a Social Ethic* (New York: Macmillan Co., 1968), passim; and by Berger and Luckmann's *The Social Construction of Reality* (n. 3 above), whose perspective is strongly Schutzian.

16. Mead's views are given convenient treatment in the exposition of Schutz in Gibson Winter (n. 15 above).

17. This expression paraphrases a formulation by John Howard Yoder in his

privately circulated but as yet unpublished manuscript, "The Possibility of a Messianic Ethic" (1968).

18. In his article "Jews and Gentiles: The Social Character of Justification in Paul," *Journal of Ecumenical Studies* 5, no. 2 (Spring 1968): 241-67. Barth bases his interpretation largely upon Gal. 2: 11-21.

19. Peter Berger uses the expression *nomos* for an established legitimation of social structure or practice (see *The Sacred Canopy* [Garden City, N.Y.: Doubleday & Co., 1967], passim).

20. This is one of the principal strands of argument in the early chapters of *Moral Man and Immoral Society* (New York: Charles Scribner's Sons, 1932), esp. pp. 7ff.

3

Ecclesia as Counter-Consciousness

Amid the theological confusions of our time, the central issue may turn out to be one of ecclesiology. But, if so, the discussion will demand ecclesiology in a new key. Informed by the social sciences yet focused on the emergence of a new humanity, the new ecclesiological debate will raise the question of how, if at all, transcendent perspectives can today be socially embodied. It will consider the consequences of different sorts of ecclesial embodiment. It will confront a situation in which "belief" and "unbelief," "inside" and "outside," in their traditional senses, have become problematic, and in which the gathering of community around biblical meanings may take unprecedented and unexpected forms.

This essay seeks to sketch what this new kind of ecclesiological reflection might involve. In doing so, it borrows both a certain perspective and a certain terminology from the social sciences. For whatever else may be said of our time, it is one in which we have come to a kind of deliberate self-consciousness about the workings of our institutions and symbols. No longer are the social structures, including ecclesiastical structures, in which we live our lives simply seen as givens. We are more aware than before of the processes by which such structures come to be what they are. We know that we are free, within limits, to make them what we will. And we know that in doing so we make ourselves and our perspective on reality, again within limits, what we will as well.

This situation need not, and in the present essay does not, lead to a kind of reductionism which limits the significance of attempts to find historical embodiment for the biblical notion of peoplehood to what empirically minded social scientists are able to categorize and measure.

The object is to make sociologically informed self-awareness the servant of faith, not a substitute for faith. Never before have Christians or Jews had the opportunity to examine old ecclesiological models, and to consider new ones, with such a degree of conscious understanding of what goes on when the attempt is made to give faith a tangible communal form.

Disabled Denominations, Experimental Communities: The Rise of "Counter-Consciousness"

In such a perspective one begins to suspect that important roots of the self-doubt and confusion rife among modern theologians lie in the fact that no very adequate social embodiment of biblical faith appears to exist in contemporary culture. Perhaps none can exist. Yet symbolic constructions representing the shape and meaning of faith must have some kind of social constituency as their ground. This is the testimony both of social theory and of the biblical stress on incarnation.

The disabilities of the existing churches in this regard have been endlessly analyzed. Two factors stand out. The churches, as a result of social differentiation, have been forced into the position of being institutions which specialize in "religion," however modern culture, for its own reasons, may choose to define it. And, at the same time, the different denominations perpetuate the various social metaphors which informed the shape of faith at the times and places of their foundation, metaphors which in modern dress are anachronistic and alienating. Saddled with outdated conceptual patterns, subject to systematic misunderstandings, it is not surprising that the churches struggle and die.

The Barthian version of dialectical theology, so influential for forty years, helped obscure these issues. The sharp distinction between "faith" and "religion," whatever its other merits, tended to make us indifferent to the inevitable interaction between the content of faith and the shape of its social expression. Furthermore, an ecumenically motivated willingness to admit a variety of church forms (an impulse not unconnected with the Barthian formulation) tended to suppress the question whether any of these structures, or anything like them, could be an answer to the ecclesiological question.

It may be doubted whether the more recent burgeoning of

experimental communities, "underground" churches, and innovative liturgies has done much to clarify the theoretical issue of how social embodiment of biblical meanings can take place in the modern world. That such gatherings, under certain conditions, have lived the messianic reality with intensity is not to be doubted. They have added fascinating details to the picture, but not solved the basic conundrum. Hence the issue remains: What sort of social reality is, or could be, a contemporary embodiment of faith as the Bible understands it? Have we the conceptual tools to think clearly about such a social reality, much less the resources to work it out in practice?

The expression "social reality" is deliberately used here instead of the word "church," because it is not clear at the outset that the meanings of "church" in our language come near enough to the point to be semantically serviceable. This paper maintains that the answer does not lie in any known variant among existing ecclesiological themes, nor in any conceivable reformation of strategy or structure. It lies, rather, in a new way of conceiving the ecclesiological problem. The social reality with which the biblical tradition must interact today is not institutional or organizational in character. The social reality genuinely open to being an embodiment of biblical tradition today is best described as a kind of shared symbolic awareness which lives in, with, and under existing institutional forms, religious and otherwise, and anticipates forms and styles of life yet to come. This shared awareness can be called a "counter-consciousness."

The resemblance of this notion to Theodore Roszak's well-known concept of "counter-culture" is obvious enough,[1] and a debt to Roszak should be recorded. But the reader will soon discover that my plea is not for a canonization of the "hippie church" or for the use of communes, rock festivals, or organized drug-taking as simplistic models for ecclesiastical reconstruction. The point is rather that the word "consciousness," when its history in social theory and its implications in present social process are carefully analyzed, may turn out to be useful in illuminating the nature of that pre-institutional level of social awareness at which the human future is constantly taking form, and at which, therefore, a special openness to the Word may exist. The writer prefers the word "consciousness" to Roszak's term "culture" precisely because the former does not tend to stress particular preferences in art, music, dress, and life-style. A counter-consciousness has begun to emerge among persons of highly diverse institutional and cultural commitments. This is where the opportunity for a new kind of ecclesiological understanding may lie.

Consciousness, Social Metaphor and Church Polity

More than a century ago, Karl Marx explored the relation of group or class "consciousness," in the sense of collective self-understanding, to the reality of historical experience. He concluded that much of the time people thought in categories and frames of reference which obscured the real nature of their situation, and he called such inadequate systems of understanding "false consciousness." "False consciousness" deprived men and women of the capacity to be effective actors on the historical stage. It sentenced them to a collective disempowerment which Marx called "alienation."

The fact that Marx believed that "religion" as practiced by both capitalists and workers furnished much of the content of "false consciousness" need not detain us, for the specific conditions under which he wrote have changed and the shape of our problem is different. Our purpose is to apply Marx's insight about the relation of consciousness to circumstance to the questions besetting modern religious communities. With this in mind we will ask whether the way we formulate the ecclesiological question does not involve "false consciousness," and therefore a disempowerment of both the believer and the tradition he or she represents.

All forms of church organization tend both to reflect and to legitimate the basic social metaphors at work in their environment.[2] By social metaphors I mean not only models for the administrative structures of church and state (monarchy, heterarchy, etc.) but also the symbolic constructions that go with every kind of corporately defined activity (growing up, getting married, earning a living, dying, etc.). Thus the subject matter of "ecclesiology" is not simply church government. It is the sum total of social interaction of every kind that owes its genesis and its meaning to the particular way in which the biblical tradition finds concrete expression. Thus so "theological" a notion as "salvation" (to take but one example) gains its effective meanings in any given instance from the whole bundle of metaphors thrown up by the encounter between tradition and culture. And one can see that this interaction may generate symbolic consciousness which is adequate to the historical situation, or it may, for various reasons, generate a consciousness that is false, or alienating. In the first case, the content of tradition may be more or less adequately communicated in and through its social expression. In the second, it will hardly be communicated at all.

It is useful to think of the purpose of social interaction as human empowerment. People cooperate to augment their power, and in doing so they generate symbols which define the meanings and ends of power, as well as conceptual devices for controlling it. The primordial issue in all human collectivities, then, is whether the way power is conceived and applied really does enhance and augment the human, or whether it leaves men diminished, enslaved. There has been a close relation between the social functioning of biblical meanings and this empowering or disempowering process in the West. One may say that where biblical meanings are symbolized in such a way as to wrestle with historical realities--bringing them under judgment, offering them new life--there the empowerment implied in the notion of "salvation" is concretely alive. Where, on the other hand, biblical meanings fail to wrestle with real historical circumstances and merely serve as a cover for processes of quite another kind, there the tradition is an accessory, an accomplice, of society's self-deception. The believer, and not only he or she, lives in a state of false consciousness and becomes an instrument of his or her own disempowerment. Bluntly put, his or her system of symbols, and hence the rationale of his or her personal and corporate activity, has little to do with what is really going on.

We thus have to ask whether our inherited structures of church life, with all the symbolizations of the meaning of human activity that go with them, may not amount to "false consciousness" in present historical circumstances. When a given metaphor of human empowerment is implicit in some emerging social process, some conception of humanity that is "on the make" (Europe at the coronation of Charlemagne, England at the rise of the Puritan ethic), that metaphor indeed empowers those human beings so situated as to be within its scope. But when the same metaphor is perpetuated (in the form, say of inherited church polities) into situations whose dynamic is different, the result is profoundly alienating, and no amount of explanation, strategizing, reforming or renewing can help. We seem to be in the latter predicament now. The kinds of symbolic interaction out of which our polities grew and which they still inevitably imply no longer correspond with the terms in which we live our lives.

To illustrate. The "catholic" type of church polity is based on an organic notion of society in which direction and integrity are guaranteed by the symbolic head, monarch, archbishop, Pope. A complex and intimate interaction between the organized church and the civil realm within a common network of "Christian" values is implied here. If the polity and its presuppositions are transplanted to some other situation however, it will not give the tradition a foothold from which to grapple with human activity as it actually is. The difficulties may be illustrated by the delusion, fostered by this ecclesiological model, that all races and classes are truly included by the church because they are all, at least in token fashion, to be found within its nominal boundaries. On the organic, Christendom model, this might make sense. In modern Europe or America, the very formulation of the question is somehow wrong. Who is to include or exclude? Where is the church?

Or consider the "heterarchic" model which informs the bodies of Calvinist provenance, both "church" and "sect." Here God is conceived to be so majestically removed from the mundane details of human affairs that "he" is virtually the "invisible hand." A balance in society is thought to be achieved by the interaction of many organized interest groups (craft and merchant guilds, classes, corporations, parties) and people are free to pursue the logic of any given enterprise to its appropriate conclusion (productivity, profit, power, or whatever the case may be). Success is evidence that one is of the elect. What *can* be done thus must be done, and we are again enslaved. For in an advanced industrial society it is illusory for me to suppose that the enhancement of my power as I autonomously define it automatically enlarges the humanity of all. It is an illusion to think that a version of the biblical message capable of being squeezed into such a frame can in fact be empowering for anyone in the real world today. What is salvation? Who is to decide?

In our slavery to outworn metaphors of human interaction, we make the empowerment implicit in biblical meanings unavailable to human beings as they are. Our ecclesiologies, with the action metaphors they imply, are empty. And this makes the churches vulnerable to those who would define their functions for them. The sad picture of churches conforming to popular stereotypes for the sake of institutional survival is a sign of this weakness, a sign that we have little idea of the fundamental nature of our problem, and much less of what to do about it.

Clearly we must take a step back from the immediate problems of church strategy and try to find some new conceptual equipment. Here contemporary social science may help. There exists a rich array of heuristic devices for grasping the nature of social interaction which the churches have barely begun to use. For our immediate purpose we will try to clarify and improve upon Marx's notion of "consciousness," false and otherwise.

Social theorists such as Talcott Parsons, Robert Bellah, and many others have been pointing out for years that human interaction is vastly more multi-leveled and complex than the operative political (and thus, ecclesiological) metaphors of any given society may suggest. This has always been true, but it has not until the present generation been systematically understood. Political-ecclesiastical metaphors (monarchic, heterarchic, etc.) are crystallizations at particular points of time of certain understandings of social interaction reached for the purpose of making decisions of a certain type. But below the level of manifest polities a complex symbolic process is going on out of which new formulations will in time be thrown up in response to new sensitivity, needs, and pressures. The total human action system, including all that is involved at the levels of organism, personality, society and culture, involves much more than any given polity can contain or express. There is a vast (but, of course, finite) range of possibilities in the form of available symbols and metaphors which may or may not coalesce into social structures, depending on the vision of human purpose, or intentionality, which runs through the system.

The social reality about us may usefully be grasped, therefore, on the analogy of a system of energies and communication links which somewhat resembles the popular image of the computer. Hence the label "cybernetic" often applied to social theories developed in this direction from Talcott Parsons' basic "structural-functional" model. A cybernetic model for social interaction has been elaborated in detail by Karl W. Deutsch in his book *The Nerves of Government*.[3] Deutsch argues in fact that in the cybernetic model we have more than a mere analogy for grasping social process; we have a conceptual scheme or paradigm which is as revolutionary in its potential as the theory of evolution was for biology. The cybernetic model draws attention to an aspect of social process never systematically understood before. Society can be seen as based on constantly reproduced, yet varied, patterns of "information," systems of symbols connected by communications links. What is more, the cybernetic model offers the possibility of accounting for direction and purpose on the social level. Certain impulses activate certain social "circuits." New combinations of symbols become socially potent. Old combinations break up. The social system works through "input," and "feedback." Given enough flexibility it can be to a degree self-corrective.

It is no accident that the cybernetic paradigm suggests the comparison between the social network and a system of "consciousness." Not only is the science of cybernetics constructed on the analogy of physiological brain function (in which "consciousness" consists of internal messages, symbols, or labels for states of the system itself), but the functioning of shared symbols in society is inseparable from its "consciousness" as we experience it. One even finds in Deutsch a cybernetic restatement of Marx's idea of "false consciousness": a network of inadequate symbols and feedbacks which lead to highly misleading ideas about the real state of the social system. Unquestionably, the processes of "consciousness" in nations, classes, or other social groups are of vast importance for understanding manifest institutions and behavior. We have only begun to use this tool.

But now we reach the second step in the argument. Precisely at the level of "consciousness" in modern society something new is happening. The systems of shared symbols by which increasing numbers of people live are beginning, so to speak, to come unstuck from established social structures and ideologies. "Consciousness" is less than ever before the mere product of economic circumstances or systems of production. Here we are beyond Marx, for this liberation of consciousness from economic determination is apparently happening apart from any single or specific revolutionary theory. Increasingly, creative imagination is being brought to bear, not upon engineering modifications of existing political hardware, but upon creating new kinds of inter-personal sensibility, new responses to external social reality.

All this means that we can be in touch with consciousness at a level which anticipates more concrete social and historical developments. We can study the storehouse of symbols where the human future is made. It has often been observed that some forms of modern art anticipate general public sensibility and style by twenty years. The new consciousness now emerging, if its circuits can be mapped, might enable us to do this for a still wider range of human phenomena. Nothing guarantees, of course, that events will echo conscious anticipation, or that we are in touch with the right levels and sectors of consciousness. But here, at least, is a tool capable of breaking the hegemony of the given. If the process of consciousness were well enough understood, one might even hope to influence it constructively: not by means of propaganda (for Goebbels, like Machiavelli, would have understood this) but by dealing therapeutically with the kinds of alienation and the kinds of possibility the new consciousness contains.

As it exists in the Western world now, the new consciousness is a highly diversified phenomenon with what is nevertheless a certain underlying unity. Movements as varied as the now splintered "New Left," the commune movement among both young people and others, the rock and drug cultures, are certainly included. But so is the new kind of unrest and openness which grips many men and women, young and old, which seemingly has little to do with the movements mentioned. Yet there is also a kind of network of recognition (for the sensitive, not limited to outward and visible signs like long hair) among persons who share the new awareness, a network which tends to bypass channels of communication in the established social system.

It would probably be safe to say that the new consciousness is as pre-theoretical as it is pre-structural. It has as yet thrown up no really coherent or persuasive analysis of social and personal alienation. It has produced no stable program for overcoming human disempowerment. Both Marxist and mystical (both Eastern and Western) patterns are discernible, of course, but by and large the new consciousness is an openness in search of meanings, not a movement with an established world-view. Such openness makes the movement vulnerable to ideological hucksters, of course. But this vulnerability is different from that of church leaders who internalize extraneous meanings out of emptiness and despair. It would be better to call the openness of the new consciousness a vulnerability to hope: provided, of course, that a genuinely infectious hope is available.

New Consciousness and Ecclesial Embodiment

If the vision of human society and possibility found in the Bible has anything to offer, that fact is now obscured by the alliance between this tradition and anachronistic, alienating frames of reference. The future of the biblical tradition in the West may well depend on whether deeply traditioned people can both learn from the new consciousness and speak to it. By becoming part of the new sensibility, and at the same time influencing it, the bearers of tradition might make this revolutionary movement aware of its own world-historical nature, thus forging out of counter-consciousness a new kind of *ekklesia*.

The Bible and the new consciousness have in common the conviction that the root of human difficulty lies in a collective, largely self-imposed, disempowerment. People alienate themselves from their human birthright of responsibility by projecting the image of power upon the collective, its symbols, its processes and its products. Power becomes extrinsic to human beings in their daily thinking, working, and loving. They become blind to the disempowering consequences to others of what they do, because they are not aware of the power that is in their hands in the first place. The biblical vision and the trend of the new consciousness agree that human history must move toward a realization in which both the generation and the use of power can be intrinsic to the constantly rewoven fabric of human sharing.

Creation, creativity, the thrust of history. The power of God seeks embodiment in covenant, incarnation in community. In response, people grope together toward a network of symbols, a shared awareness, adequate to contain both the vision and the responsibility. They know that the only authentic power is in the sharing, and that the sharing is the authentic source of new empowerment. The power of God-ruling enters into the Body of Christ, and yet the Body looks forward to the Holy City that is not yet. At the center of everything is the "we-relation" of the Messiah together with his people, inseparable as they are in Jewish eschatology, given, as in the New Testament vision, to be an ecstatic anticipation of the Messianic age in the midst of human beings for whom the Messiah is yet to come.

These biblical traditions can live if those who bear them can grasp the nature of the pre-structural intersubjectivity of human communities today and enter into it. It is one thing, of course, to call for dialogue, but another to envision its practical form. For if the dialogue is to be more than occasional conversation it must be embodied in concrete relationships. Only so can it generate a social reality tangible enough to be called *ekklesia*. The *ekklesia* we seek must emerge out of continuing practical interaction between those who know the content of the tradition, and those who, without knowing its content, are nevertheless living out some of its meanings. We propose that this interaction consist (at least as it is seen analytically) of two basic movements, a kind of systole and diastole, which can be called coalition and reflection.

Coalition means what it says. The bearers of tradition must enter into long or short-term alliances with crystallizations of the counter-consciousness wherever it can be discerned that biblical meanings, however symbolized, may be potentially present. Concretely such meanings may be found in the peace movement, in efforts of varying ideological commitment to achieve racial justice, in moves toward a more responsible use of the environment, and so on. The point is that tradition must enter into material, working coalition with such movements. Only so can those who know the content of the message earn the right to a hearing. The alliance actually entered represents, in fact, the only historically meaningful interpretation of the tradition's meaning. The commitment to action in itself is a necessary step through which the bearers of tradition themselves begin to learn its contemporary sense.

Coalition involves risk, above all the risk of identification between biblical tradition and secular ideology (in the sense of ideas which are an expression of class, party, racial, or other interest). Yet apart from taking this risk, there can be no link between tradition and the power of historical transformation. The decision to enter this or that coalition is, in effect, the decision that this or that ideological interest for the moment coincides in practical terms with the general human interest. And if this is so, the ideological character of the movement in question cannot be absolute. Rather it is a trait of limited self-understanding which the biblical tradition may possibly help to enlarge. The tradition may be a catalyst through which the consciousness of the movement becomes more aware of its true world-historical (that is, eschatological) nature.

But at this point the dialectical movement of reflection must begin. Involvement with some particular historical expression of counter-consciousness will not leave the content of the tradition unaffected. The bearers of tradition will begin to experience a certain "feedback," indicating how the tradition is being heard and understood. This "feedback" will inevitably modify the self-understanding of the originally traditioned people. The tradition-bearers will discern not only the meanings of "significant others." They will also be hearing echoes of significant (and perhaps previously repressed) levels of their own consciousness. The result will be a new chapter in tradition, a new set of meanings related to the old not merely (or even mainly) by verbal congruity but by passage through a process of variously committed intersubjectivity.

Clearly this means, in so many words, that tradition will come to owe a significant debt to non-believers. Metaphors of human empowerment whose origins lie entirely outside the circle of faith will begin to play a role in faith's self-awareness. This may, in turn, make easier new commitments to coalition which will elicit still more feedback, still more metaphors. And all this without lessening the tension between "belief" and "non-belief." Such tension, in the present cultural situation, is essential to the dialectic, for it defines the risk which belief must now run to recover its own content.

The reader will now recognize two things. What has been sketched here in effect extends the cybernetic paradigm to describe the input of a new, yet traditionally wired, component into the symbol-circuits of the counter-consciousness. And, true to the cybernetic analogy, the character of this component, as well as that of the entire system, is modified by the interaction. But understand this symbol network as containing the thresholds of historical awareness today, envision this intersubjective consciousness as the place where future events and structures take form, and the input of the Christ-tradition becomes a modern reenactment of incarnation in a new fullness of time.

Second, the reader may discern that what has been sketched here could serve as a description of interactions that are already going on in typical local congregations. Every man and woman in the pew experiences some awareness of alienation, some sense of unactualized possibility, some sharing of a configuration of symbols that points beyond what is. However much the church as institution may legitimate the status quo, to be in church at all is to participate in a rudimentary counter-consciousness. To celebrate, to counsel, to preach, moreover, is to enter into risky coalitions with the hundreds of ideologically self-interested life projects lived out by "church members," in the hope that self-interest, by the aid of the Word, may recognize community with the interest of humanity. And as for non-belief, theoretical, operational, or any other kind, it is present in both pulpit and pew. But tradition is often best understood as non-belief hears it. For what passes for belief among us is often nothing but a misplaced loyalty to the institution which refuses to hear the message being spoken as it really is: either as expression of false consciousness or as a Word of life.

Thus "ekklesia as counter-consciousness" is not a model for a new kind of church organization. It is a proposal for a new way of thinking about what ecclesial embodiment involves. The level at which we have been speaking is pre-structural, and the strategy involved, if that is the right word, will not in the nature of the case produce new visible forms. It will rather, for the moment, "unpack" what the interaction between tradition and society already means. It will seek out those points in common human awareness where the future is being made, and thereby place the biblical vision in a position to participate in shaping the social forms that in fact emerge. These forms, ecclesiastical structures among them, may or may not resemble the arrangements we now know. It is important only that they have a quality of openness to the message, which must be re-symbolized again and again as living social reality in the midst of history.

Notes

1. See *The Making of a Counter-Culture*, Doubleday, 1969. Likewise, there is a link between this idea and Charles Reich's "consciousness III" in *The Greening of America* (Random House, 1970) which appeared after the present paper was completed and in the hands of the editors. My remarks about Roszak also apply to Reich. My concern is with "consciousness" as a heuristic category for getting at a particular level of social reality and only secondarily with specific manifestations of new consciousness in contemporary life. The latter, of course, offer symbols which may be indispensable for the theologian who wishes to grasp the pre-institutional social reality in its present forms.

2. Extensive documentation of such relationships has recently been furnished by Guy W. Swanson in his book *Religion and Regime* (University of Michigan Press, 1967). Swanson classifies "religions" and "regimes" in terms of the degree to which they understand the ultimate power to which they are related as immanent in the structures and symbols of the society. The scale of immanence ranges from the divine-right monarchy in which every social institution is seen as a direct expression of the ruler's personality and will, to the heterarchic social order in which political decisions are made by the interaction of many organized interest groups, and in which no person, institution, or symbol is identified with the power the society represents. Roughly speaking, the monarchic sort of regime produces metaphors which lead to hierarchical, sacerdotal polities, such as that of the medieval church at its zenith, while the heterarchic sort of regime produces metaphors which lead to polities of the Presbyterian or Congregational type. Between the two extremes, for Swanson, lie a series of other possibilities, "commensal," "limited centralist," and "balanced," which tend to produce intermediate ecclesiastical possibilities, such as the Anglican or Lutheran.

3. MacMillan, 1963.

II

Hermeneutics

4

The Servant Lord and His Servant People

The themes of church conferences are often no more than umbrellas which, if they conveniently gather together the business to be discussed, also tend to shelter the discussions too effectively from sunlight and storms. Fortunately, the more cloying slogans are generally short-lived, and therefore harmless. Truth will out in the long run even if it does not appear at a given ecumenical meeting. On the other hand, if a conference theme does express a biblical truth uncommonly well, the fact that the meeting is soon over may render that insight quite prematurely out of fashion. Perhaps it is no service to a really good idea for it to be made the watchword of an international conference. Yet there is the possibility that time, place and thinking may coalesce in such a way that the insights of a congress may become a permanent gain for Christian thought.

Presbyterians and others have every right to turn such suspicious, yet hopeful, thoughts toward the theme which the World Presbyterian Alliance has chosen for its 18th General Council this summer in Sao Paulo, Brazil. "The Servant Lord and His Servant People" is obviously a carefully drawn formulation. But what are its chances of leading the Reformed churches to a vital discussion of the issues facing the Church? What are its chances of promoting Christian truth now and later, rather than acting to confuse the issue with words which have only a temporary usefulness?

The hypothesis of this article is that the power of a theme to open our eyes and press us forward depends not on the publicity program connected with it but on the extent to which it is a thought-galvanizing window into biblical revelation for our day. If it is the latter, then there is no need for people to remember the exact form of words, or even the name of the organization that set up the meeting. The New Testament itself, speaking to a Church newly sensitized to apprehend this aspect of its message, carries the program forward. The question we need to ask, then, is not: how catchy and alliterative is this theme? but: how deeply does it penetrate into the thought of the Bible? How truly will the thought underlying it body itself forth from the New Testament when the carefully selected, though human, words chosen to express it are forgotten?

Probed from this perspective, the Alliance theme stands up well. But critical readers will want the point proved, as far as can be, from the exegetical standpoint. This article is intended to indicate some of the exegetical considerations that led to the choice of the Sao Paulo theme, and to suggest some paths that further research might take.

Surveying the Critics: Skepticism about Skepticism

Any survey of the vast literature on the Suffering Servant must reach the conclusion that the servant motif is pervasive in the Bible, and unquestionably christologically important. Yet a closer reading of the literature will indicate that no biblical category is as confusing as this one when it comes to specifying how, exactly, the motif fits into the structure of scriptural thought. Our interest is particularly in the New Testament evidence. Is the servant theme to be classified there as a messianic title, or merely as a prophetic figure of speech? Is Jesus Himself responsible for the New Testament use of it, or is this usage primarily the work of the early Church? And what *is* the New Testament usage? The references are surprisingly vague. One might indeed ask the question, What are we talking about when we speak of the "servant motif"? Do we mean the use of one or more Hebrew or Greek words? Or do we mean an idea or circle of ideas? Or do we mean references to a certain set of passages in Isaiah--themselves not certainly delimited?

Literature which devotes itself to answering such questions is remarkably sparse. One must mention T. W. Manson's *The Servant Messiah*, and L. L. Carpenter's *Primitive Christian Application of the Doctrine of the Servant*, along with the interesting treatment of the subject that appears in Lohmeyer's monograph, *Gottesknecht und Davidsohn*. There are also the studies of individual Greek terms in the

Wörterbuch, the most notable of which, on *pais*, by Zimmerli and Jeremias, has appeared in English as a separate volume, *The Servant of God*. A useful independent word study is at hand also in Brandt, *Dienst und Dienen im Neuen Testament*. But this virtually completes the list of books, of which the writer is aware, which dwell substantially on the New Testament problem. Very useful references to the subject, of course, appear in a host of other volumes. Among the most useful are W. Manson's *Jesus the Messiah*, and the writings of Vincent Taylor, including his latest, The *Person of Christ in New Testament Teaching*. And one must not forget certain sections in H. Wheeler Robinson's *The Cross of The Servant*. But a book which does justice to the significance of the servant theme in New Testament thought as a whole has yet to appear.[1]

In spite of the difficulty of this problem from the technical standpoint, it is impossible to escape a very powerful impression that the servant motif is central to the New Testament message. Many scholars have offered this opinion. The most recent, and perhaps the most important, is Oscar Cullmann who, in his *Christologie des Neuen Testaments*, puts the matter very strongly. For him, the servant motif is the classical expression of what Jesus meant in the New Testament age as the one in whose earthly work and in whose sacrificial death the whole *Heilsgeschichte* comes to its central point (p. 80). Cullmann's general impression furnishes us with a text. Our task, therefore, is to ask whether this impression can be defended. The best way to begin is to weigh the impression against the case that has been made on the other side.

First of all, two facts are evident about the biblical materials, for all to see. The first fact is that the allusions to the servant motif in the New Testament are surprisingly few in number and vague in their actual reference to the Isaianic poems. And not only that, but in the Gospels, where the most important references are found, the passages in question often occur in strata which the form critics ascribe to the secondary reflection of the early Church. The second fact is that very little use of servant christology is apparently made in the later development of New Testament theology. In particular, we do not find it--at least in its original form--on Greek soil. As Jeremias puts it, "The title *pais theou* was at no time on Gentile Christian territory an accepted designation of the Messiah (it is not found in Paul); the titles *kyrios, christos, huios tou theou* were there preferred" (*The Servant of God*, p.

84).

With these data in mind, scholars such as F. C. Burkitt in *Christian Beginnings*, W. Bousset in *Kyrios Christos*, the editors of *The Beginnings of Christianity* (F. J. Foakes-Jackson and Kirsopp Lake), and such contemporary writers as W. G. Kümmel, in *Promise and Fulfillment*, have tended to play down the importance of the servant motif. Instead of the full-blown servant christology of which Cullmann speaks, they have seen in the New Testament references to suffering and humiliation the rather embarrassed attempt of the hellenistic church to construct a credible account of the ministry of the Son of Man in the light of the crucifixion. Isaiah 53 is used only to the extent that it is useful in constructing sayings which make sense of the passion. This usage may be very minimal indeed, as Foakes-Jackson and Lake would have it, and this may explain the vague and scattered character of the references to the servant songs in the Gospels. Moreover, this theory also explains the absence of a later and more developed servant christology. There never was any true servant christology, these writers in effect argue, for there was no need of one. Once a coherent life of Jesus had been constructed, there was no further reason to use Isaiah 53 for theological purposes.

It is worth noticing how consistent this skeptical position is. It insists that there is no clear reference to the Suffering Servant in the early strata of the Gospels, and that Isaiah 53 cannot then have had any influence on the mind and action of Jesus. It accounts for the defection of the disciples at the time of the crucifixion by insisting that the eleven could not have been in any way prepared for the fate of their Master. The later disappearance of references to Isaiah 53 is explained by considering the contribution of this passage to New Testament thinking to have been almost incidental. The influence of the servant motif upon the Testament is localized and encapsulated at a single point: the very earliest historical rationalizations of a Christian community on which Hellenistic influences were increasingly being brought to bear.

One cannot but feel dissatisfied with this. Indeed, Bousset himself finds it remarkable that the influence of Isaiah 53 upon the Christian imagination was so momentary and so slight (*Kyrios Christos*, pp. 69-72). There are many points at which the judgment of these skeptical writers might be attacked. These critics may not be correct about the historical stratum of certain sayings in the Gospels. There is always the question of why the early Church, if it was determined to inject an explanatory category into its accounts of Jesus' ministry, did not do so more definitely and clearly. But all such considerations--persuasive or not as they may be--are matters of exegetical preference and personal judgment.

The point at which the detractors of a servant Christology are really vulnerable lies in their use of a gratuitous presupposition about what the "servant motif" means, and how it is used. They assume that the question the Church tries to answer is always: how can it be explained that the Messiah, the Son of Man, had to suffer? This is indeed the way the question would have presented itself to both Jews and Greeks outside the Church. And it is the form in which we habitually pose the question today when examining the development of the messianic consciousness of Israel. We assume that we are dealing with the juncture of two previously incompatible ideas: messiahship and suffering. But there is very little evidence in those texts which may contain references to the Isaianic servant songs that the problem looked at all this way to the apostolic community itself. The servant motif, in brief, is not used in the manner which the skeptical hypothesis requires. In fact, we may go on to say something else. The assumption that "servant" passages appear only where the stock question of reconciling messiahship with suffering is raised, greatly narrows our vision of the possible influence of the Isaianic songs on the Gospel text. Not only may there be references to the servant figure in contexts where other motifs are also at work, but servant passages other than Isaiah 53 (the only one in which the servant's suffering is particularly emphasized) come into view. Once we shake off the quite unjustified critical assumption that everything may be traced to the early community and its intellectual difficulties, a whole new world of interpretation opens up. The possibility that Jesus Himself may have had something to do with the introduction of the servant theme into Christian thought is immediately revived.

A Second Look at the Evidence

What impressions do we get if we examine the various NT allusions to the servant idea just as they stand? Repeatedly, we find that the messiahship of Jesus is expressed so naturally and integrally in servant language that the servant motif itself is made to express the full implications of divine Lordship. From the earliest moment to which we can trace references to the servant songs, the ideas of messiahship and service are already perfectly fused. The Gospels do not speak of a Messiah who must, under the circumstances, suffer. They speak of a Messiah whose service to God is broader than suffering, whose service is the very substance of his messiahship rather than an apparent contradiction of it. To paraphrase William Manson, the servant motif is itself a phase of the messianic idea; the phase appropriate to Jesus' own place in the *Heilsgeschichte* (*See The Servant Messiah*, p. 174)

This interpretation is in harmony with the fact that nowhere in the Gospels is "Servant of God" used as a title to be placed alongside other possible messianic titles. As William Manson has pointed out (Ibid., p. 111), the servant motif is always a "predicate", and, one might add, an inseparable one. That is to say, the servant motif is always used to specify what Jesus has in mind when one of the recognized messianic titles is used. Mark 10:45 is typical: "For the Son of man also came not to be served but to serve, and to give his life as a ransom for many." Although this "prediction" of the passion--with its parallels and other similar passages--is one of the chief pieces of evidence for those who trace the whole matter to historical rationalization by the early Church, no saying could be less appropriate for the purpose the critics suggest. Service and suffering are not ideas rudely juxtaposed with the doctrine of the triumphant, heavenly Son of Man. They are inseparable from the Son of Man's fundamental nature. It is remarkable, too, how often the servant motif is used in connection with the verb "to come," an expression having quasi-technical status in the language of messianism. This again implies that service and suffering are not defined as the temporary vicissitudes which a heavenly being meets during his earthly sojourn. To say that "the Son of man came...to serve..." is to connect this service integrally with the Messiah's essential eschatological function, and to suggest that the Messiah is always in some sense a servant both in heaven and on earth.

The scope of a short article will not permit detailed treatment of many similar passages. The same pattern of thought, however, is clearly present in the Synoptic accounts of Christ's baptism, where, quite apart from the importance of this incident for understanding the attitude of the Church to the "coming" of the Messiah, we find the ideas of messiahship and service inextricably intertwined in the combined reference to Psalm 2:7 and Isaiah 42:1 in the words, "Thou

art my beloved son (*pais*); with thee I am well pleased." Again, a similar collocation of thought appears in the account of Jesus' appearance in the synagogue at Nazareth, in which He reads Isaiah 61.1-2, a passage listed by many scholars among the servant songs:
"The Spirit of the Lord God is upon me, because the Lord has anointed me to bring good tidings to the afflicted; he has sent me to bind up the broken-hearted, to proclaim liberty to the captives, and the opening of the prison to those who are bound...."

But perhaps the most notable and unmistakable example of all is the Johannine presentation of the washing of the disciples' feet: "Jesus, knowing that the Father had given all things into his hands, and that he had come from God and was going to God, rose from supper, laid aside his garments, and girded himself with a towel. Then he poured water into a basin, and began to wash the disciples' feet, and to wipe them with the towel with which he was girded' (John 13: 3-5). All the elements are here. The footwashing is recounted as the act of Him who "had come from God and was going to God." It is thus precisely a messianic act. No theological backtracking is needed to connect an *idea* of the Suffering Servant with an *idea* of the Messiah. This is the Messiah in action "in the form of a servant."

The result of this very brief survey is to suggest that there is ground for giving the servant motif a central position in the primitive christology and to suggest that Cullmann's impression is precisely right. In the broadest sense, the service of the Son of Man is His coming into history. It is His part in the *Heilsgeschichte* taken as a whole. The "form of a servant" may not be a temporary vesture at all, but only that aspect of His eternal messiahship that is most appropriately brought out in our present epoch. Hence the formulation of the first part of the theme for Sao Paulo is an appropriate one: 'The Servant Lord....' What is expressed in these words is not merely a dramatic contrast, and not merely the paradox of grace. It is the proclamation of the Christian message in the form of an image which can once again grip the human imagination, as it did in the life and death of the Servant Himself.

From Christology to Ecclesiology

On the basis of our present knowledge of the history of the New Testament text, the question of how much of the servant Christology is to be ascribed to Jesus and how much to the early Church is impossible to answer. Nor is it theologically very important to try to find out. If the remarks we have made about the meaning of the servant figure in early Christian thought are close to the truth, we must credit at least some contribution to the process to both Jesus and his followers. To ascribe everything to the rationalizing reasoning of the primitive community, as we have seen, is to interpret the servant texts with unjustifiable shallowness and artificiality. Yet to say that Jesus himself interpreted His messianic mission in servant terms is not to say that the servant motif did not pose a serious challenge to the primitive Church. It was one thing for the disciples to have grasped the significance of a Servant-Messiah. It was quite another for them to work out the terms of their own existence as a Servant People.

The argument, then, that since the disciples fled in confusion at the time of the crucifixion, Jesus could not have spoken of His ministry in servant terms, falls to the ground. The servant sayings were not intended to prepare the disciples in a practical way for the Master's death. They were intended to state the nature and meaning of His messiahship. Hence, with the crucifixion, the problem of interpreting the servant christology was just beginning. That christology now had to live in the fabric of the messianic community.

We must start by insisting that the existence of this messianic community was, in principle, included in the Servant *kerygma* from the beginning. The Messiah was, by definition, the supreme exemplification of the existence of Israel in world history. (The *ebedh* material from which the kerygmatic imagery is drawn clearly has both individual and communal significance.) To proclaim the Messiah was to proclaim the messianic people as well. Not that the people was to be identified with the Messiah, but that the two were included in the same continuous act of God. Paul expresses this point very clearly in 2 Cor. 4-5: "For what we preach is not ourselves, but Jesus Christ as Lord, with ourselves as your servants for Jesus' sake." Here both "Christ" and "ourselves" are direct objects of the verb "we preach." Thus there is some kind of carry-over in the servant motif from Christology to ecclesiology. How is this understood in theological terms? Certain passages in the Gospels express the relation between the Messiah and His people in terms of a kind of repetition of form. The disciples are asked, for example, whether they can share the baptism with which Christ is to be baptized. There is an analogy between the service of the

Messiah and the service of His people. Yet it is also clear that this form is not to be repeated in any one-dimensional way. Nowhere is it suggested that the disciples should have exposed themselves to execution on Golgotha with their Lord. The Church does not occupy Christ's unique place in the *Heilsgeschichte*. The people of God must work out the meaning of its service in terms of its distinctive role in the history of salvation. There is, therefore, room within the servant motif both for saying that the Church shares and continues Christ's work, and for saying that Christ's work uniquely and vicariously makes the work of the Church possible.

The earliest evidence we have of reflection by the primitive community on its own nature appears in the opening chapters of Acts. It is extremely significant that the basis of this reflection is a view of the history of God's actions in which the servant Christology plays a central part. The well-known *pais* christology of Acts 3: 12-26 and 4:23-30 is cast precisely in the role of furnishing a historical and eschatological background for the Church's self-understanding. "Men of Israel," Peter says, "why do you stare at us, as though by our own power or piety we had made him walk?' There follows a rapid history of Israel culminating in the crucifixion and followed by a call to repentance. The whole is anchored between two references to the *pais theou*, Jesus (vv. 13 and 26). It is because the apostolic community takes part in this salvation history, and knows Him who is Lord over it, that the acts of healing in Solomon's porch are possible.

Acts 4: 23-30 is a further instance of the same complex of thought. The whole of salvation history is again sketched in as background to the life of the Church. The *pais* christology is explicitly connected with the messianic hope of Israel by way of a quotation from Psalm 2: 25, and by the phrase "thy holy servant Jesus, whom thou didst anoint" (v. 27). Yet this passage marks a development over the *pais* passage in Acts 3 in that it is even more concerned to establish an organic connection between the servant role of Jesus and the life of His people. The strong community concern of the passage is indicated at the outset: "When they were released they went to their friends" (v. 23). Further, there are two very significant innovations in the use of language here which are worth our attention. In the first place, the word *pais* is now applied to David (v. 25) as well as to Christ. In effect, this is to give the *pais* Christology a firmer grounding in the history of Israel: to say in a new way that Christ and His people are theologically inseparable, and to prepare in schematic form for more precise applications of the servant motif to the life of the New Israel, the Church. The second innovation is the use of a word which can be translated, "servant" with reference to the apostolic community itself, the word *doulos* (v. 29). This is the beginning of a most important process by which the New Testament writers broaden the servant motif in order to use it in connection with various aspects of the Christian life.

The word *pais* is used in the New Testament only to refer to Jesus (Matt. 12: 18 in addition to the above), and, by extension of the messianic idea through the line of salvation history, to David (Luke 1:69; Acts 4:45) and to Israel (Luke 1:54). Christians are never called *paides theou*, nor is the Church ever specifically designated a *pais*. But it is against the background of the *pais* christology, linked as it is with the history of God's dealing with Israel, that the New Testament writers use a number of other words to relate the servant motif to specific situations: words such as *doulos, diakonia, leitourgia, latreia, huperetes*. *Doulos*, for example, is used very often to speak of Christians in terms of their individual careers in such contexts as Rom. 1:1, Phil. 1:1, and so on. *Leitourgia*, with its sacrificial background, often designates the cost to the individual of relating him or herself meaningfully to the Christian community, as in 2 Cor. 9:12, Phil. 2:17 and 2:30. *Latreia*, most notably in Rom. 12:1, has a similar meaning, with a special emphasis on the contrast between the world and the Church. *Diakonia* is used mainly in contexts dealing with discipline within the ecclesial community in passages such as Acts 6, Mark 10.45 and parallels, and seems to reflect the idea of mutuality in service by using a conception that has a definite eucharistic flavor. *Huperetes*, finally, appears to have the fascinating meaning of one who is grasped by God's word for some special mission, as in Luke 1:2, and I Cor.3:5.

By the use of such terms, the messianic actions of Jesus are carried over dynamically into the life of the Church, while undergoing changes appropriate to the fact that the Church is not to be identified with Christ, but has its own place in salvation history. In interpreting these various Greek words, we must then remember the matrix out of which they come. The relation of these terms to the Isaianic *ebedh* is certainly not by way of direct philological equivalence. Nor is it due to the influence of the Septuagint. Apart from *pais*, only *doulos* is significant among the Septuagint translations of *ebedh*. The relation is the pragmatic result of the fact that such terms are used in a living community in an attempt to specify the relation of that community to the work of a Messiah understood in *ebedh* terms.

We are not surprised, either, to find that the circle is completed. Some of these terms that first came into prominence in community situations are eventually applied to Christ. This is no doubt true of *diakonia* and its cognates in Mark 10:45, Luke 18:27 and Matt. 20:28, and of *leitourgia* and its cognates in Heb. 8:6. In one most important passage, which we will discuss later, *doulos* also appears to be used this way. The servant christology, in short, grows along with the growing development of the servant community.

Paul's Innovation: The *Soma* Figure

If all this is true, we can see how false it is to say that the *ebedh Yahweh* christology makes no impact on the later development of New Testament thought. It is true that the word *pais*, as applied to Christ, rapidly disappears. But in the use of this word, we are seeing only the basic, fundamental, kerygmatic image of messiahship as it was early understood by the apostolic fellowship. With that point established, the thinking of the Church moves on to a fuller expression of what it means to be a messianic people. Yet its thinking still moves within a Servant Lord-Servant People complex.

For this movement, some new conceptual equipment is needed. Christology and ecclesiology can only proceed along these lines if the Church finds a terminology for denoting the concrete reality that has entered into the world with God's Messiah, in such a way that the participation of the Church in that reality is made manifest, and in such a way that the servant character of the Messiah and His Church is clearly indicated. Such a terminology, it may be proposed, is provided by St. Paul in his image of the "body of Christ." Both the need for such a figure, and its appropriateness for the use suggested are evident upon a moment's reflection. In addition, a few less well-known facts about the use of the term *soma* in Paul, and its background in the Septuagint, will make this appropriateness even more evident.

Soma in Paul without exception denotes a kind of neutral, though living, continuum in which various positive or negative influences may act. *Soma* never stands alone, nor is it ever, except in one doubtful instance, the subject of a sentence. The word is always the direct or indirect object of a verb or preposition.[2] Thus such expressions as "the body of Christ" and "the body of this death' are common in Paul. Such usages indicate that the "body" may serve either God's purposes or some other purposes depending on the way it is oriented. When we add to this the interesting fact that in the Septuagint *soma* can mean a person who is a servant or slave,[3] and that in the book of Job the word is supplied by the Septuagint translators where there is no Hebrew equivalent in contexts apparently having to do with suffering brought on by the will of God,[4] the usefulness of the term for carrying out a theological extension of the servant motif jumps into immediate prominence. It may be proposed, indeed, that this is the fundamental need which lies behind Paul's use of the word.

It is not surprising, either, that this theological extension of the servant motif would have been Paul's work. As the one Apostle who had not been part of the apostolic circle from the beginning, Paul would naturally have seen the theological presuppositions and assumptions of the apostolic community a way that the original eleven could not. He would unquestionably have been interested in thinking out the meaning of the Servant Lord-Servant People motif for the life of the individual, and for questions of life and death; and equally unquestionably he would later have been concerned for applying this thinking directly to problems of church organization. Both concerns are found most prominently in Paul's use of the word *soma*. Perhaps the genesis of his thinking is indicated in I Cor. 15. The first eleven verses of this chapter describe Paul's relation (through the Damascus Road experience in which Christ and the Church are already identified) to the basic *kerygma* of the apostolic community, a message expressed here in "suffering servant" terms: "Christ died for our sins according to the scriptures....' The remainder of the chapter seeks to understand the meaning of this message for the problem of personal resurrection that both Paul and the Corinthians found most pressing. And just here the breadth of the motif as the early Church understands it becomes clear. God does not only let his Servant die for humanity's sins. He raises his Servant up to newness of life. So it is in the *soma* we share with our fellow Christians. If it is indeed the body of Christ that we share, God raises us up in Christ's own resurrection. Servanthood is not left behind. The Servant Lord thus rules in the heavens.

A progression from the basic kerygmatic servant theme to its reexpression in the *soma* figure is equally evident in Paul's handling of the problem of church organization. Here our basic text is Rom. 12: "1 appeal to you therefore, brethren, by the mercies of God, to present your bodies as a living sacrifice, holy and acceptable to God, which is your spiritual worship" (v.1). Again the individual Christian is implored to allow him- or herself to be grafted into the continuity of the Servant Lord and His Servant People (chs. 9-11). The result in this case is that Christian's service is articulated in accordance with his place and function in the "one body" which has "many members." The introduction to this Pauline reflection, with all its momentous ecclesiological consequences, is expressed in terms of service and sacrifice (*latreia*). The respective roles of Christ and his people in this total work are their true service, and all of this comes to a specific focus in the communal relations to which Paul then turns his attention.

It may be conjectured that thinking of this sort also lies behind the christological "hymn" of Phil. 2:5-11, whether or not Paul is its author. It must not be overlooked that the hymn itself is set in the context of a discussion about the life of the Church. In this chapter as a whole, we thus have precisely the same pattern of thought as that of which we have been speaking: the basic kerygmatic utterance around which is built a theology of messianic peoplehood. The proclamation of Christ is never complete unless both the Messiah and his people are included. Our special interest in this passage is of course aroused by the unique use of the word *doulos* in verse 7. Nowhere else in the New Testament is this term used of Christ Himself. As we have seen, it is generally employed by the early Church to characterize the service of the individual Christian. Yet we need not be surprised, for *doulos* translates *ebedh* no less than 327 times in the Septuagint. Of course, the expression here is "the form of a servant." *Doulos* falls short of being made a messianic title in the strict sense. The word is used--just as so many of the servant terms in the Gospels are used--to describe a specific mode or form in which the significance of the Messiah appears. In this case, the stress appears to be on the utter identification of the Messiah with the lot of humankind, bound down as we are to ignorance, temptation and mortality. But the reference of Phil. 2 to the servant christology does not depend on this one word *doulos* alone, but on the form and structure of the whole passage. The hymn in its entirety reflects the kerygmatic image of which we have been speaking. The whole of the descent, humiliation, suffering, death, resurrection and exaltation of the Son of Man is his "service." So it is that the full significance of *doulos* is the meaning the word gains from being taken up into a wider context. "Slavery" to human conditions is transformed into divine "sonship." By implication, something similar may be the destiny, in Christ, of the *douleia* we experience in our own humanity.

Theological Consequences

These suggestions must suffice to indicate the role which the servant figure may possibly have had in the development of New Testament thought. If what has been said is near the truth, the implications for a revitalization of theology--and Reformed theology in particular--may be considerable. Some of these implications may be briefly listed: not in such a way as to conclude a discussion, but to open one. Jeremias remarks that *pais* disappears as a christological term in the devotional language of the patristic Church after the fifth century (*The Servant of God*, p. 84). It is not too much to say that it has been generally overlooked in christological usage ever since. Bishop Stephen Neill in his recent book *Who is Jesus Christ* proposes that "the explanation" is probably to be found in the fuller understanding of the meaning of the resurrection that came to the Church as it lived in fellowship with the risen Jesus. "There must be no turning back from this experience to that which the disciples had had before the resurrection" (p. 53). This may be a true assessment of the inclination to spiritualize the faith that has marked Christian thought in all ages, but one may wonder whether it is theologically sound. The servant christology of the New Testament is really more than a reflection of the experience which the disciples had had before the resurrection. The evidence presented in this article at least suggests the appropriateness of the servant christology for Christ risen and ascended, as well as for Jesus in the flesh. It suggests that because Christ takes humanity with Him to the right hand of God, the servant Messiah becomes a permanent part of Godhead. It may even be that this terminology can be applied equally well to Christ preexistent. Surely this is no place for dogmatism, and it must be admitted that explicit scriptural evidence for such assertions is hard to come by. Nonetheless, such passages as Luke 24:30-31 ("He took the bread...and gave it to them. And their eyes were opened....") and I

John 4:2 ("Every spirit which confesses that Jesus Christ has come in the flesh is of God...") seem to point in this direction. It is heartening indeed to find that many expositors of our time, notably Karl Barth, have reached the conclusion that the servant christology points toward an essential aspect of the doctrine of God.

If so, we are in the presence of a most interesting avenue of approach to the whole question of mythology and meaning the Bible. From the standpoint of the servant figure, there need be no separation between the cosmic descent and ascent of God and the life of his people through history. It is not a question of relating the one to the other by some sort of philosophical schematism. The two are proclaimed as one thing. To preach God's people is to preach the Messiah and vice versa. God's power is revealed by, and is materially (somatically) present in, their shared servant life. Moreover, the Suffering Servant is then the Lord of history, and God's people, by their participation in his work, have the key to the meaning of events now and for ever.

There is material here for recovering the majesty of the heritage of Calvin and the other reformers, and also for deepening that heritage where it has been shortsighted. Without the slightest degree depreciating God's sovereignty, we may perhaps be led to say that humanity can share the cosmic service through which God's sovereignty is revealed on this earth. Without in any way dulling the cutting edge of the doctrine of sin, we come to see how God can transform the meaning of our human slavery by wrapping it in a garment of His encompassing purpose. The whole of human culture, religious and otherwise, indeed may become open to us in a new way when we grasp the fact that God once knelt at the feet of human beings to point them toward a destiny in heaven. Perhaps these are some of the consequences Karl Barth had in mind *The Humanity of God* when he wrote, "If Calvin had only carried his thoughts further on this subject, as far in his christology and in his doctrines of God and of predestination, and in his ethics, Geneva would not have become such a gloomy matter" (pp. 26-27).

Notes

1. A new work, *Jesus and the Servant*, by Morna D. Hooker (S.P.C.K., 1959) has come to the writer's attention since this article was set in type. Miss Hooker argues that Isaiah 53 as such makes no doctrinal contribution to New

Testament christology above and beyond the general New Testament use of the whole Old Testament servant motif. There is, Miss Hooker claims, no "servant figure" in either the Old Testament or other Jewish writings with which Jesus could have been "identified". Rather the meaning of the "servant songs" is one with the pattern of suffering and exaltation characteristic of Israel's history, as that pattern is interpreted by the prophets. The writer is warmly appreciative of Miss Hooker's careful study, and especially of the progress she makes toward showing the connection of the servant motif with the whole history of God's people interpreted as *kerygma*. He cannot quite agree, however, with her systematic elimination of Isaiah 53 from a position of doctrinal influence in the New Testament apart from a few late passages, e.g. some in I Peter.

2. See Rudolf Bultmann, *Theology of the New Testament*, vol. 1, p. 197.

3. See Gen. 36:6; Tobit 10:10. 2 Macc. 8:11, and also, on this whole question, Kendrick Grobel, "Soma as 'self, person' in the Septuagint," in *Neutestamentliche Studien für Rudolph Bultmann*, Alfred Töplemann, Berlin, 1954, p. 52.

4. Compare the handling by the Septuagint translators of the Massoretic Text at Ps. 39:6; Job 6:4, 33:24, 40:32; and the references to "my servant job" in ch. 4:2.

5

Paul Ricoeur on Biblical Interpretation

"Beyond the desert of criticism, we wish to be called again.[1] So wrote Paul Ricoeur toward the end of *The Symbolism of Evil* (1960). This longing is shared today by the many for whom historical- critical method remains indispensable, but at the same time insufficient to bring us to a "post-critical moment" of openness to the biblical summons. Is there an intellectually responsible way through the critical sands, always shifting, sometimes abrasive, to an oasis where bedrock, with its springs of water for the spirit, once again appears?

The Promise of His Work

Ricoeur's commitments, associations, perspective, and program combine to make us turn to him with hope. "Listener to the Christian message,"[2] occasional preacher,[3] dialoguer with biblical scholars, theologians, and specialists in the history of religions,[4] Ricoeur is above all a philosopher committed to constructing as comprehensive a theory as possible of the interpretation of texts.[5] A thoroughly modern man (if not, indeed, a neo-Enlightenment figure) in his determination to think "within the autonomy of responsible thought,"[6] Ricoeur finds it nonetheless consistent to maintain that reflection which seeks, beyond mere calculation, to "situate [us] better in being,"[7] must arise from the mythical, narrative, prophetic, poetic, apocalyptic, and other sorts of texts in which human beings have avowed their encounter both with evil and with the gracious grounds of hope.

Ricoeur's work approximates positions often seen as poles apart. With biblical "conservatives" he shares reverence for the sense of the given text, the "last" text.[8] He is not concerned to draw inferences from the text to its underlying history, to the circumstances of writing, to the spiritual state of the authors, or even to the existential encounter between Jesus and his followers.[9] Indeed, Ricoeur, in his own way, takes the New Testament for what it claims to be: "testimony"[10] to the transforming power of the Resurrection. Moreover, all the literary genres of the Bible, not just certain passages of special theological import, are media for this revelation."[11]   On the other hand, Ricoeur attracts "liberals." With them, he opposes every form of "dogmatic mythology,"[12] political or ecclesiastical authoritarianism, intellectual obscurantism or false consciousness. Moreover, he shares the liberal concern that interpreters of the Bible should be in dialogue with all that has gone on in "the great romance of culture"[13] and all that is happening in contemporary experience. In Ricoeur's hands, interpretation is always confronted with the perspective of "counter-disciplines": physiology, psychoanalysis, sociology, anthropology, linguistics, the history of philosophy.[14] The sense of the text is taken seriously in the midst of other constructions of the human condition that enter into dialogue with it.

In this writer, then, we have a combination of elements which could be fruitful in assisting a critical, yet post-critical, biblical theology into being. But the expectations we bring to Ricoeur's work must not betray us into holding him responsible for matters outside his professional vocation. Ricoeur's chosen task is not the exposition of the Bible within the community of faith. It is, rather, the rational clarification of human existence in the world. The famous "wager" to which Ricoeur has given currency is a philosophical wager that, following "the indication of symbolic thought", "I shall have a better understanding of man and of the bond between the being of man and the being of all beings." And, he continues, "I bet at the same time that my wager will be restored to me in the power of reflection, in the element of coherent discourse."[15] Yet biblical texts play an indispensable role in this philosophical program. They, above all, provide the "indication" out of which Ricoeur's thought comes.

We must not expect, however, that reading Ricoeur will be an experience comparable, say, to reading Paul Tillich. Tillich the theologian addressed himself directly to problems of faith. Moreover, he often did this in a way accessible to the general reader, or at least to the student of religion or theology. Ricoeur, particularly of late, has written mainly about philosophical problems for the philosophically trained. His contributions to biblical hermeneutics must be extracted from these sometimes difficult writings. The difficulties of Ricoeur's writing stem from his singleminded pursuit, with appropriate terminology, of whatever intellectual issue is at hand, often beginning somewhere near the middle of the argument. Seldom does he pause to take stock, or to explain his overall perspective. Often his essays and lectures traverse a field of complex allusion. Woe to the reader who does not at first recognize the set of concerns packed into such a phrase as "a post-Hegelian interpretation of Kant." He or she will not be told: at least not outright, although the context will help. The field of reference which is Ricoeur's intellectual habitation ranges over the whole history of Western philosophy. Perhaps the most commonly mentioned names are Aristotle, Kant, Hegel, Husserl, and Heidegger. Spinoza, Gabriel Marcel and Karl Jaspers are not far behind. One meets some theologically famous names, too: Rudolf Bultmann, Karl Barth, Gerhard von Rad, Jürgen Moltmann, and others.

The theologically concerned reader of Ricoeur will be helped if he or she can see some paths through the philosophical thickets, some relations between the different Ricoeurian ideas, some connections with familiar intellectual landmarks. In the work of this uncompromising thinker, who is also in his own way a believer, we may find important clues to unraveling the conundrums of contemporary consciousness, and particularly to understanding how people today may be "called again" by texts which, to their surprise, summon them to reckon with realities whose existence they had forgotten.

The Problem and the Project

We are deaf to the Word today. Why? The root of the problem, for Ricoeur, lies in a general loss of sensitivity to symbolic language in modern Western civilization. We construe the world in terms of the Cartesian dichotomy between the self as sovereign consciousness on the one hand, and an objectivized, manipulable nature on the other. We conceive ourselves as authors of our own meaning and being, set in the midst of a world there for us to interrogate, manipulate, and control. We make language our instrument in this project in a way that sees artful equivocation, richness of meaning, or metaphysical range as a liability to be overcome rather than a gift to be treasured. We dismiss realms of meaning beyond the literal either as confusion to be cleared up by the logician or as emotional embellishment to be kept in check. It is hard for us to see scriptural language, full as it is of figure, metaphor, vision, and myth, as having to do with reality.

What lies behind this literalism? Not merely the need of science and technology for precise terminology. The language of empirical inquiry has its indispensable place. Behind our deafness to biblical language, rather, lies the fear that such language alienates us from our hard-won modern autonomy and freedom. Ricoeur repeatedly refers to a triad of writers--Marx, Nietzsche, and Freud--who have taught us to suspect that religious language may not mean what it appears to say at all: that it may be a coded version of something else of which we would prefer not to be aware. The problems we have with the mythological vehicle of the scriptural message, with the cultural distance between ourselves and the biblical texts, are relatively surmountable in comparison with the fear, before we even begin to "translate" scriptural language into modern terms, that there may be nothing behind it but the ideologizing of the class status of its authors, the resentment felt by losers in a power struggle, the outcome of oedipal conflicts in persons whose desires are repressed by cultural prohibitions. And even if scriptural language is somehow exempt from such suspicious reductionisms, we suspect our own hidden motives for cleaving to it. Details of the Marxian, Nietzschian, and Freudian criticisms have since been revised, and even discredited, on economic, anthropological, or psychological grounds. But in their basic thrust and convergence, these thinkers have become part of our culture. They still accuse us and all transcendence-language users, of "false consciousness." Marx, Nietzsche, and Freud continue to have power for us, indeed, because they are instigators of a positive affirmation of the human which we are bound, if we are honest, to respect. In different ways they seek to overcome the domination-submission-alienation syndrome of which religious language in the past has been a vehicle. In this they both anticipate and echo Feuerbach, who taught that we, by articulating our consciousness in religious language, are in fact emptying our human substance into an illusory absolute. Theologically, we should call this idolatry. Hence we are bound to agree that any new articulation of faith must pass through and beyond the "hermeneutics of suspicion," not slide around it.

But how is this to be done? There are many contemporary forms of protest against unidimensional interpretations of the human, against the insistence that all properly cognitive discourse must reflect a univocal subject-object Cartesian mentality. Many of these forms of protest are theories of the interpretation of the signs human beings produce in the business of being human: poems, dreams, fantasies, myths, works of art, patterns of culture, and so on. The trouble is that there are today so many conflicting theories of the interpretation of human signs that we do not know where to begin. The debate about the symbolic dimension of expression, about the relation between literal and figurative uses of language, is an academic battleground. The realm of language, Ricoeur writes,

> is an area today where all philosophical investigations cut across one another.... Language is the common meeting ground of Wittgenstein's investigations, the English linguistic philosophy, the phenomenology that stems from Husserl, Heidegger's investigations, the works of the Bultmannian school and other schools of New Testament exegesis, the works of comparative history of religion and of anthropology concerning myth, ritual, and belief--and finally, psychoanalysis."[16]

We live in a time in which there are many different realms of hermeneutical discourse isolated from each other, a "conflict of interpretations" of human expression no one of which can grasp the human condition as a whole. Thus Ricoeur must not only seek, through his own hermeneutic, to open our ears to the scriptural call. He must work out his theory of interpretation in dialogue with a hundred others. He must search for something like a "unified field theory" of the explication and understanding of texts. An early program for his attempt to do this appears in the final chapter of The Symbolism of Evil. Ricoeur there proposes a philosophical analysis of symbolic and metaphoric language intended to help us reach a "second naïveté" before such texts.[17] The latter phrase, which Ricoeur has made famous, suggests that the "first naïveté," an unquestioned dwelling in a world of symbol, which presumably came naturally to men and women in one-possibility cultures to which the symbols in question were indigenous, is no longer possible for us. But we may approximate that state: of course with a difference.

> For the second immediacy that we seek and the second naïveté that we await are no longer accessible to us

> anywhere else than in a hermeneutics; we can believe only
> by interpreting. It is the "modern" mode of belief in
> symbols, an expression of the distress of modernity and a
> remedy for that distress.[18]

How can philosophy help? In two ways. First, the philosopher, so to speak, follows the believer through, trying to model conceptually what is involved in staking one's life on the message. "The philosopher adopts provisionally the motivations and intentions of the believing soul. He does not 'feel' them in their first naïveté; he re-feels them in a neutralized mode, in the mode of 'as if'. It is in this sense that phenomenology is a reenactment in sympathetic imagination."[19]

Then, secondly, the philosopher tries to account conceptually for the lived possibility of the believer's symbolic world. In The Symbolism of Evil this endeavor takes the form of a "transcendental deduction" of symbols in the Kantian sense. Transcendental deduction "consists in justifying a concept by showing that it makes possible the construction of a domain of objectivity."[20] The philosopher tries to show that the symbol is in fact a reality detector, that it enables us to discern a human possibility that could not be discerned in any other way. "In fact, the symbol, used as a means of detecting and deciphering human reality, will have been verified by its power to raise up, to illuminate, to give order to that region of human experience...."[21]

It is instructive to compare this project with that of Bultmann, who in Ricoeur's view does not take the expressive power of scriptural language, with all its mythological content, seriously. Bultmann, the philosopher argues, jumps directly from the kerygma stated in the barest terms, "that God has drawn near to us in Christ," to faith understood equally starkly as the surrender of my self-will that I may stand radically before God.[22] This leap ignores the question of how the actual language of the Bible--in its various literary forms--conveys content, sense, meaning, to which we respond.

Bultmann defines myth as the application of subject-object language to realms where it does not belong. He thereby capitulates conceptually to the Cartesian perspective instead of asking what myth is in its own nature. His own statement, "God has acted," Bultmann maintains, is not itself mythological. That is, it is not inappropriately "objectifying" in the way much biblical language is. But then, having reduced the fullness of biblical discourse to bare kerygma, Bultmann feels no need to ask how the actual language of the Bible functions as a vehicle of meaning. The sheer statement that "God has acted" in this or that event is, for Bultmann, not subject to historical or hermeneutical inquiry, because such language does not convey meaning to faith in and through what it says. Rather it derives meaning from my radical response in faith to it. I do not apprehend a sense, a content, independent of my response. There is thus no concern on Bultmann's part about how the language of the gospel refers to transcendent reality. His exposition jumps over the question of how biblical language conveys sense.[23]

Bultmann has been betrayed into this refusal to deal with biblical language, Ricoeur thinks, in part by a misreading of the modern situation. It is not the case that our familiarity with technology and science renders us incapable of responding to myth. It is not the case that we must reduce myth to some modern, nonmythological conceptuality such as Heideggerian existentialism (which, after all, escapes neither Marxist, Nietzschian, and Freudian suspicion nor the contemporary conflict of interpretations) in order to be grasped by what it is saying. On the contrary, we desperately need the "fullness of language," the whole range of scriptural expression, to find ourselves. Myth's literal function must be suspended, but its symbolic function must be affirmed.

If anything, Ricoeur's position is closer to Karl Barth's. It is not the mythological vehicle of the gospel message that prevents us from hearing. It is the message itself that we cannot hear, because our linguistic impoverishment has deprived us of the possibility of articulating such realities as radical evil or grace-empowered hope. Symbolic, metaphorical, mythological language gives us the capacity to bring experiences of a certain kind to awareness, thereby creating the basis for reflective reasoning. Without the Word which comes to us from beyond ourselves, we cannot know the realities the Word conveys. Ricoeur denies the notion of an independently existing conceptuality in us, ready to receive the message once it is demythologized, which plays so large a part in Bultmann's thought. We need the texts of Scripture to activate the questions, to generate the experience, in us. As he puts it,

> ...to preach is not to capitulate before the believable and unbelievable of modern man, but to struggle with the presuppositions of his culture, in order to restore this interval of interrogation in which the question can have meaning. If we consider the problem of secularization no

longer only as the end of mythology and the religious era
...but as an estrangement from the kerygmatic situation
itself, then the whole problem of myth will from this point
of view become immediately changed.[24]

The Philosophical Background

We must now examine more closely the perspective in which
Ricoeur carries on his project of opening the way for the text of
Scripture to restore the "interval of interrogation" in which the question
of faith can be heard. In the philosopher's own words, his thought,
early and late, has led him to

> a permanent mistrust of the pretensions of the subject in
> posing itself as the foundation of its own meaning. The
> reflective philosophy to which I appeal is at the outset
> opposed to any philosophy of the Cartesian type based on
> the transparency of the ego itself, and to all philosophy of
> the Fichtean type based on the self-positing of that ego.
> Today this mistrust is reinforced by the conviction that the
> understanding of the self is always indirect and proceeds
> from the interpretation of signs given outside me in culture
> and history and from the appropriation of the meaning of
> these signs. I would now dare to say that, in the coming to
> understanding of signs inscribed in texts, the meaning rules
> and gives me a self. In short, the self of self-understanding
> is a gift of understanding itself and of the invitation from
> the meaning inscribed in the text.[25]

This passage repays careful reflection. A recent expositor has called
the perspective set forth here and elsewhere a "hermeneutic
phenomenology."[26] In what sense, first, is Ricoeur's thought a
"phenomenology"? And second, in what way is this phenomenology
"hermeneutic"?

Ricoeur has been both translator and critical expositor of the writer
generally credited with founding modern phenomenology, Edmund
Husserl.[27] He represents a particular form of phenomenological
movement which brings him into dialogue with thinkers such as Gabriel
Marcel, Karl Jaspers, Maurice Merleau-Ponty, Martin Heidegger and
others. Phenomenological philosophies have in common a procedure

clearly palpable in the above quotation: an approach to reality through the structure of consciousness, through the way we constitute every object in the act of consciousness directed toward it. Consciousness is not locked up in itself. The content of consciousness always consists of "intentions," that is, it is always consciousness of *something*. We approach the world through the reality the world has in consciousness. In order to understand how this takes place, we must "think away" all the assumptions we have derived, let us say, from the method of the natural sciences, about what is or is not "real," and attend to the way consciousness "constitutes" a world of distinct essences, of this and that, out of the manifold impressions given in awareness. And when we ask how our world takes shape we are at the same time asking how the self takes shape. The phenomenological method, although it begins on Cartesian ground, questions Descartes's dichotomy between the self as inquirer and manipulator and the world as object to be studied and manipulated. The self takes shape in its way of giving shape to the world which appears in consciousness.

Such a method can obviously be applied to phenomena of any kind, and can investigate any sort of self- or world-constituting activity. Maurice Merleau-Ponty applied the method to the problem of perception, wrestling with the complexities arising from the fact that we are embodied consciousness: we perceive and constitute the world through an instrument that is also a part of the givenness of that world. Ricoeur, in *Freedom and Nature*,[28] adapted the phenomenological method to an inquiry into the will. The philosopher thereby announced a theme that has run in various ways through all his subsequent work. The choice of will as subject matter has been providential for Ricoeur's dialogue with theologians and biblical scholars, for this question opens up that with which the ancient Hebrews were concerned, in contradistinction to the Greek preoccupation with knowledge. Out of concern for the will one reaches not only the whole range of existential issues, but also those questions which arise from human involvement on the one hand with evil, and on the other hand with hope.

But what makes Ricoeur's use of the phenomenological method "hermeneutic"? It has already begun to be so incipiently in the author's explorations of the will. Ricoeur thinks away naive, subject-object oriented, assumptions about willing, to explore the way both "self" and "world" are constituted in the movements of decision, action, and consent. Over against the phenomenon of willing is something we call nature: the realm from which the phenomenon of consciousness arises, a realm which can be studied by various objective, i.e., non-phenomenological, sciences valid and useful within their own spheres of discourse. Biology, physiology, sociology, and psychology all study the phenomenon of willing in objectivizing ways. There is, Don Ihde argues,[29] an implicit hermeneutic here. Ricoeur is saying that we "read" our limits in the objectivities we meet, by consulting the signs that are generated as these givens of the human situation are explored by "counter-disciplines." Such disciplines limit the disciplines of phenomenology, and are themselves limited by the phenomenological.

This "reading" of the meaning of my consciousness by reference to objective accounts of that consciousness sets up a relation which Ricoeur calls "diagnostic," a designation which rests on a reversed medical analogy. The doctor supplements his objective observations by my accounts of how I feel. But in daily life, my consciousness is illumined and given symbolic form by systems of discourse which deal objectively with what I experience. The most striking example is my own birth. I have no memory of that experience, thus I can hardly constitute it phenomenologically, but I have made my birth a part of my consciousness by internalizing what I have been told about it. So it is that the perspectives and vocabularies of the empirical sciences may illuminate my understanding of the world I constitute in consciousness, just as 1, by inquiry into my world-constituting intentionalities, may disclose some of the implicit phenomenologies these sciences contain.

Here, it seems, are the conceptual roots of Ricoeur's conviction, expressed in the quotation at the head of this section, "that the understanding of the self is always indirect and proceeds from the interpretation of signs given outside me in culture and history and from the appropriation of the meaning of these signs." It is fundamental to any adequate understanding of Ricoeur to note that his phenomenology is so constructed as to be open to the "signs" generated by "counter-disciplines," and indeed to read the meaning of human existence "on" a world full of such expressions generated by the natural and social sciences, as well as in the history of culture. Ricoeur's approach, then, to disciplines such as the history of religions (as represented by his friend Mircea Eliade and others), psychoanalysis (with particular reference to Freud), linguistics (de Saussure, Jakobson), and anthropology (Lévi-Strauss and various other structuralists) is set within this diagnostic relationship. The "signs" through which we constitute our being arise in realms of discourse which can and must be studied objectively to see how such "signs" work. Hence Ricoeur's conversation with the "counter-disciplines" is ultimately controlled by his phenomenological concern with respect to the authentic figures of the will, a concern which deserves also to be called existential.

The nature of Ricoeur's existentialism will be seen more clearly if it is contrasted with Heidegger's. While Ricoeur believes that I situate myself in being by appropriating its "signs" in texts such as those also studied by counter-disciplines, Heidegger takes a short cut. The latter defines our being as that being which asks the question of being, as the being which has its being in understanding. Ricoeur comments,

> One does not enter [Heidegger's] ontology of understanding little by little; one does not reach it by degrees, deepening the methodological requirements of exegesis, history, or psychoanalysis: one is transported there by a sudden reversal of the question. Instead of asking: On what condition can a knowing subject understand a text or history? One asks: What kind of being is it whose being consists of understanding? The hermeneutic problem thus becomes a problem of the Analytic of this being, Dasein, which exists through understanding.[30]

By contrast, Ricoeur takes the long route. He proceeds by way of the hermeneutical "detour." Repeatedly in his writings he has recourse to a formulation derived from Jean Nabert:

> Reflection is the appropriation of our effort to exist and our desire to be, through the works which bear witness to that effort and desire.[31]

And again:

> The ultimate root of our problem lies in this primitive connection between the act of existing and the signs we deploy in our works; reflection must become interpretation because I cannot grasp the act of existing except in signs scattered in the world. That is why a reflective philosophy must include the results, methods, and presuppositions of all the sciences that try to decipher and interpret the signs of man.[32]

There is a further dimension to this hermeneutical turn. Something about this "effort to exist and desire to be" forces us to have recourse to symbols. The "self-positing ego" ends in futility because in our being there is a structural "disproportion" which makes us fallible, and, in the end, involves us inevitably in "fault." Here we have a perspective that challenges traditional phenomenology deeply. In *Fallible Man*[33] Ricoeur argues that our desires--for possessions, for power, for honor--overrun the limits of our finitude. Happiness is the presence to human activity of the end which will fulfill it. But there is never any proportion between desire and its ends. When will I have enough? When will my authority be sufficiently established? When will I be sufficiently appreciated?

> Human life is in danger of forgetting or of losing its goal
> by reason of the indeterminate character of the threefold
> demand where the self searches for itself; and the strange
> thing sometimes happens that the more our action becomes
> precise and even technical, the more its goals become
> remote and elusive.[34]

Hence I am subject to a "self-infinitization" in which I may lose myself. I can only articulate this experience symbolically.

In The *Symbolism of Evil*, Ricoeur traces this avowal from the primitive symbol of "stain," through the incorporation of symbols into narratives we call myths, and into a dialogue among great cycles of myths. He finds that the Adamic myth recapitulates and synthesizes many of the themes of other myths, and thus functions as the most fully adequate imaginative expression of what is involved in our implication with evil. The myth enables us to say what our conceptual equipment cannot say. On the one hand, we know evil acts as our own: they are expressions of our freedom. Yet at the same time we experience evil as something already present in our finite situation in nature and history. The dialectic of freedom and nature is repeated. Only a work of the imagination can reconcile, and enable us to grasp, this antinomy. The philosopher is thus given, for further reflection, what he or she cannot arrive at by reflection alone: the notion of "the servile will," the will that uses its freedom to abdicate freedom, being both responsible and not responsible for the outcome.[35] Experience is read not directly but through its figurative expression.

But not all symbols function at the conscious level. Ricoeur interprets

Freudian psychoanalysis as a hermeneutic discipline in its own right, a hermeneutic which suggests that certain symbolic forms conceal from everyday consciousness more than they reveal. Yet, through interpretation, these forms may be made to disclose repressed aspects of our being. Ricoeur's *Freud and Philosophy* details the psychoanalytical critique of the pretensions of the cogito. Symbols, especially those derived from the reconstruction of dreams, are the forms in which primitive experience, opaque desire, come to expression. As Ricoeur writes of this work,

> It is with *Freud and Philosophy* that I broke away from the illusions of consciousness as the blind spot of reflection. The case of the symbolism of evil is not an exception, one tributary of the gloomy experience of evil. All reflection is mediated, there is no immediate self-consciousness. The first truth, I said, that of the "I think, I am," remains as abstract and empty as it is invincible; it has to be "mediated" by the ideas, actions, works, institutions and monuments that objectify it. It is in these objects, in the widest sense of the word, that the Ego must lose and find itself. We can say, in a somewhat paradoxical sense, that a philosophy of reflection is not a philosophy of consciousness, if by consciousness we mean immediate self-consciousness."[36]

But, if this is so, Ricoeur can counter Freud's "hermeneutic of suspicion" with a "hermeneutic of belief." The philosopher demythologizes the naturalism of Freud's model of the unconscious, and finds in the resulting language field a ground for the reintroduction of Hegel's idea of "spirit." just as there can be, through interpretation of symbol, an inquiry back toward the origins of consciousness, so there can be in the figures of language, of the intersubjective, of culture, a forward movement of humanity toward its limits. We can have eschatological, as well as primordial, symbols.

In this procedure there is the same decentering, even "dispossession," of reflective immediacy we have previously observed: a demand that we must make a "detour" through the symbolic world. If we do this, learning from Hegel, we will discover that the world of the symbolic is expressive of humanity's relation to being. Myth contains more than philosophy can comprehend. In the end, certain privileged myths may speak to my broken condition. "I describe this new dimension as a call," Ricoeur writes, "a kerygma, a word addressed to me.... To believe it is to listen to the call, but to hear the call we must interpret the message."[37]

Interpreting Biblical Texts

With this haunting quotation, we are ready to see what Ricoeur does with biblical texts. But we must approach this subject with a reflection on what is involved when the interpretation of texts is carried on in the context of a philosophy which leaves the ego chastened, dispossessed. From the start, Ricoeur rejects the assumption that to understand a text is to understand the intention of the author, or, alternatively, to grasp the text's meaning as it was grasped by the first hearers or readers who shared the author's cultural situation. This view, worked out in the nineteenth century by such writers as Schleiermacher and Dilthey, Ricoeur calls "romanticist hermeneutics." He is opposed to it on the grounds that it fails to account for the difference between acts of consciousness and written texts.[38]

Reading a written document is different from being part of a living dialogue. Even in dialogue we can never, except by inference, penetrate the interiority of other persons. But there is at least a common situation, a common cultural context.

When discourse assumes written form, however, it begins a new career. The meanings of written discourse are no longer bound, if they ever were, to the intentions of authors or the apprehensions of first readers. Written communications have a logical, as opposed to a psychological or existential, sense. "Sense" is not a mental event, but an ideality capable of actualization in an infinite series of mental events. Here the philosopher is following the Husserl of the *Logical Investigations*, as well as the logic of Frege, in an antihistoricist trend which favors "the objectivity of meaning in general." As Ricoeur puts it, unmistakably,

> Not the intention of the author, which is supposed to be hidden behind the text; not the historical situation common to the author and his original readers; not the expectations or feelings of these original readers; not even their understanding of themselves as historical and cultural phenomena. What has to be appropriated is the meaning of

the text itself, conceived in a dynamic way as the direction
of thought opened up by the text.[39]

But, as the end of this quotation shows, Ricoeur does not intend
simply to oppose "romanticist hermeneutics" with a theory as one-sided
in the other direction turning on a purely objectivizing approach to the
text and the data it contains. Whereas in Schleiermacher and Dilthey
"interpretation" means *Verstehen* understood as a kind of empathy with
the writer, Ricoeur is in search of a theory of interpretation in which
"understanding" seeks help in objective "explanation" and returns
deepened and enlarged. Indeed this dialectic, worked out in the context
of Ricoeur's general theory of discourse in *Interpretation Theory*,
underlies what the philosopher now tells us about understanding biblical
texts.

In developing his ideas Ricoeur has a habit at first disconcerting but
in the end helpful: he constantly reoccupies familiar ground with new
conceptualizations and terminologies. Throughout what follows we see
again and again the fundamental notion of a "divestment" or
"dispossession" of the sovereign self and a search for signs through
which to "appropriate the effort to exist and desire to be." The total
self-implication of the subject in such signs is now called "testimony."
Testimony generates forms of discourse which can be called revelatory.
"Revelatory" discourse is "poesis" which we, given the needed critical
judgment, can receive and live out as "testimony" in turn.[40] We will
try to show that this dialectic, carried out over generations, closely
corresponds in the retrospective mode to Ricoeur's account of Gerhard
von Rad's "tradition history" and, looking forward, to the philosopher's
understanding of Jürgen Moltmann's "theology of hope."

Let us follow each step of this dialectic in turn. What, first, is the
nature of the process which produces a text which claims to be a
revelatory witness to truth? What, secondly, goes on as we today try
to judge whether, and in what way, such a text fulfills its claims? And,
finally, what happens when we receive such texts as the Word to us,
making the testimony of the text our own? In tackling the questions this
way we must, as always, make connections. We must elicit from
Ricoeur's writings an order of presentation not explicit there but
nevertheless justified by the structure of his argument.

Testimony in the Making

First, then, how does a revelatory text come to be? At first sight, this question seems to violate Ricoeur's stringent prohibition against looking behind the written document to some process of consciousness. It is clear that the philosopher will allow no inference from text to author's personal inwardness. For the text to be taken as testimony, as revelatory, judgment must be made about objective characteristics, above all what Ricoeur calls in *Interpretation Theory* its "self reference," its claims to represent an "I" or a "we" engaged in a certain past "event of discourse."[41] All discourse is articulated as event, and understood as meaning. In the initial moment, there is a dialectic between the event and the meaning. Afterward the event is surpassed by the meaning. As Ricoeur says, "The experience as experienced, as lived, remains private, but its sense, its meaning, becomes public."[42] Yet, "We are able to give a non-psychological, because purely semantic, definition of the utterer's meaning. No mental entity need be hypothesized or hypostasized. The utterance meaning points back toward the utterer's meaning thanks to the self-reference of discourse to itself as an event."[43]

We can say, then, that in elucidating how biblical discourse comes to be as "testimony" we are not psychologizing but interpreting the text's self-reference. What then does the claim of biblical discourse to be "testimony" mean? It claims to be discourse in which, in a moment of total unity between event and meaning, an individual or community has found its "effort to exist and desire to be" interpreted to the point of total dispossession or divestment of the claims of the self. Every attempt of the self to be a source of meaning in its own right has yielded before the question, "Who is God?" And the event or combination of events in which this has happened has been interpreted as a "trace" of the Absolute at this historical moment. The event of testimony is set down in discourse which claims, by its own self-reference, to be of this character.

It is important to see that no individual or community comes to the moment in which the event and meaning are fused in witness without some existing symbolic tradition with which to express the meaning of this fusion. Indeed we may say that, even within the period of production of the biblical documents, the lived juncture of event and meaning repeatedly evaporates. Event and meaning must then be reconnected through recourse to mediating meanings. ". . . It is always reconnected through recourse to mediating meanings. "...It is always possible," Ricoeur writes, "to mediate the relation of meaning and event by another meaning which plays the role of interpretation with regard to their very relation."[44] Charles Sanders Peirce furnishes Ricoeur a model of this triadic relation. Every relation between a sign and an object, Peirce says, can be explained by means of a sign which plays the role of interpretant with regard to their relation. An open chain of interpretants is thus possible. The manifestation of the absolute in persons and acts may be indefinitely mediated by means of meanings borrowed from tradition, a process which in turn generates new tradition.

This quiet philosophical account inadequately conveys the passion with which Scripture itself bears witness to the interpretative process. For the issue is always, "God or an idol?" The adjudication of this question in Scripture often takes the form of a rhetorical trial, in which the prophet calls upon the true witnesses to come forward. Ricoeur is particularly fond of Isaiah 43:8-13.

> Let them bring their witnesses to justify them, and let them hear and say, It is true. "You are my witnesses," says the Lord, "and my servants whom I have chosen, that you may know and believe me and understand that I am He" (9b-10a).

And, of course, the ultimate testimony is understood to be the total engagement of a life, as in the case of the New Testament understanding of Jesus as faithful witness, variously portrayed in the different Gospels, and of the witness of the primitive community to him. The entire ministry of Jesus is portrayed as a trial, culminating in the trial before Pilate which is, especially in the Fourth Gospel, only an episode in the great cosmic trial of truth, an immense contest between God and the "prince of this world."

In all this, Scripture makes metaphors of the process by which the sacred text itself takes form. The interpretative process is a life or death matter for the faith community. The process, which clothes every juncture of event and meaning with means for an articulation which will faithfully transmit the meaning, closely corresponds to Gerhard von Rad's account of the rise of historical consciousness in "tradition-history." Ricoeur's interest focuses on the "intellectual activity which presided over this elaboration of traditions and led to

what we now call Scripture."[45] This intellectual activity generates
"history" in at least three senses. First, it joins diverse traditions of
testimony (the Abraham, Jacob, and later Joseph cycles, for example)
to the original core of Deuteronomy 26:5b-6b, thus creating a saga
celebrating the historical founding action of Yahweh. Second, the
theological work needed to do this is itself a historical process which
illuminates the sense in which the founding traditions are apprehended
as historical. In its own way, indeed, this theological work involves a
certain critical awareness: "sources are juxtaposed, schisms maintained,
and contradictions exposed..."[46] "The tradition corrects itself through
additions, and these additions themselves constitute a theological
dialectic."[47] And third, it is through this work of reinterpreting its
own traditions that Israel as a community develops a historical
consciousness, thereby becoming a historical reality. If it is true, as
critical scholarship suggests, that Israel did not exist as a unified entity
until the amphictyonic period after the settlement of Canaan, then we
can say that "by elaborating this history as a living tradition, Israel
projected itself into the past as a single people, to whom occurred, as
to an indivisible totality, the deliverance from Egypt, the revelation on
Sinai, the wandering in the desert, the gift of the Promised Land."[48]
Israel's identity as a people is "inseparable from an endless search for
a meaning to history and in history."[49]

The third approach to historicity generated by Israel's intellectual
activity is, of course, the stage of the interpretation of tradition: its
critical (sometimes prophetically critical) reworking which is precisely
what keeps the community going. We can thus graft onto Israel's
traditioning the critical process by which that tradition is reinterpreted
as a living testimony that produces the New Testament, and in which
the New Testament is in turn interpreted in the life of the Church.

For Ricoeur, "the Christian fact is itself understood by effecting a
mutation of meaning inside the ancient Scripture."[50] The kerygma is
a rereading of the Old Testament. Furthermore, "the kerygma, by this
detour through the reinterpretation of an ancient Scripture, enters into
a network of intelligibility...Jesus Christ himself, exegesis and exegete
of Scripture, is manifested as *logos* in opening the understanding of the
Scriptures."[51] But secondly, and already within the New Testament,
a correspondence is effected between "the interpretation of the Book
and the interpretation of life."[52] "Saint Paul creates this second
modality of Christian hermeneutics when he invites the hearer of the

word to decipher the movement of his own existence in the light of the Passion and Resurrection of Christ. "[53] In this way scriptural understanding is related to the community's "total understanding of existence and reality." And finally, we see that the process just described produces a text which itself must be interpreted. This third stage of interpretation takes up into itself the preceding stages, with the additional problem generated by modern historical consciousness, that we must distinguish "what can be understood and received as word of God, and what is heard as human speaking."[54] In this modern perspective we discover that what we have to interpret is the testimony not for the most part of eyewitnesses and followers of Jesus in the days of his flesh, but "the witness of the apostolic community. We are related to the object of its faith through the confession of its faith."[55]

The Critical Moment

With this observation we find ourselves in the midst of the second question raised by Ricoeur's philosophy of testimony. On the one hand, we modern interpreters of Scripture may see ourselves as part of the traditioning process at work from the start. Event and meaning are constantly re-fused by the introduction of interpretative categories which reactivate previously unused strands of tradition, categories which must withstand the prophetic-cosmic "trial" to determine whether God is speaking through them. But is the cultural problem the same for us as it was for the ancients? Is there not a different kind of historical distance between ourselves and the events on which the original testimonies were based? Ricoeur, in his interpretation of von Rad, fastens on the German scholar's insistence that understanding Scripture today is a matter of "recreating the intellectual activity born of this historical faith."[56] Is the "intellectual activity" of the modern critic anything like that of the prophets of old, or of those who recorded the great trial of truth between Pilate and Jesus? Or, let us put the matter still more pointedly. In *The Historian and the Believer*[57] Van A. Harvey uses the metaphor of judicial proceedings to illuminate the different relationships between evidence, warrants, and conclusions involved in the "field encompassing" discipline practiced by the modern scientific historian. Is there any relationship between this critical discipline and the theological trial of truth which distinguishes true and false testimony for the modern reader of the Bible?

This extremely difficult question may not find a direct answer in

Ricoeur. The philosopher's procedure is not to confront the text with the question whether it bears testimony to "what really happened" in the modern sense, but rather to ask what the text means by its assertions about the testimony it bears. He wishes to ask how Scripture witnesses in its various literary genres. Does prophecy work the same way as narrative? Does a wisdom saying witness in the same way as a hymn, or miracle story, or parable? The question posed to us, the issue at our trial of truth, is whether we are confronted to the point of divestment of self by the claims of Scripture, rather than simply informed by schemas of the meaning of "revelation" derived from our culture, or from various forms of ecclesiastical authority. The phenomenological procedure of thinking away extraneous reality claims is of course palpable here. But in Scripture we confront a counter-reality-claim. which demands that we reappropriate our "effort to exist and desire to be" in terms which propel us into a new world of "freedom in the light of hope."

How does this happen? We come to the text with some kind of preengagement. In *some* sense we hear a call, but we cannot hear it authentically because we have forgotten the very questions around which the biblical text turns. I would conjecture that this preengagement constitutes our lived form of "first naïveté. " Never, as modern human beings, can we experience the one-possibility consciousness of a primitive or archaic culture in which myth quite simply is the received construction of the world. *Our* "first naïveté" is surely the condition of being in some sense "called," but unable to distinguish the authentic message from the reality apprehensions of our culture or from the dogmatic and ecclesiastical framework in which we hear it.

Thus, as Ricoeur develops the importance of critical explanation of the text, it is not to destroy faith but to open the way for it. If one of the motives of the nineteenth-century historical-critical scholars was to free the Bible from dogmatic ecclesiastical interpretations, Ricoeur in turn seeks to free the Bible from culture-bound, subjectivizing interpretations, as well as from fundamentalist, objectivizing interpretations, by asking us to listen carefully to what biblical discourse testifies. We have no alternative today to working through criticism toward a second naïveté because the first naïveté available to us in our culture is so deeply idolatrous.

It is not difficult to follow the writer in his rejection of the "opaque and authoritarian" understanding of revelation associated with ecclesiastical authority and theological dogmatism. "[58] Such understandings lead to the mistaken idea that there are propositions which count as "revealed truths." Ricoeur does not question the importance of systematic theology, but the real action, for him, comes in dialogue between the philosopher and "the believer who is informed by the exegete." When we begin to examine the array of different sorts of texts found in the Bible, we discover that one type, prophetic discourse, provides the model of "inspiration" by the voice of Yahweh, on which the traditional dogmatic view of revelation has been constructed. But there are many other genres of biblical discourse: narrative discourse, prescriptive discourse, wisdom discourse, and hymnic discourse among them. We must develop an understanding of the Word which takes into account the ways in which all these literary forms convey sense to our self-reflection. In this larger context the idea of revelation as a voice speaking behind the voice of the prophet is too narrow. It separates the prophetic mode from its narrative context, tends to tie prophecy to the still more ancient genre of the oracle, and hence to the idea of an unveiling of the future. This chain of reasoning, in turn, leads to an idea of revelation which concentrates on the notion of a disclosure of "God's plan" for the end of history. Revelation, in short, is reduced to "the dimensions of a divination applied to 'the end of time.'"[59]

Ricoeur, in contrast, stresses the variety of sorts of content which may be called revelatory because they are the literary products of various interpretings of the tradition in testimony. In interpreting the Bible we must stick close "to those modalities of discourse that are most originary within the language of a community of faith,"[60] without neutralizing the variety in order to extract a theological content. What the testimony is is modulated by the form of discourse in which it is expressed. It is not "inspiration" in the sense of a psychologized version of the doctrine of the Holy Spirit that makes Scripture revelatory, but rather "the force of what is said." Hence the use of critical study for the recovery of the revelatory power of testimony is a matter of close attention to how the various genres work: to what they do say and what they do not say, and therefore to the great variety of human situations in which testimony has been borne.

One generalization is possible. The sense in which all these forms of discourse may be said to be revelatory turns on what Ricoeur calls their "poetic function." Building upon his understanding that written texts can burst the world of the author, and indeed that of the reader as well, and upon his understanding that different genres accomplish this in different ways, Ricoeur comes to his understanding of "the world of the text" or, in other citations, "the world in front of the text," by which he means "the...world intended beyond the text as its reference."[61] This referential function differs from the referential function of ordinary language or of scientific discourse. If by the latter we mean the description of familiar objects of perception or of the objects which science defines by its methods of observation and measurement, then the reference of poetic language projects "ahead" of itself a world in which the reader is invited to dwell, thus finding a more authentic situation in being. Ricoeur writes,

> My deepest conviction is that poetic language alone restores
> to us that participation in or belonging to an order of things
> which precedes our capacity to oppose ourselves to things
> taken as objects opposed to a subject. Hence the function
> of poetic discourse is to bring about this emergence of a
> depth-structure of belonging-to amid the ruins of
> descriptive discourse.[62]

But is it not an abuse of language to call such a function revelatory? Ricoeur answers no. The poetic function of biblical language suspends the criteria of falsification and verification to manifest "a proposed world, a world I may inhabit and wherein I can project my ownmost possibilities."[63] We see this by giving primacy to *what is said* in all the variety of biblical literature. Instead of beginning with an image derived from prophetic discourse, that of another voice behind the prophet's voice, and extending it by analogy to narration, prescriptive saying, wisdom literature, hymnic compositions, and so on, we are delivered from psychologizing interpretations of revelation to a sensitivity to the sense of the text, to the world-reference it opens up before it. To see the text as revelatory *poesis* is to understand that it "makes sense" by projecting a reference as a possibility for me.

Ricoeur has studied this revelatory *poesis* in special detail in the gospel parables. His exposition is a particularly good illustration of his use of a linguistic discipline, in this case the theory of metaphor, to show concretely how a certain literary genre "projects a world." A parable, Ricoeur tells us, is a metaphorical process in narrative form. A parabolic metaphor, in the strangeness of its plot, institutes a shock which redescribes reality, and opens for us a new way of seeing and being. The Kingdom of God is like "what happens" in the story. What happens, despite its everyday setting and circumstances, is "odd." More, it is "extravagant." This form of metaphorical process opens an otherwise matter-of-fact situation to an open range of interpretations and to the possibility of new commitments.

Fully to consider the applicability of the theory of metaphor for this purpose would require more space than is available here. The reader may consult the treatment of parables, proclamatory sayings and proverbial formulae in *Semeia* IV (1975). Here the referential power of the text, in the sense that it opens a "world in front of it" which we may inhabit, is likened to the power of the "model" in the natural sciences. A "model" in this sense is a heuristic device, an instrument for the redescription of reality, which breaks up an inadequate interpretation of the world and opens the way to a new, more adequate, interpretation. We are helped to see things otherwise by changing the language we use. Similarly, a metaphor is a heuristic fiction, an instrument for the redescription of lived experience that permits us to see new connections in things, or, as Ricoeur says elsewhere, to "decode" the traces of God's presence in history.

For more on this subject we should look at Ricoeur's large recent volume, *The Rule of Metaphor*,[64] in which his theory is radicalized to place metaphor at the root of all linguistic disclosure of being. Suffice it to say that the parables, particularly when they are seen in their "intersignifications" with the gospel proverbs, miracle stories, and eschatological sayings, and even more when they and these other genres are connected with the passion narrative in an intertextuality, illustrate what Ricoeur means by a *poesis* that is revelatory. Far from mounting a reductive argument, that what we used to call revelation is "only poetry," Ricoeur ties revelation to all the text says, and even more, to what it does in us as it is read.

The Post-Critical Moment

And so we come full circle: from our initial naïve fascination with texts in which testimony is preserved in *poesis*, through the critical disciplines which help us overcome idolatry and dogmatism, to the post-critical moment when we ourselves begin to testify in a divestiture of consciousness, which implicates our lives in the world "in front of" the text. We earlier asked if our "intellectual activity" in doing this is anything like the "intellectual activity" of the ancient authors as seen in von Rad's tradition-historical hypothesis. The differences are obvious. But so are some similarities. Just as the prophetic reformulation of Israel's earlier traditions generates a form of historical awareness, so our critique of the pretensions of consciousness in the critical study of texts gives us historical sense. Ricoeur speaks of the

> distanciation without which we would never become conscious of belonging to a world, a culture, a tradition. It is the critical moment, originally bound to the consciousness of belonging-to, that confers its properly historical character on this consciousness. For even a tradition only becomes such under the condition of a distance that distinguishes the belonging-to proper to a human being from the simple inclusion of a thing as part of a whole.[65]

The standpoint of contemporary historiography gives precedence to one of the illusions of consciousness: that the perspective of our own historical moment must be autonomous. But to receive the biblical text as testimony is to "dismantle" this fortress, "and to restore a historical dimension to studies otherwise purely literary." Testimony

> introduces the dimension of historical contingency which is lacking in the concept of the world of the text, which is deliberately nonhistorical or transhistorical. It throws itself therefore against one fundamental characteristic of the idea of autonomy; namely, not making the internal itinerary of consciousness depend on external events.[66]

At the very least, however, our modern task needs new tools. Our continuation of the "intellectual activity" of the prophets and of the early church, responding to the suspicion of a Marx, a Nietzsche, or a Freud, takes us through the "speculative Good Friday" which declares that the God of the transcendental illusion, the God of "dogmatic mythology" is indeed dead. To participate in the history of testimony we must convert our naïve faith through criticism into the register of hope.

A salient example of the author's self-implication in the history of biblical testimony through use of modern critical procedures occurs in his essay "Freedom in the Light of Hope."[67] This essay is centrally important because it ties the theme of freedom, so basic to Ricoeur's early studies of the will, directly to the imagery of hope contained in and inspired by the Resurrection texts. The strands of thought leading to this essay are thus both philosophical and hermeneutical.

The analysis of freedom implicit in Ricoeur's early phenomenology of the will, just because it is carried out in awareness not only of the many possible objectivizing counter-methods but also of all the contradictions in the long and by no means concluded history of philosophical inquiry, is limited by the notion of a total meaning which is thought but not known. This is the philosophical category of hope. But not only is the philosophical idea of freedom full of antinomies: the lived experience of freedom contains a basic contradiction. Evil is an invention of freedom which abdicates freedom. Thus, in some of his early essays, Ricoeur is already giving this philosophical hope a hermeneutical turn, referring to it as "the Last Day," which, in its original context in the Hebrew Scriptures, is a symbol of the hope of the community of faith for fulfilled righteousness and justice.

"Freedom in the Light of Hope," then, explores how humanity's self-sufficient effort to achieve autonomy is challenged, even "divested" of its credentials and conceptual clothing, by the powerful imagery of Resurrection, when this is received as a *poesis* which bodies forth testimony. We are, precisely, delivered into a modern form of tradition -historical awareness by this confrontation.

"For my part," Ricoeur begins, "I have been very taken with--I should say, won over by--the eschatological interpretation that Jürgen Moltmann gives to the Christian *kerygma* in his work *The Theology of Hope.*"[68] We will argue, indeed, that what von Rad is for Ricoeur with respect to the theology of Israel's traditions looking back toward the accounts of origin, Jürgen Moltmann is for Ricoeur in the gathering of Jewish and Christian traditions looking forward to "the Last Day." Moltmann sees the Resurrection *kerygma* not as referring to a completed foundation event in the past, not as symbolizing an existential state to which we can aspire in the present, but as set "entirely within the framework of the Jewish theology of the promise."[69] Once this kerygma is disentangled from Hellenistic epiphany religion, we see that "the Resurrection, interpreted within a theology of promise, is not an event which closes, by fulfilling the promise, but an event which opens, because it adds to the promise by confirming it."[70] The principal meaning of the Resurrection is that "the God of the promise, the God of Abraham, Isaac, and Jacob, has approached, has been revealed as He who is coming for all."[71] This Resurrection symbolism gives us a content for hope, which otherwise remains simply a regulative idea of reason in the Kantian sense. The phenomenology of freedom can now be further worked out "in the light of" an interpretation of the Resurrection texts, which give us something more, and something different, from what we find in the Adamic myths.

Here is our entry into the history of the interpretation of the traditions of the people of God as von Rad understands that process. The Resurrection passages control the entire New Testament, and the New Testament, in turn, is an interpretation of the traditions of Israel. We become part of that history of interpretation by submitting our own "effort to exist and desire to be," which is nothing other than our thrust toward the realization of freedom, to the hope projected by the Resurrection stories. Here, above all, we are invited to live in the world which the texts project "in front of" them. "What is freedom in the light of hope? I will answer in one word: it is the meaning of my existence in the light of the Resurrection, that is, as reinstated in the movement which we have called the future of the Resurrection of the Christ."[72]

But now a dialectic arises between this "kerygmatic nucleus" and elements in our experience which are, inevitably, also subject to interpretation by the familiar Ricoeurian "counterdisciplines." In this context, Ricoeur mentions the realms of psychology, ethics, and politics. Psychologically, the power of hope encounters us by opening up the imagination. "Freedom in the light of hope, expressed in psychological terms, is nothing else than this creative imagination of the possible."[73] Ricoeur contrasts this eschatological opening of imagination to the tendency of existential interpretations of Scripture to stress an "instantaneousness of the present decision at the expense of the temporal, historical, communitarian and cosmic aspects contained in the hope of the Resurrection."[74] Ethically and politically, we move beyond what the Law imposes to what the promise proposes. We are called to a mission which is "inseparable from the deciphering of the signs of the new creation."[75] We are here still further from the existential interpretation. "A freedom open to new creation is in fact less centered on subjectivity, on personal authenticity, than on social and political justice; it calls for a reconciliation which itself demands to be inscribed in the recapitulation of all things."[76]

Reading these words, we wonder how directly Ricoeur believes that he can move from the Resurrection *kerygma* to the determination of concrete actions. There is no doubt of the direction of his commitments. In a recent work he has described "the principal function of religious discourse" as being "to establish through the Gospel a life lived for others, and to anticipate, ethically and politically, a liberated humanity."[77] And, he continues, "I too am ready to speak of the Gospel as a project of a liberated humanity and to develop the political implications of this project."[78] But still, Ricoeur refuses to identify the "kerygmatic center" of freedom with social and political action. This "kerygmatic center" is the "in spite of" and the "how much more" with which we "decipher the signs of the resurrection under the contrary appearance of death."[79] We must "decipher" this "economy" of freedom "in work and in leisure, in politics and in universal history," thus giving communitarian, historical, and political expression to the hope projected by the Resurrection texts, without allowing the hope to be reduced to that expression.

> What I am saying is that the properly religious moment of all discourse, is the "still more" that it insinuates everywhere, intensifying every project in the same manner, including the political project. Political discourse therefore is no less oriented, disoriented, and reoriented than any other form of discourse; and the specific way in which it is oriented and disoriented is that it becomes the place for the insertion of an impossible demand, a demand that we can validly interpret in utopian terms, meaning by this a quest that cannot be exhausted by any program of action. Paradox then does not strike *praxis* any less than it does *theoria*, political *praxis* any less than the *praxis* of private morality. It just prevents us from converting religious discourse entirely into political discourse--for the same reasons that it forbids its conversion into moral discourse, even if this morality is elevated to the dignity of proverbial wisdom.[80]

Thus the threat of the text to "decenter" the self and its aspirations, to strip us of our desire for power, possession, and honor, applies even to the political and religious enterprises we enter because we believe the Gospel calls us to. The fact of evil threatens all our achievements, including pious ones, insofar as they are expressed through "fraudulent totalizations" of our being. As Ricoeur says, "the true malice of man appears only in the state and in the church, as institutions of gathering together, of recapitulation, of totalization."[81] In the end, the gospel is not an action program but an "impossible demand," for which the perspective of "freedom in the light of hope" is the only valid frame of reference.

The Role of Conceptualization

"The symbol gives rise to thought." The "approximation" of the New Testament message in a conceptual framework is the final step in its interpretation. For Ricoeur, this is a philosophical task, and hence "within the autonomy of responsible thought."[82] The biblical message presents a new starting-point for thinking and exerts a continually reforming pressure upon it. But yet thinking, once it begins, is autonomous. If the philosopher is "converted," he is converted "within philosophy and to philosophy according to its internal exigencies."[83] Ricoeur thus is saying that thinking to which the biblical message gives rise must make its own way in the intellectual world. It must function "within the limits of a reason alone." At the same time, this does not mean that the philosopher who also happens to be a Christian may dispense with the biblical text. Thought, autonomous on its own account, must constantly seek to "approximate" the message in fresh ways. What it is as a constituting of the world of experience must be intelligible to all, whether accepted by all or not.

What is the theological use of this philosophical quest? Its purpose is not primarily apologetic. Rather, Ricoeur is trying to be sure that the gospel message everywhere has the same sense. The concrete possibility of "freedom in the light of hope" rests on our ability to specify the "innovation of meaning" given us in Scripture as reliably the same innovation in all circumstances and vicissitudes. The innovation begins as "a-logical." It begins as an irruption into a closed order and seems a-logical not only in relation to this order, but also because it represents a cognitive excess. "But if this novelty did not make us think, then hope, like faith, would be a cry, a flash without a sequel."[84] Ricoeur is saying that we cannot distinguish authentic "freedom in the light of hope" from the utopias that are merely ecstatic projections of the thinking of this or that time or place unless the novelty of this *kerygma* is "made explicit by an indefinite repetition of signs," and "verified in the 'seriousness' of an interpretation..." The *kerygma* is to be grafted onto "real [historical] tendencies..."[85] deciphering the signs of the Resurrection wherever they are, we must find the form of conceptual universality given by the *kerygma*'s content. As Ricoeur says, "It is necessary...that the Resurrection "deploy its own logic..."[86]

The conceptual framework in which this is worked out, described as "a post-Hegelian Kantianism," will be more understandable to the technically equipped philosopher than to the student primarily interested in biblical hermeneutics. But it is worthwhile to sketch the main elements. Let us begin by noting what Ricoeur finds to his liking in Hegel, and then go on to show how Hegel must be corrected by Kant.

As Ricoeur puts it, "The positive and permanent value of Hegel's phenomenology of religion is to have attempted to trace the stages through which religious 'representations' point toward their speculative achievement."[87] The progress of the figurative toward the conceptual is actually the progress through the history of culture of the figurative expressions of desire. Hegel is concerned not with the ethics of duty in the abstract, but with the confrontation of will with will, with the adjudication of rights in concrete communities, the family, the economy, the state. Ricoeur willingly calls Hegel's philosophy the philosophy of the will. "Its greatness derives from the diversity of problems that it traverses and resolves: union of desire and culture, of psychology and politics, of the subjective and the universal."[88] Ricoeur's concern to find a transcendental deduction of freedom in the light of hope "cannot but be in dialogue" with Hegel, so close is Hegel's thought to being an account of the conceptualization of hope and freedom in process of realization.

The problem with Hegel's thought is that the fullness of life, of conflict, of culture, out of which the imaginative representations of the will come, is progressively swallowed up until only the concept survives. Moreover, the concept emerges when the living forms of life that led up to it have ceased to be living. Philosophy always "arrives too late" to preach "what the world ought to be like." It records "gray in gray" forms of life that have become old.

It is here that Ricoeur must abandon Hegel and seek help in Kant. Hegel's understanding of the forward progress of the will through the history of culture is richer than Kant's, but it leads to a notion of the completion of the will in "absolute knowledge," a metaphysical abstraction which Hegel's critics, Ricoeur among them, find pretentious and impossible. Kant puts a limit on our ability to "complete" our conceptual knowledge of what is involved either in human knowing or human striving. For Kant, the role of religious symbols and representations is imaginatively to represent the limit beyond which the demand of conceptual knowledge for completeness cannot pass.

For Kant we can *think* beyond the world of objects, but we cannot *know* that which is unconditioned by the object world. To suppose that we can *know* the realm of the unconditioned is, as we have seen, what Kant calls the "transcendental illusion." But in the practical realm of our willing and doing--the realm of society and culture--we experience a demand for completeness of meaning. This demand is a moral pressure that human nature should be fulfilled, that human effort should be capable of attaining the good, and that the attainment of this good should be accompanied by happiness. The problem is that if we try to think out what this means, we run into impossible conflict between our concepts of the good and the actual circumstances of appetite, desire, political and personal compromise, and the like. If our redescriptions of the world of everyday life under the sign of the Resurrection have helped to fuel this desire for goodness and happiness in this life, if they have helped us formulate, with Kant, the notion of a human society understood as a "Kingdom of ends" (in which each human being, including oneself, is treated as an end in him- or herself), we find that the effort to realize such hopes requires us to postulate" realities which we cannot *know*: freedom, immortality, God. Precisely this moral pressure to go beyond the limits of objective knowledge calls for a reintroduction of symbol.

Biblical symbols, then, serve to limit, but also to break open, our reasoning process. It is "the task of hermeneutics to disentangle from the 'world' of the texts their implicit 'project' for existence, their indirect 'proposition' of new modes of being.... Hermeneutics has finished its job when it has opened the eyes and the ears, i.e., when it has displayed before our imagination the figures of our authentic existence."[89] Thus Ricoeur proffers "a transcendental inquiry into the imagination of hope." In Kant, a transcendental inquiry asks what formal conditions must be satisfied for us to have a realm of objectivity such as, for example, the realm of objective relationships described in Newtonian physics. Since Heidegger, the notion of a transcendental inquiry has been broadened: how, we now ask, is a certain way of seeing and acting in the world possible? Ricoeur seems to be suggesting that the figures of hope function in the interpersonal world somewhat as Kant's categories of substance, causality, and so on, function in the interobject world.

There is a difference, of course. While the Kantian categories are pure concepts, the figures of hope correspond most closely to Kant's "schemas" which serve as a bridge between empirical objects and the concepts under which these objects are subsumed. The schema is not simply an image, but a product of the imagination. I reach toward the concept of substance, for example, through the notion of the permanence of the real in time. Kant calls this a "representation of a general procedure of the imagination by which a concept receives its image."[90] This notion of the "productive imagination" which reaches toward concept is further developed by Kant in his treatment of "aesthetic ideas" in *The Critique of Judgment*. In Ricoeur's words,

> At the moment of accounting for the aesthetic productions
> of genius, Kant invokes that power of the imagination "to
> present" (*Darstellung*) those ideas of reason for which we
> have no concept. By means of such representation, the
> imagination "occasions much thought (*viel zu denken*)..."
> Historical testimony has the same structure and the same
> function. It, too, is a "presentation" of what for reflection
> remains an idea, namely the idea of a letting go wherein
> we affirm an order exempt from that servitude from which
> finite existence cannot deliver itself.[91]

Ricoeur wants to give this "transcendental inquiry into the imagination of hope" an autonomy that it does not have in Kant, just as he wishes to move ethics, the question of the will, to center stage as the realm of realization of our relationship to being. Hence ontology, of a kind, enters through the question, "What may we hope?" The imagination functions transcendentally to give us a world in which certain fulfillments of our being are possible. The fact of evil threatens this fulfillment because evil is expressed in our lives as "fraudulent totalization" of our being. Under these circumstances, the conditions for the "regeneration" of the will "cannot be deduced from the formal condition of Freedom."[92] And, for the same reason, "the narratives and symbols which 'represent' the victory of the Good Principle over the Evil Principle are not expendable."[93] That is, if our being is to be fulfilled, not in fraudulent totalization but out of what Ricoeur early in his career called its "originary affirmation," symbols of "regeneration" must be at work in the "productive imagination."

For, as Ricoeur points out, in the *Dialectics* in Kant's Second Critique we find the question of the "full or complete" object of the will. This involves "the reconciliation of freedom and nature, i.e., the achievement of Man as a whole."[94] Precisely, that is, the question that began to open up in his early work. How can we speak of an authentic actualization of freedom unless we can articulate in productive imagination the content of the hope underlying such freedom? Such an ideal, presumably, would be a counterpart of the articulation of self-abdicating freedom, the "servile will." It would be an articulation of the symbols and metaphors of humanity as regenerate and fulfilled. This articulation has begun, but only barely, in Ricoeur's treatment of the texts of the Resurrection. Are we to expect that the long-awaited *Poetics of the Will* will complete the needed "symbolic of regeneration"? The direction of Ricoeur's work to date suggests that it could. So Ricoeur may fulfill the promise implicit in his early recognition that we hope for "a recreation of language." We, citizens of postmodernity, "wish to be called again."

Notes

1. Paul Ricoeur, *La Symbolique du mal* (Paris: Aubier, 1960). The Symbolism of Evil, Emerson Buchanan, trans. (Boston: Beacon Press, 1969), p. 349.

2. See the preface to the first edition Paul Ricoeur, *Histoire et vérité* (Paris: Editions du Seuil, 1955). *History and Truth*, Charles A. Kelbley, trans. (Evanston: Northwestern University Press, 1965), p. 5.

3. Ricoeur has preached from time to time in the Rockefeller Chapel of the University of Chicago, and elsewhere. Among his published sermons are "You Are the Salt of the Earth," in *Political and Social Essays by Paul Ricoeur*, David Stewart and Joseph Bien, eds. (Athens: Ohio University Press, 1974), pp. 105-24, and "Listening to the Parables of Jesus," in *The Philosophy of Paul Ricoeur*, Charles E. Reagan and David Stewart, eds. (Boston: Beacon Press, 1978), pp. 239ff. Ricoeur was the preacher at the eucharistic service uniting Protestants and Roman Catholics in the midst of the uprising of workers and students in Paris on June 2, 1968. His sermon, as summarized in *Christianisme social* (Nos. 7-10, 1968), may be found in translation in Lewis S. Mudge, *The Crumbling Walls* (Philadelphia: Westminster Press, 1970), pp. 30-33.

4. Ricoeur has recently been colleague and collaborator, in particular, with Norman Perrin, David Tracy, Mircea Eliade, and others, at the University of Chicago.

5. See Loretta Dornisch, "Symbolic Systems and the Interpretation of Scripture: An Introduction to the Work of Paul Ricoeur," *Semeia* IV (1975): 17f.

6. See "Freedom in the Light of Hope," in *The Conflict of Interpretations: Essays in Hermeneutics*, Don Ihde, ed., (Northwestern University Press, 1974), reprinted in Lewis S. Mudge, ed., *Essays on Biblical Interpretation* (Philadelphia: Fortress Press, 1980) p. 156.

7. *The Symbolism of Evil*, p. 356.

8. Ricoeur, "Biblical Hermeneutics," *Semeia*, IV (1975): p. 29.

9. E.g., Paul Ricoeur, *Interpretation Theory: Discourse and the Surplus of Meaning* (Fort Worth: Texas Christian University Press, 1976), p. 92.

10. See "Toward a Hermeneutic of the Idea of Revelation," in *The Harvard Theological Review*, Vol. 70, No. 1-2 (Jan.-April), 1977, and "The Hermeneutics of Testimony," in *The Anglican Theological Review*, LXI, 4, reprinted in Lewis S. Mudge, ed., *Essays on Biblical Interpretation* (Philadelphia: Fortress Press, 1980), pp. 73ff. and 119ff.

11. "Toward a Hermeneutic of the Idea of Revelation," Ibid., pp. 73ff.

12. See "The Hermeneutics of Symbols I," Dennis Savage, trans., in Paul Ricoeur, *The Conflict of Interpretations: Essays on Hermeneutics*, Don Ihde, ed. (Evanston, Ill.: Northwestern University Press, 1974), p. 299.

13. Quoted in the Editor's Introduction, *The Conflict of Interpretations*, Ibid., p. xxii.

14. See Paul Ricoeur, *Freedom and Nature: The Voluntary and the Involuntary*, Erazim V. Kohak, trans. (Evanston: Northwestern University Press, 1966) and *The Conflict of Interpretations, passim*.

15. *The Symbolism of Evil*, p.355.

16. Paul Ricoeur, *Freud and Philosophy* (New Haven: Yale University Press, 1970), p. 3.

17. *The Symbolism of Evil*, p. 351

18. Ibid., p. 352.

19. Ibid., p. 19.

20. Ibid., p. 355.

21. Ibid., p. 355.

22. See "Preface to Bultmann," in *The Conflict of Interpretations*, Ibid., reprinted in Lewis S. Mudge, ed., *Essays on Biblical Interpretation* (Philadelphia: Fortress Press, 1980), p. 65.

23. Ibid., pp. 65-66.

24. Paul Ricoeur, "The Language of Faith," in Reagan and Stewart, *The Philosophy of Paul Ricoeur*, p. 227.

25. Paul Ricoeur, Preface to Don Ihde, *Hermeneutic Phenomenology: The*

Philosophy of Paul Ricoeur (Evanston: Northwestern University Press, 1971), p. xv.

26. Ihde, Ibid., pp. 4ff.

27. Ricoeur began the study of Husserl's work while a prisoner of war in Germany in World War II, subsequently publishing a number of translations and studies in French. Some of these have been gathered in English in the volume, *Husserl: An Analysis of His Phenomenology*, Edward G. Ballard and Lester E. Embree, trans. (Evanston: Northwestern University Press, 1967).

28. See note 14, above.

29. So Ihde, pp. 26ff.

30. "Existence and Hermeneutics," in *The Conflict of Interpretations*, p. 6.

31. *Freud and Philosophy*, p. 46.

32. Ibid., p. 46.

33. Paul Ricoeur, *Fallible Man*, Charles Kelbley, trans. (Chicago: Henry Regnery Co., 1965).

34. Paul Ricoeur, "The Antinomy of Human Reality," in Reagan and Stewart, The Philosophy of Paul Ricoeur, p. 33.

35. *The Symbolism of Evil*, pp. 151 ff., *et passim*.

36. "Toward a Hermeneutic of the Idea of Revelation," in Mudge, ed., *Essays*, p. 106.

37. *Freud and Philosophy*, p. 525.

38. *Interpretation Theory*, passim.

39. Ibid., p. 92.

40. See "Toward a Hermeneutic of the Idea of Revelation," in Mudge, ed., *Essays, passim*.

41. *Interpretation Theory*, pp. 8ff.

42. Ibid., p. 16.

43. Ibid., p. 13.

44. "The Hermeneutics of Testimony," in Mudge, ed., *Essays*, pp. 110ff.

45. "Structure and Hermeneutics," in *The Conflict of Interpretations*, p. 45.

46. Ibid., p. 46.

47. Ibid., p. 46.

48. Ibid., p. 46.

49. Ibid., p. 46.

50. "Preface to Bultmann," in Mudge, ed., *Essays*, p. 50.

51. Ibid., pp. 51-52.

52. Ibid., p. 52.

53. Ibid., p. 52.

54. Ibid., p. 56.

55. Ibid., p. 56.

56. "Structure and Hermeneutics," in *The Conflict of Interpretations*, p. 45, Ricoeur's italics.

57. Van A. Harvey, *The Historian and the Believer* (New York: Macmillan

Publishing Co., Inc., 1966).

58. "Toward a Hermeneutic of the Idea of Revelation," in Mudge, ed. *Essays,* pp. 73-74.

59. Ibid., p. 77.

60. Ibid., p. 90.

61. Ibid., p. 100.

62. Ibid., p. 101.

63. Ibid., p. 102.

64. Paul Ricoeur, *The Rule of Metaphor*, Robert Czerny with Kathleen McLaughlin and John Costello, S. J., trans. (Toronto and Buffalo: University of Toronto Press, 1977).

65. "Toward a Hermeneutic of the Idea of Revelation," in Mudge, ed., *Essays*, p. 107.

66. Ibid., p. 109.

67. "Freedom in the Light of Hope," in Mudge, ed., *Essays*, pp. 155ff.

68. Ibid., p. 157.

69. Ibid., p. 159.

70. Ibid., p. 159.

71. Ibid., p. 159.

72. Ibid., pp. 159-60.

73. Ibid., p. 161.

74. Ibid., p. 160.

75. Ibid., p. 162.

76. Ibid., p. 162.

77. Paul Ricoeur, "The Specificity of Religious Language," *Semeia* IV (1975): 127.

78. Ibid., p. 127.

79. "Freedom in the Light of Hope," in Mudge, ed., *Essays*, p. 164.

80. "The Specificity of Religious Language," p. 127.

81. "Freedom in the Light of Hope," in Mudge, ed., *Essays*, p. 180.

82. Ibid., p. 156.

83. Ibid., p. 157.

84. Ibid., p. 165.

85. Ibid., p. 165.

86. Ibid., p. 166.

87. "The Specificity of Religious Language," p. 140.

88. "Freedom in the Light of Hope," in Mudge, ed., *Essays*, p. 168.

89. "The Specificity of Religious Language," p. 144.

90. Immanuel Kant, *The Critique of Pure Reason*, Max Muller, trans. (New York: Macmillan Publishing Co., Inc., 1927), pp. 115f.

91. "Toward a Hermeneutic of the Idea of Revelation," in Mudge, ed., *Essays*, p. 116.

92. "The Specificity of Religious Language," p. 145.

93. Ibid., p. 145.
94. Ibid., p. 145.

III

Ecclesiogenesis

6

Church and Human Salvation:
The Contemporary Dialogue

In what way is the Church an agent of ultimate human well-being, of that state we have traditionally called salvation? How do we conceive of the role of the Church in relation to humanity's fate at this moment in world history, and how does our conception influence the way we do theology? Is there such a thing as an "ecumenical theology of church life"? These are some of the topics suggested for this essay. I welcome the invitation to write because I believe that the way we think about the role of the Church in relation to the salvation of the world tends to shape our conception of theological method. By the question of "method," I mean the roots of our sense of what is theologically authoritative, convincing, or persuasive. One can hardly embark on a theological essay today without some notion of what constitutes, for oneself or one's readers, a persuasive theological argument in the first place. What "makes sense" to us today depends upon our view of the context in which we are thinking.

It is striking that today, possibly for the first time, we are close to being able to give an exhaustive empirical description of "humankind." It is well within the state of the computer art at this moment if not actually accomplished, to be able to enumerate the earth's population by name, date of birth, place of residence and much else besides. The existence of the transistor radio in every tiny village could make it possible, even, to address all the earth's people simultaneously. Never before have we been able so concretely to say what we mean by the word "humanity." Yet we are as far as ever from having a universally held idea of what it means to be human. Our ideas of "humanity" are only projections of our respective cultures, constructs of the different human sciences, implications of our interpersonal behavior.

Suppose that we did have the greater part of humankind on a transistor hookup. What would we have to say? Would it be "What hath God wrought?" Or something more personal like "Watson, come here. I want you!"? In fact the existence of such a communications network would not at first guarantee anyone's right to speak, much less suggest what to say. For we would have to decide who owned the network, and why the initial message should go in one direction rather than another. It has been suggested by one of my students that the first words which the whole of humankind should hear might as well be those of the allegedly traditional Chinese greeting: "Have you eaten?" For us to ask first about the well-being of our companions on this planet, for them to ask the same of us, would perhaps be the most meaningful beginning there could be. For Christians, the Eucharistic overtone would be patent. And thus, whether recognized or not, our first words to our fellow human beings could well concern what we have traditionally known as "salvation."

Church and Salvation in Ecumenical Debate

At the recent meeting of the Commission on Faith and Order of the World Council of Churches at Lima, Peru, and even more recently at the WCC Assembly in Vancouver, our fundamental differences about the meaning of "salvation" were dramatized. On both occasions, the matter, roughly speaking, came down to a debate between those who seem satisfied to remain within the traditional Western academic paradigm of theological reasoning and those for whom such reasoning has become almost totally contextual, hence relative to the preconceptions and imagery of the culture and social situation where the theologizing is done. In the first camp are the traditional laborers in the vineyard of Faith and Order, the bilateral dialogues and the routine pursuit of theological teaching in the seminaries of Europe and North America. In the other camp are the proponents of such movements as Black theology, Feminist theology, the Latin American theologies of liberation, and the contextual thinking often quite unique, of contemporary Africa and Asia.

This methodological debate was dramatized, indeed, by the encounter at Lima between Wolfhart Pannenberg and José Miguez-Bonino. The issue was precisely a version of our own concern for the role of the

Church in human salvation: the issue, as Faith and Order put it, of "The Unity of the Church and the Renewal of Human Community." Although debate on this issue already has a long history in the ecumenical movement, the effort at Lima to find a common method for pursuing it broke down in disagreement on several fundamental presuppositions. A steering group brought in a methodological proposal which came under attack from both directions. In the "cloakroom" outside the meeting hall Pannenberg was heard to say in English heavily accented enough to satisfy any theological pedant, "If this were a dissertation proposal, I would say: it is not yet ready!"

How, then, can we even begin to talk about church and salvation? The most fruitful approach to a method probably lies through the effort to see the fundamental nature and unity of the Church through various "prisms" (a phrase interestingly used in the work of Mary Tanner, an Anglican theologian from Great Britain) of practical human experience. The question of ecclesiology can be seen through the "prism" of the problem of race, or of the experience of women, or of the struggle of handicapped persons. It can also be seen through the "prisms" provided by different experiences of culture. Above all, it needs to be seen through the diffractions connected with differing human experiences of power: the powerful and the powerless obviously see matters in different ways. In all this there needs to be a growing understanding of what Dietrich Bonhoeffer meant when he spoke of "never understanding the reality of God apart from the reality of the world." It is clear that we face ecclesiological conundrums today not only because of traditional differences between "protestant" and "catholic" understandings, but also because the issues which divide humankind cut directly through the life of the Church. The notion of seeing old issues through new "prisms" helps us realize that we do not abandon the old issues but rather see them in fresh perspectives which, today, are indispensable for understanding the import of these issues in the first place.

Ecclesiology: Toward New Methodological Paradigms

As we try to do this, however, traditional frames of reference in ecclesiology are going to be strained. When one asks why a given theological argument is persuasive, we are less and less satisfied to refer to ecclesiastical authority and to leave the matter there. Authority, of course, is not merely "magisterium." All of us have to contend with that in different ways, and if we provoke our respective authorities sufficiently, we will hear about it. But what is far more important is the traditional and psychic authority residing in certain patterns of reasoning which represent the forms of tradition at work in our heads. Edward Farley, in his recent book *Ecclesial Reflection,* has done what he calls, after Michel Foucault, an "archaeology" of the forms of reasoning which have prevailed in the Church over the last few hundred years. Farley lays bare the assumptions concerning biblical authority, the role of doctrine and the frame of reference of the *ekklesia,* in which all of us to a greater or less extent work. He suggests that this combination of factors, which he calls the "house of authority" is now eroding: not because we are becoming Enlightenment persons two hundred years after the fact, but because the Church's calling to bear witness in the world is bringing new factors to bear upon theological reflection as such. The present disarray of the field of "systematic theology" may well be evidence of the truth of Farley's thesis. While we cannot afford to abandon the task of interpreting and reinterpreting Tradition, we may well in the next decades discover that our fundamental paradigms of authority and persuasiveness no longer work.

More recently, Farley has written another work, *Theologia: The Fragmentation and Unity of Theological Education,* in which current assumptions about the nature of theological thinking are traced to the social and institutional contexts in which, for the last two hundred or more years, this enterprise has been carried on. Farley's argument makes clear that at least two things have happened to abstract theological reflection from the living practice of faith. The growth of the self-sufficient "guilds" or "fields" of Old Testament, New Testament, Church History, Systematic Theology, and so on, has created realms of inquiry in which the basic criteria are not those of the faith-community but those of the professional guilds and of the critical standards of the secular university. And the struggle of theological faculties as such to maintain their standing in the university, or the world of higher education generally, has been achieved largely by turning theological education into professional training on the model of the faculties of Medicine or Law. Thus the *telos* of theological work has been organized around what Farley called "the clerical paradigm," or training for leadership tasks in the Church as such. In both cases, the shape of theological reflection has been determined by considerations of power and conceptual generality. rather than by the needs of the lived faith for clarity about a "cognitive disposition toward divine things."

Thinking about these matters, I was fascinated to come across a recent essay by Michel Foucault in his book *Power/Knowledge*. Foucault is noting the fact that "global" or "totalitarian" theories of the human have been far less successful than many hoped in explaining what actually goes on in human life in all its detail. In fact, such theories are deeply "inhibiting." It is not that such things as Freudian theory or Marxist criticism are useless. But theories of the human which, as theories, occupy positions of power in the intellectual world tend precisely to suppress those forms of knowledge which are personal, communal and local. We are seeing now what Foucault calls "an insurrection of subjugated knowledges." And, he continues, "We are concerned...with the insurrection of knowledges that are opposed primarily not to the contents, methods, or concepts if a science, but to the effects of centralizing powers which are linked to the institution and functioning of an organized scientific discourse within a society such as ours."

There are things we can only learn by consulting human experience not just in general, but rather in the particular forms it takes in particular places. This is even true in the writing of history. There is such a thing as local history, the history of villages. the history of particular communities over against which the private experiences of individuals and groups are worked out. Such regions of meaning have little to do with universal theories of the meaning of epochs, or of the overall direction of history as such. For Foucault, such subjugated meanings above all have to do with human struggle. "What emerges out of this is...a painstaking recovery of struggles together with the rude memory of their conflicts." The memory--and present reality--of such imaginative wrestling with the realities of power will stand us in good stead in the latter part of this analysis.

The Church can learn much from Foucault's insights. We need to devise ways of permitting ecclesiologies which tend toward universal formulations to be corrected by the experience people have had of seeking to be the Church in the immediate circumstances of human need. We do not as yet know enough about how to do this. I would suggest that one approach might lie through an attempt at critical re-covery of what I call theology in its primary mode. By this I mean the thinking which actually goes on in congregation as the Church seeks to be the Church in this or that particular place for the salvation of human beings there. I am suggesting that the congregation no longer be either the object of theological definition or of sociological study as it has so often been in the past, but that the thinking of the congregation be critically honored and studied. This is not to say that academic theology no longer has a place. It is rather to say that academic theology must proceed in a dialogical relationship with thinking in actual situations: aiding and abetting that thinking, providing critical norms for it and at the same time being criticized by it. I have come across a fascinating small book that tries to suggest ways in which this may be done: Ian Fraser's *Reinventing Theology as the Work of the People*. This short work is based on experiments in dialogue between theologians and congregations recently made at the Selly Oak Colleges in Birmingham, England. If we could try to do what this book suggests, the needed ideas and paradigms would eventually come.

The Church as Salvation-Sign

The practice of dialogue between theologians and people should precede our attempt to comprehend such dialogue theoretically. We should experience the dialogue first and then see what we have on our hands. But if one has thoughts about what the dialogue might mean, it is only honest to have them on the table: if only to permit them to be criticized in practice.

I remain fascinated by the words of *Lumen Gentium*: "The Church is a kind of sacrament or sign of intimate union with God, and of the unity of all (hu)mankind." These words of Vatican II were taken up by the World Council of Churches at Uppsala in 1968 with a slightly more eschatological twist: "The Church is bold in speaking of itself as the sign of the coming unity of (hu)mankind." In both cases the key is the use of the word "sign," a term much bandied about since but not, so far as I know, adequately explored. What might we make of this word in search of a means of articulating insights concerning the Church as agent, or medium of salvation in our world?

The notion of the Church as a "sign" suggests that the theologian might turn for help to the relatively new field of semiotics, or theory of signs as they operate in the human environment. While extremely technical in its more esoteric philosophical forms, semiotics, as a way of analyzing the action-world, is becoming increasingly familiar in the popular journals, especially since the French writer Roland Barthes began his studies of the signification of common elements in life experience. Styles in clothing, social habits, and even the configuration of institutions, all have sign value for us: that is, they activate the store of signs present in our culture in particular ways to convey messages. A person who habitually wears cowboy boots is sending signals of a sort. So is the Christian congregation which habitually enters into relation ships with marginalized persons in its immediate environment. The human world may be looked upon as an extremely complex configuration of signs which wait to be activated in the chains of meaning, corresponding to sentences, which we inscribe in the world by what we do. Might not the Christian theologian try, in dialogue with the congregation, to decipher the signals which that congregation is sending out through its patterns of activity? Could not the theologian use semiotic and semantic method to ascertain whether the congregation functions as a "sign" of the coming renewal of humankind under god's rule?

What would one look for? Two things above all. Bonhoeffer said that the Church should be "Jesus Christ existing in the form of a community." One would know such community by the fact that, given its cultural and social setting, the "sign" of Jesus could be "read" there. The cross, of course. But how might one recognize that? Not in self-immolation for its own sake, but rather, following a suggestion in Jan Sobrino's book *Christology at the Crossroads*, the kind of signification generated by the community's comportment in relation to the power realities around it. The Church could convey the "signature" of Jesus Christ through being related redemptively to power the way He was related to power.

Secondly, the congregation that bears the sign of Jesus Christ is one whose behavior conveys "signals" through which members and others are able to see a world of possible action stretching ahead into the future. This is an idea derived from Paul Ricoeur, who argues that in reading the Bible we can see "possible worlds" stretching out "in front of" the text. A parable, for example, reexpresses the signs present in its situation in such a way as to offer us new possibilities for being and for action. The Church in the midst of the world should function in much the same way. It should be a configuration of signs capable of energizing the imagination to see what is possible in the situation concerned, rather than leaving human beings to settle only for the possibilities provided by the prevailing structures of power in that situation. Here, perhaps, is a semiotic analog to the combined notions of resurrection and eschatological expectation. Through the sign of the cross we see, not an end to our possibilities, but rather entirely new possibilities.

The use of semiotic method suggests that when we act in the world we are always resolving in some way, through the use of a productive imagination, the question of all that implodes, restricts, or limits us. "Power realities" mean not only human structures which either enable or oppress. They refer also to the boundaries and horizons of life experienced as restraints upon the spirit: our particular settings in time and space, our particular bodily endowments, the facts of illness and death. To be related to power as Jesus was related to power, and to transcend the finite powers as he did, is to relate ourselves to the ultimate Power with which we have to do. Richard R. Niebuhr, in his book *Experiential Religion*, describes contemporary Western humanity as "radial man," in the sense that we experience ourselves encompassed by impinging forces we do not control. Here is the modern shape of Foucault's history of "struggles." The experience is no doubt intensified by the sense that with contemporary technology we should be able to control more than we do. Somehow our capacity to imagine ways of fulfilling human possibilities in this situation has been outrun by the sheer power we exercise but have not rationally mastered, so that we have made the power of nature even more our enemy than it was in pre-industrial times precisely by our tamperings with its nuclear foundations. What is needed in this situation, as Ricoeur argues, is not merely moral precept but moral imagination. Morality should suggest possibilities. It should help us see what might be, and draw us toward the enactment of such possibilities.

Hence the force of the idea that the Church could function as "sign" in our situation by being the sort of parabolic community, or lens, or prism, through which human beings might be summoned to new possibilities of moral imagination in relation to power. The "sign-ature" of Jesus Christ could and should be acted out. The work of the theologian could and should be both to participate in that acting-out and critically to examine it in dialogue with the faith-community in order to be sure that what is signified is indeed the salvation of human beings in the context of God's rule, not some lesser or idolatrous sign. What has come to be called "ideology criticism" could well take semiotic form: the criticism of what we articulate and communicate by the configuration of our lives, to be sure that what we say is not merely a justification either of our privileges or of our pain.

The perspective offered here, of course, does not stand or fall with the semiotic method as such. The dialogue between theologians and those in our congregations who seek clarification of the thinking that leads them to action in the world can go on in other ways. The important thing, whatever the method used, is that this dialogue, which has already begun, should vigorously continue. Both our theological faculties and our parishes deeply need the results that such dialogue can afford. We need a deeper understanding of what is involved in making such a dialogue possible. New thinking about the church as agent of salvation in the world, can, in turn, lead to new insights about theological method for the years of ecumenical discussion ahead of us.

7

Thinking in the Community of Faith:
Toward an Ecclesial Hermeneutic

Practical theologians, whatever their viewpoint or approach, need ways of thinking about the thinking that goes on in the shared life of faith. Faith communities both grow out of and generate symbolic interactions, and therefore involve thinking processes. Those who seek to reflect upon these processes, perhaps to bring them into relation with norms or to assess their faithfulness, need categories that permit the reasoning intrinsic to shared faith to speak for itself, while encouraging critical judgments concerning it to be made.

What is the nature of the thinking that underlies, accompanies, and sustains faithful life-together? Several writers have recently sought to describe it. Edward Farley's notion of "theologia," of theology as "habitus,"[1] despite its elusiveness and tendency to individualism, surely moves in the right direction. Robert Bellah and his associates perhaps come closer to the lay mind and to the actual phenomena of collective awareness with their Tocquevillian term "habits of the heart."[2] But Saint Paul long ago identified and addressed the same notion of community-embedded thought. "Have this mind among yourselves," he wrote to the Philippian church, "which is yours in Christ Jesus..." (Phil. 2:5). And to the Romans, "...be transformed by the renewal of your mind..." (Rom. 12:2). What is this way of thinking, this making of a common mind, but the deliberation that contextually forms and carries forward the life of shared discipleship? It is certainly not what we now call "systematic theology." It is, rather, that which systematic theology needs to thematize and study if it wishes to recover its ecclesial vocation.

If the truth be told, academic theologians have typically set little store by the symbolic exchanges, linguistic and otherwise, that actually constitute the fabric of the faith community. Best, we think, to give a wide berth to all such regions of intellectual chaos. Yet here lie the primary thought movements that actually shape the community's decisions, and therefore its social form. Here lie the mostly unspoken patterns of signification that account for the way some things "make sense" to us in congregational meetings or in daily life, while other things do not. To the extent that the theologian is rooted in a faith community, these sign sets will influence his or her more explicit intellectual inclinations--the sorts of things that "make sense" in his or her academic theological discourse--as well.

This essay seeks a fresh approach to the description and analysis of the faith community's primary thinking processes. The approach sought is hermeneutical in genre, but follows the lead of those who have extended the scope of hermeneutic from the world of texts and text-like products to the human life-world as such, seen as an arena of activated, interrelated, signs. It argues furthermore that there is such a thing as lived, and not merely discursive, exegesis. A community of faith may be understood as such an exegesis, following certain rules or norms, of the signs of the world around it. And by being such a lived exegesis of the world, the community becomes a signifying element *in* that world. The embodied and normed exegesis of signs itself becomes a new sign. Because this process is practical and communal, and not merely academic, it is itself a process of symbolic interaction. Hence it involves a kind of thinking-in-action which is precisely that which we are trying to understand. To the extent that this thinking is exegetical in nature, critical reflection in the midst of and on behalf of it will need to be an ecclesial hermeneutic. The task of this essay is to begin to sketch the kind of hermeneutic required.

Our Inquiry in the Present Theological Situation

But why are we doing all this? If this inquiry is to be properly understood, it must be not only grasped in its own right but also seen as part of a larger quest. The search for a hermeneutic of primary thinking in the faith community is a response, not merely to the church's practical problems, but to a series of crises in the Christian theological enterprise. Every essay in this book affirms this in one way or another. But the present writer believes it makes a difference how one comes to the question of the faith community's practical reasoning. How and why is the traditional academic way of doing theology breaking down? The writer was brought up theologically in a Barthian context. Hence he tends to see the present crisis--if that can be done--in Barthian terms. This essay will argue that the present deconstruction. of the Christian theological edifice parallels, and may even be said to continue, the deconstruction. launched by Karl Barth with his Romans commentary after World War I.[3] Barth's series of moves marked not only his personal intellectual development and his ongoing attempt to meet changing political and spiritual concerns; it also pointed to a series of shifts in the implied social and cultural locations for theological work. Barth journeyed from a nineteenth-century culture protestantism. that had its home among educated elites and in the universities, to a theology of "infinite qualitative distinction"[4] in which the preacher proclaims the Word to a congregation of solitary existers, and finally to "theology as a function of the Church":[5] the disciplined testing of the "language about God" peculiar to a confessing community seeking its independent identity and voice in the face of worldly powers.[6]

Taken together, Barth's moves overcame the nineteenth-century marriage between theology and the spirit of the age and reaffirmed dogmatics as a "science" (in the German sense of *Wissenschaft*) in its own right. But they were worked out in a manner which assumed that both the ecclesiastical and the cultural conditions needed for confident theological construction were still relatively secure. Barth, for example, could consult the Christian past with confidence that his work stood in demonstrable continuity with it. He could presuppose the existence of the institutional church without questioning the sufficiency of his Swiss, bourgeois, context for modeling its mental habits. And, above all, he could develop a "doctrine of the Word of God" without serious doubt about the nature and role of language in human life, and therefore of dogmatic constructs dependent upon it. Today each of these assumptions has been radically shaken.

We live in a crisis of sources and of our relation to them. What sources are authoritative, and why? What connects us with these sources, and how? What guarantees the identity and continuity of the faith community? We speak of appropriating tradition but we cannot (despite ecumenical achievements in this area) give a common account of what tradition is or of how it works over time. Our sense of the integrity of tradition and of its transmission has rested, Farley says, on the maintenance of a notion of the church as "house of authority" and of Christian thinking as requiring a "principle of identity."[7] But neither frame of reference is tenable under the actual conditions of contemporary Christian life on this planet. Moreover, we cannot take the institutional church we know as normative setting even for a critical "dogmatics." Instead, we face a situation of radical religious pluralism: so much so that we cannot say whether the different expressions of Christian faith across the cultures and across the globe have any single essence. Contextuality rules. Not only does Christian faith appear to have radically divergent meanings in different venues, but within Western cultures alone there have appeared theologies representing women, minority groups, groups with special interests, and the like. At this historical juncture, this is as it should be. It is in the interests of justice that different human communities come to self-awareness and achieve their voice: appropriate too that the church become a vehicle for such self-expression. But with what result for Christian faith? In what sense can all these expressions of the faith be thought to represent one church? What confessional norm or norms can be said to be present in all? Is there in fact any practical limit to such diversity? May contextually situated forms of faith diverge to the point of being beyond the possibility of mutual communications? *Is* there one gospel for the whole world?

And, finally, we face a radical loss of confidence in the means of theological conceptualization. To the extent that such conceptualization, even of the Barthian kind, depends on the integrity of the European university and literary language-worlds, it must today be called in question. The deconstructive attacks of a Foucault,[8] or of a Derrida,[9] have been devastating to the assumption that our academic discursivities place reality at our disposal. If language speaks us rather than the other way around, it cannot be the medium for a theology of the Word. We now see that language as we know it in the lecture hall or library is an expression of the human power situation, and perhaps not capable of being a medium for the expression of a Word beyond that situation.

The methods employed in *Church Dogmatics* are not workable where impassable gulfs separate past from present, here from there, language from intentional consciousness. We are left unable to account for the community of faith, or to think coherently about it. Each of the three factors of tradition, context, and contextuality has become almost infinitely variable in its own right. Any combination of these variables into a particular form of life is probably *sui generis*: unique, forming a class of one. To put this another way, for any given instance of the *ekklesia* we cannot confidently make connections to the Christian past, or to other contemporary forms of the church. And we cannot generalize in thought what we see. With tradition, context, and conceptuality simultaneously problematic, the ecclesio-social form of life that takes shape in any given case will probably be, at least humanly speaking, a *bricolage*, an adventitious combination of elements lashed together on the spot. The actual configuration of the faith community will seldom, if ever, reflect exactly any standard ecclesiology found in the history of Christian thought or in current denominational manuals. It will not correspond, either to the dogmatic "Church concept" with which Barth, so his critics write, replaced the notion of God's action in history.[10]

Perhaps it is only now that the full implications of Barth's original deconstructive move can be worked out, and the question raised whether *Church Dogmatics* represents the only possible outcome of the original initiative. The issue, of course, is whether the encounter with the God of "infinite qualitative difference," which negates all human aspirations and achievements, leaves any concrete sociocultural, yet not idolatrous, place in the world for the gospel to stand. Yet if there is any act of faith inherent in the present essay, it is that God has not left the world without a witness. Despite the fact that we cannot account for them in traditional theological terms, recognizably Christian communities of faith continue to exist, in fact in many cases to thrive. Like the "subjugated knowledges" proffered by Michel Foucault[11] and the "local knowledge" analyzed by Clifford Geertz,[12] the ways of thinking worked out by thousands of Christian communities in their contexts defy academic attempts at regulation or classification. Yet, just by existing, they demand recognition. We must adopt a theological perspective through which we can be open to this demand: when, where, and as it happens. We need a perspective through which we ourselves can be open to being the ones through whom it happens.

Hence, the proposal for what could be called a "humble hermeneutic" or a "hermeneutic of recognition." We need a hermeneutic capable of detecting and identifying the forms of situational exegesis, and therefore the significative configurations, characteristic of particular forms of faith-in-situation. To see the situational shape of faith, we must bracket out, or deconstruct, the established institutional and conceptual forms in order to see what is there prestructurally. That can perhaps be done through a form of "hermeneutic phenomenology"[13] that sees the social world as "text-like" and thus can study different lived "readings" of that text. The value of semiotic method for this purpose is that it renders the world ready to be read. It helps us see how the social world, below the level of established institutions and concepts, remains "readable," and hence an arena in which human action makes sense.

Could it be that the encounter with infinite qualitative difference might be described in sociolinguistic rather than existentialist terms? The "new quest for the historical Jesus" contended that "history" in the Gospels was essentially an arena for existential encounter. Why not conjecture that such an encounter took place for the followers of Jesus as their secure frames of self-and-world reference were exchanged for a precarious, yet tangible, form of existence known as discipleship? This new form of being-in-the-world was not confined to the existential moment. It was not purely inward and dimensionless. It is describable today as a set of relationships to the powers of this world and to the forms of imagination by which the powers are sustained, such that these powers become penultimate to the power of the kingdom. There can, in short, be an exegesis of the situation that exists when the disciples leave everything to be with Jesus. The hermeneutical principles that govern this exegesis underlie the codes and rules which regulate and sustain the faith community.

The community-forming power of such a hermeneutic must rest upon the thoroughness of its inherent deconstruction and reconstruction of common "sense." Written texts are far from the only sources to be "read": the reading must penetrate to the constituent "signs" of the world, the fundamental building blocks of meaning. The coming of Jesus Christ introduces just such a radical deconstruction and reconstruction of the signs which, at that time and place, have sustained the world of power and meaning.

Is the gospel then an instrument for the "insurrection of subjugated languages"? May it be that the Word of God comes to us through signs which the forms of expression in power normally exclude and repress? May it come in messages that disrupt the structures constructed to domesticate them? Is language capable of being the vehicle of such disruption? May the Word of God speak in the wordlessness of what it is to be a *campesino*, or an asylum inmate? Can we reach such a level of understanding by permitting our hermeneutic of the human sign-world to be controlled by a christological metaphor: that of the Suffering Servant of God?

Semiotic Method in the Worlds of Power and Imagination

The emerging discipline of semiotics is the logical discussion partner for our attempt at an ecclesial hermeneutic, for it demonstrates how both society and culture are generated and maintained by human interactions involving the signifying elements in the situation concerned. Culture is, in effect, a set of codes along with the rules for using them. A hermeneutic of ecclesial existence requires semiotic analysis of the signifiers and codes among which the faith community functions as a living, expressive exegesis.

The best brief account of the theory of signs as grist for a theological method is no doubt to be found in Robert Schreiter's *Constructing Local Theologies.*[14] Semiotics is an approach to the study of the human lifeworld in which that world is seen as an interconnected array of "signs." Semiotic theory sees culture as a vast communication network in which virtually every element, both of the natural and of the human-made environment, may function as the bearer of signification. Hence, the term "semiotics" from the Greek *semeion* or "sign." Different writers may use different terms: "symbols" or "signifiers" may convey approximately the same meanings, depending upon the point of view intended. Seen semiotically, a culture is a system of signs whose usage is governed by still other signs functioning to denote the relationships between signs. These usage indicators are often tacit rather than explicit. Yet they constitute much of what the culture is about. They make it possible for the signs to be understood correctly. Just as native speakers of any given language know implicitly the rules for how that language goes together, and thus can speak, for practical purposes, unlimited numbers of correct sentences, so a culture consists of signs functioning within a silent syntax so that its members can not only speak but act understandably in a vast variety of ways. The task of semiotics is to describe and explain these signs, their interaction, and the rules that govern these interactions, thereby delineating the cultural complex that emerges as a result.

But where do these sign networks come from? Each person is born into an already-existing universe of significations, but also generates his or her own inner sign network. Perhaps it is true here, as in other matters, that ontogeny recapitulates phylogeny: that the child's acquisition of signifying capacity is a product of an active and imaginative struggle for selfhood in relation to the meanings conveyed by the environment. Signs and their syntaxes arise in the individual and the collective imagination. And imagination, then and now, is preoccupied with the reality of power. Human beings form mental images of the world that are more than merely diminished or evanescent copies of what has registered on their optic nerves. Our images have to do with ourselves as actors and with the world as either inviting or resisting our actions. We see the world and ourselves in terms of what we can and cannot do. The slave's world image is different from the master's. If we feel imploded and disempowered we form images that interpret the world, as they reflect it, accordingly. The same if we are empowered in a position to shape our own and others' lives. The reality of power (as distinguished from mere energy or force) in human affairs is always to some degree a matter of the imagination. Political power rests on a collective sense that confers it and defines it in certain terms. To resist power that rests on shared social imagination may not only be to invite retaliation but also to violate the world image that underlies the symbolic and conceptual ordering of one's universe. It is a conjecture, but certainly an attractive one, that signs of every kind, functioning to constitute culturally maintained codes or sets of rules, rest upon each culture's reigning configurations of power and the imaginative constructs that define and sustain them.

Clearly there are different ways of construing power imaginatively, and hence different sets of culture-maintaining signs. In his book *Religion and Regime*,[15] Guy E. Swanson sets out the range of possibilities that seems to have been present in Europe in the period following the Reformation. His point is to show that the different ecclesiastical polities that settled out of sixteenth-century religio-political conflict reflected the power metaphors current in the cultures concerned. Swanson offers a spectrum from "immanental" social metaphors at one end to "heterarchic" ones at the other. In the "immanental" metaphor, power is conveyed throughout the social organism from the sovereign to whom it properly belongs. To have power is to be in symbolic touch with its source. In modern terms, it is to be "In Her Majesty's Service:' The society's sign complex, then, conveys this notion even in its most apparently insignificant details. The social organism becomes a construct of corporately maintained imagination, carried by its significative liturgies, uniforms, heraldry, royal ciphers, and all the rest.

In the "heterarchic" metaphor, on the other hand, power does not flow from a royal source. It is rather the outcome of some form of adjudication of competing interests: as in the stock exchange, in litigation, or in business contract negotiation. Again the social-cultural context for this view of power is a work of the collective human imagination maintained by a complex of signs with the rules for their use. The potent signs now tend to be the symbols of success in the conflict of interests: signs related to status, wealth, and political influence. Such signs are, as in the preceding example, both massive and subtle. Public life-styles make unmistakable statements. But, lacking obvious clues, we still look for indicators of manner, dress, accent, and the like which tell us how a person has fared in the struggle. A systematic study of such sets of signs will reveal the manner in which they convey and maintain an imaginatively construed syntax of power.

In either of these semiotic contexts, or in a world which embodies some combination of them, it is possible to imagine religious communities that "read" the signs in their own either legitimating or counter-cultural ways. In the first case we have the makings of Troeltsch's "church type" and in the second his "sect type." But such ideal-typical analysis is already a form of abstraction from the notion of the faith community as itself a living exegesis. The semiotic method proposed here suggests that the faith community is a "reading" of its environment in the sense of a principled translation or paraphrase of that environment's signs. It is not just a "type," but something unique to be appreciated in its own right. Perhaps the most pertinent analogy is to an interpretation of a plot by a subplot, or the exegesis of a play by a play-within-a-play. The faith community can be made aware by its own semiotically trained theologians of how it is living out its subplot within the world's larger story, and hence realize what sort of sign in the world it is itself becoming.

The transformative energy of the church's lived exegesis in the sign system will depend, of course, on how close the norm or principle of this exegesis comes to the roots of signification as such. This essay has argued that significative syntaxes arise, both in the individual and in society, out of the interplay of imagination with power. An expression

of the Christian message which gets at this power/imagination nexus
has the potential to make a difference. Consider the possible impact in
culture and society (whether of the ancient world or our own) of a
community whose being rests on a situational exegesis such as this:

> Who has believed what we have heard?
> And to whom has the arm of the Lord been revealed?
> For he grew up before him like a young plant,
> and like a root out of dry ground;
> he had no form or comeliness that we should look at him,
> and no beauty that we should desire him. (Isa. 53:1-2)

These words, with their well-known continuation, speak for themselves.
Clearly there is a challenge here to the common power-world's
fundamental meanings, to the way the sign complexes of ancient Near
Eastern societies were put together. If a community of faith exists in
such a power-world as carrier of such a subversive set of significations,
it is in effect using the signifiers of the old world to make present a
different world. To be part of such a community is to give voice to
those "subjugated knowledges" that tacitly influence the manifest forms
of knowledge. By reshaping human society down to the level of its
foundational dialectic of power and imagination, down to the region of
the origins of its signifiers, it effects a fundamental semiotic
transformation at the roots of thinking and knowing.

The Servant Signifiers in the New Testament:
An Illustration

We can infer from the Synoptic Gospels how this may have
happened for the members of the early Jesus community. Consider,
first, the scriptural heritage the Jesus community brought to bear. One
thinks of the different ways in which the power of God and the
resulting possibility for God's people are bodied forth in the Hebrew
Scriptures: of how the early community of Israel in Canaan articulates
God's rule in one way, how the monarchy does it in another, and of
how the prophets recall their hearers to a covenantal sense by holding
before them an imaginative vision of the blessed commonwealth. One
then asks how the imaginative construal of God's power in relation to
penultimate powers is expressed in the early "Jesus community." In

relation to all that is going on in first-century Palestine, in relation to the various forms of symbolic valency attached to diverse elements in that social environment, what did it finally mean to become a follower of Jesus? What did the very existence of this "messianic" community communicate to those who knew it? Was there any relation between the meanings acted out in each disciple's membership and the messages conveyed by the faith community's public reality?

To have joined the early Jesus community must have meant experiencing an upheaval in one's symbolic world, especially where issues of ultimate and penultimate power were concerned. The signifying elements in the Palestinian Jewish tradition would have been read and acted out in new ways. The signs and signifiers surrounding the vision of the Suffering Servant now offered a vehicle for the expression of both shared and personal faith. They also made possible a "readable" public statement concerning the rule of God in history. The complex of signs embedded in the surrounding culture would have been taken up and put to new use: incorporated in fresh parable and metaphor so that the new community itself became a signifying medium for the message of the kingdom. The nascent church, by its very nature as a sign and bearer of signs, would have given the world of first-century Palestine and beyond not only something new to think about but something new to think with: a set of symbolic resources not previously available for wrestling with its inherent temptations and problems.

But did all this in fact happen? One reason for the elusiveness of New Testament servant imagery lies in the fact that it does not consist in a single, easily identifiable, usage. It is, rather, a perspective intrinsic to the story of Jesus and his disciples, and within that narrative takes many forms, both spoken and acted out. It has been argued by a number of scholars that the influence of this and other related passages was so taken for granted in the Jesus community that little self-conscious application of it to particular settings has survived in the Gospels. Quotations and clear allusions are surprisingly fragmentary and seem to have no consistent set of meanings. But these scattered materials may well be mere outcroppings of a massive, indeed semantically subjugated, whole.[16] The Servant Songs may have shaped the vision of power at the heart of the primitive Christian consciousness. They may have provided the initial sign set employed by the community in its exegesis of the world. The Songs may have been the imaginative form best suited to making sense of the experience the disciples shared with Jesus.

If so, these materials may have become carriers of this "sense" in a variety of subsequent expressions: each appropriate to some new situation which the New Testament also records. It appears, in fact, that the further one advances beyond the period described in the Gospels, the less intrinsic and more self-conscious becomes the usage of Isaiah 53 and related passages. Quotations become longer and more explicit. And the meanings given these excerpts become ever more clearly related to the new contexts in which they are used. While the' Jesus community's original, situational, construal of power remains the meaning core, the writers of Philippians, 1 Peter, and other later New Testament writings reexpress that core in terminology suited to the new social and cultural situations in which they are involved.[17]   This process is plainly visible in Paul's Philippian letter. Here we find an instance of faith-community formation in which a semiotic deconstruction and transformation of the power world is the chosen instrument. The famous hymn of Phil. 2:5-11, a parabolized, versified, probably liturgical, version of the Jesus story loaded with disempowerment and reempowerment terms, is a capsule summary of the results of earlier situational exegesis. The treatment has now become abstract enough in its hymnic versification to enable it to travel from its roots in the original Jesus community to the Pauline community at Philippi. Particular forms of power have given way to the universal signs of power as such. The essence of how the world looked to those who were with Jesus is captured in a few verses on the way to becoming a confession of faith.

Paul sets this hymn in the midst of his discussion of community-forming, or community-disintegrating, relationships in the Philippian church. It is to function as confessional norm for an interpretation of the Philippians' situation that will lead to certain consequences for their life together. The Philippians are to do their practical reasoning understanding that, because they are in Christ, the power relationships characteristic of the Roman world will no longer control the forms of Imagination of each other that give rise to interpersonal conduct. Factionalism, vainglory, selfishness are symptoms of the old power world. They are to be replaced by love, mercy, compassion, concern for others, the sharing of suffering. And this will be accomplished not merely by the inward transformation of individuals. It will happen because the Philippians have been led to a new kind of thinking based on the hymnic parable of Jesus the Servant-Lord. *Touto phroneite*, "have this mind among yourselves," the apostle writes (Phil. 2:5). The community is to be "of one mind" on these matters. To be so, we infer, is to permit all the levels or aspects of the reasoning, the *phronesis*, which attends community formation to be shaped by the imaginative reinterpretation of situation which is the great hymn.

Formed in this way, the Philippian church will be a "token" of both perdition and salvation to the world about them. Why is this so? Because by assuming the servant form of life they participate in and communicate the same hermeneutic of the world-historical situation that has called Paul to Rome, and is now being acted out through his imprisonment. The Philippians are in conflict with this world. Their conflict is the same one they have seen in the career and conduct of Paul. They thus represent a Power that the world has not yet acknowledged. The Philippian community is to embody in its current form of life the situation that will exist when all the principalities and powers bow the knee to the name of Jesus (2:9-11). This future situation will be a confessional event, even a language event. "Every tongue" will then "confess," *homologein*, that the world's scheme of identities and values has been rearranged in accordance with a new power geometry. The Philippians are to do their thinking, to work out their lives together, in accord with this new construal of the world now. So doing, they become a medium through which the gospel finds expression in the midst of time.

Habitus Theology in the Public World

It is clear that Paul has been speaking, in this passage, of something close to what Farley calls theology as *habitus*.[18] I take this to mean a form of thought intrinsic to the fabric of life-in-faith, bred out of lived attitudes and relationships, yet capable of rising to the level of conscious deliberation. The Philippians are not merely being exhorted: they are being challenged to think in a certain way and to be aware that they are doing so. In them the servant form of life characteristic of the early Jesus community finds reexpression, not in literal replication but in terms of its essential characteristics as an imaginative parable. To keep living so as to act out this question in each new situation, the community must engage in shared *phronesis*: must "do" theology in its primary, confessional, form.

To see the formation of the church as a gospel-shaped and shared exegesis of any given environing sign-world may be not only to think better about theology as *habitus* (Farley's term for the practice of theological reflection in the life of faith), but also to begin the reconstruction of theology as a method of critical reflection within, and upon, this formative activity. Such critical reflection will seek concepts that can both illuminate and regulate the church-formation process. Perhaps this search for categories will produce "rules for thought and action" which eventually become, on the one hand, doctrine, and on the other, polity or canon law. Perhaps such thinking will borrow intellectual categories that can enable it to draw metaphysical or ontological conclusions. Perhaps it will go on to consider what must be true about ultimate reality for such a community of interpretation to exist at all, thus constructing a transcendental argument. But such reflective activity, whatever its form, will arise within and build upon the active exegesis of the world that the faith community is by being present there.

The community of faith communicates. It acts as a sign in the wider world, because it takes up and transsignifies in its form of life signs that are already present in its situation. The church "speaks of God" as Karl Barth said, both in its characteristic language and in its social form.[19] It is the word of faith to some particular human situation in its living exegesis of that situation's signs, indeed of the depth dynamics of imagination and power that underlie these signs. The community of faith takes social and cultural materials to itself and transsignifies them just as the celebration of the Lord's Supper does with bread and wine. The materials transsignified remain recognizable. But they say something new.

The messianic reconfiguration of signs sets two questions in the midst of the power/imagination world. The first asks, in ways appropriate to the time and place concerned, Who is God? The second asks, again contextually, What may we therefore do?

How to formulate the question "Who is God?" By asking what the ecclesial reality in question signifies among the operative signs in its environment with respect not only to penultimate powers but with respect to the final Power with which we have to do. In a multitude of ways, the scriptural narratives describe tests of strength between God and the idols. The Passion Narrative is in its own way a liturgical "trial of truth." Jesus is defeated in terms of the power signs of this world, and yet Christ defeats the principalities and powers of the cosmos. The community of faith is itself an answer to the question of who God is.

And the second question is thereby also set among the signs. What may we therefore do? The messianic resignifying of the power world will have opened up previously unimagined avenues for action. The world will have been opened to new possibilities through the use of metaphors that capture the reconfiguring of signs in parabolic and narrative forms. Through such metaphors, the faith community sees new openings for creative witnessing stretching ahead into the future. Paul Ricoeur suggests that in reading the parables of Jesus we can see "possible worlds" lying beyond us "in front of" the text.[20] And not only the parables told in the text, but also the great parable enacted by Jesus and his followers, could open up that way toward the future.

Does this happen, however, in a way that contributes anything to the public weal? Does the church's presence in a situation do more than witness to an alternative form of life that some may prefer? Does such presence lead to anything useful for humankind now? The faith community must ask this question if only because it remains part of the public world and needs to behave responsibly. But there is a further reason. That of which the faith community is a sign is this present world's future possibility.

We should thus be able to transcend the distinction between those versions of practical theology that focus on the *ekklesia* as such, and those for which the field of action is the whole human community. If the church is an exegesis of the world, it cannot leave the world behind even when the visible result of its exegesis seems radically sectarian. The faith community may well be determined by all that it claims that it is not. The church as an interactive form of life is more than the church as juridical institution. The institution is merely an instrument for the faithful people to use in their worldly deployment. The people are not the institution. They are, rather, a network of signifying action and interaction, both scattered and gathered, which must be understood in much more dynamic terms. The notion of a shared hermeneutic guiding situational exegeses in a world of interacting signs is designed to help make this clear.

A chorus of voices today tells us that, in the West, the public order is losing its warrants and coming apart. Hannah Arendt, in *The Human Condition*,[21] saw this almost a generation ago in respect to the *res publica* or *polis*. Alasdair MacIntyre has said it more recently with respect to moral reasoning in *After Virtue*.[22] Michel Foucault's career traced (and, some would say, helped to bring about) the deconstruction of our confidence in the great Western theoretical constructs bearing on the nature of the human.[23] In such a world, can the church's signifying presence make a difference?

That question, of course, will be answered only in the course of events. But we have already argued that the church may be situated better than any other gathering of human beings for signifying to the world the presence and meaning of what Foucault has called "subjugated knowledges," precisely those tracts of human experience which the great, yet now crumbling, conceptual constructs of the West never did bring to the point of expression: such things as what it is to be an inmate of the Gulag, what it is to be an oppressed peasant, what it is to be a member of a group without full access to the symbol network of social and cultural power. It takes more than occasional media attention to bring such things effectively to public awareness. It takes a community that already lives a servant paradigm, and thus can take up and body forth what such experiences mean, and how they may be vehicles for seeing beyond the values of the powerful.

In short, the church may offer the world a language for grasping its own present truths and future possibilities. The fact that the church is present as a lived parable or sign may possibly give rise to forms of thought[24] that the world desperately needs. But if this is to happen, a practical theology needs to grow up that has some awareness of this possibility, that helps shape the faith community to such ends. The proposal of this essay is that the church should thinkingly constitute its presence in the world so as to add something to humankind's capacity to envision itself whole. The faith community should contribute something to the vocabulary of human self-awareness not as "mere symbol" but as a form of "real presence." By showing the world how its own vocabulary can be taken up and redeployed around a new imaginative understanding of the final Power with which humankind has to do, the community of faith may say, more convincingly, that the possibility of salvation continues to exist.

Notes

1. The notions of "theologia" and "habitus" are developed at length in Edward Farley's *Theologia: The Fragmentation and Unity of Theological Education* (Philadelphia: Fortress Press, 1983).

2. Robert N. Bellah, Richard Madsen, William M. Sullivan, Ann Swidler, and Steven M. Tipton, *Habits of the Heart: Individualism and Commitment in American Life* (Berkeley and Los Angeles: University of California Press, 1985), *passim*.

3. The possible parallel between the stance of Karl Barth's *Epistle to the Romans* (trans. Edwin C. Hoskins, 2d ed. [New York and London: Oxford University Press, 1933]) and certain features of the contemporary "deconstructionist" movement has been pointed out by Walter Lowe in an as yet unpublished article, "Barth Contra Dualism: Reconsidering the Römerbrief."

4. Barth, *Romans*, Preface to the 2d ed., 10.

5. This phrase, often used to describe Karl Barth's position in *Church Dogmatics*, does not, so far as I know, actually appear in that text. It refers, of course, to the entire exposition in 1:1, *The Doctrine of the Word of God: Prolegomena to Church Dogmatics* (trans. G. T Thompson [New York: Charles Scribner's Sons, 1936]).

6. See ibid., 1:1, p. 2.

7. Edward Farley develops the sense of these terms in *Ecclesial Reflection: An Anatomy of Theological Method* (Philadelphia: Fortress Press, 1982). The term "house of authority" is introduced on p. xiv and expounded throughout. For the "principle of identity," see pp. 34ff.

8. See Michel Foucault, *The Order of Things: An Archaeology of the Human Sciences* (New York: Vintage Books, 1973), and *Power/Knowledge: Selected Interviews and Other Writings, 1972-1977* (New York: Pantheon Books, 1981).

9. See Jacques Derrida, *Writing and Difference*, trans. Alan Bass (Chicago: University of Chicago Press, 1978), esp. chap. 1, "Force and Signification," and chap. 10, "Structure, Sign, and Play in the Discourse of the Human Sciences."

10. See, for example, Trutz Rendtorff, *Church and Theology: The Systematic Function of the Church Concept in Modern Theology*, trans. Reginald H. Fuller (Philadelphia: Westminster Press, 1971), 21.

11. Foucault, *Power/Knowledge*, esp. pp. 81ff.

12. Clifford Geertz, *Local Knowledge: Further Essays in Interpretive Anthropology* (New York: Basic Books, 1983).

13. The term "hermeneutic phenomenology" has been used by Don Ihde and others as a characterization of the philosophy of Paul Ricoeur (see Lewis S. Mudge, "Paul Ricoeur on Biblical Interpretation," in Paul Ricoeur, *Essays on Biblical Interpretation*, ed. L. S. Mudge [Philadelphia: Fortress Press, 1980],

9ff.).

14. Robert Schreiter, *Constructing Local Theologies* (Maryknoll, N.Y: Orbis Books, 1985), esp. 50ff. I am indebted to Schreiter for portions of the exposition of semiotics in this essay.

15. Guy E. Swanson, *Religion and Regime: A Sociological Account of the Reformation* (Ann Arbor: University of Michigan Press, 1967); see the theological treatment of Swanson's argument in Lewis S. Mudge, *The Crumbling Walls* (Philadelphia: Westminster Press, 1970), see esp. chap. 3, "A Contextual Look at the Churches."

16. See H. W Wolff, *Jesaja 53 im Urchristentum* (Berlin, 1949; 2d ed. 1952). Wolff argues that Isaiah 53 occupied such a central place in the life and consciousness of the apostolic band during Jesus' lifetime that seldom was it possible for the early church to use this particular passage, in the manner it used others, as a "proof text" for some particular feature of the gospel. Isaiah 53, rather, *was* the gospel. What appear to be "proof texts" are really outcroppings of a broadly held set of assumptions at the earliest stage of the history of the church.

17. It is also the case, of course, that the "Servant" christologies which appear in the New Testament later give way to other terminologies reflecting the church's encounter with Hellenistic culture.

18. See Farley, *Theologia*, passim, and also, for a different view, Barth, *Church Dogmatics* 1:1, p. 24.

19. See Barth, *Church Dogmatics* 1:1, pp. lff. "The Church confesses God, by the fact that she speaks of God. She does so first through her existence in the action of each individual believer. And she does so in the second place through her special action as a community...."

20. Paul Ricoeur, "Biblical Hermeneutics," *Semeia* 4 (1975): 101ff.

21. Hannah Arendt, *The Human Condition: A Study of the Central Dilemmas Facing Modem Man* (Garden City, N.Y: Doubleday Anchor Books, 1959).

22. Alasdair MacIntyre, *After Virtue: A Study in Moral Theology* (Notre Dame, Ind.: University of Notre Dame Press, 1981).

23. Foucault, *Power/Knowledge*, 83-84.

24. "The symbol gives rise to thought" is the famous watchword of Paul Ricoeur's *The Symbolism of Evil*, trans. Emerson Buchanan (Boston: Beacon Press, 1969).

8

Toward a Hermeneutic for Ecclesiogenesis

Churches need to think new thoughts about how they do their thinking. The social realities of faith within and around the churches today do not correspond to the expectations implicit in these bodies' formal structures. We have seen some of the reasons why. Tradition does not shape faith community the way it once did. Pluralism is rampant. Theological conceptualities are in disarray. In short, classical confessional norms for judging the authenticity of church life are more and more dysfunctional in today's world. Yet all this is happening just at the moment when new kinds of socially engaged congregations, base communities, religious orders, liberation organizations, and issue-focused associations are bursting forth with fresh spiritual energy for the church and for the human community. How are we to "test the spirits" in such a fluid situation? How are the churches to rethink their nature and calling? How are we to begin to reframe the very idea of a church universal?

A Perspective for Ecclesiology: Discernment and Vision

This chapter proposes a perspective for ecclesiology in this situation. My hypothesis is this: by their relation to Jesus Christ, Christian communities of faith are lived decipherments and expressive embodiments of the people-configuring work of the Holy Spirit in the social and cultural worlds in which the churches live. Congregations discern Spirit-formed social realities in the world and bring them into a christological frame of reference which makes them visible. Congregations thereby articulate the human communities around them as spaces in which the Spirit's people-gathering power is active. By proclaiming the gospel, celebrating the liturgy, and acting prophetically they signify that God is continually forming communities of people to be agents of justice, peace, and freedom. Christian congregations are not to be identified with the people of God. Rather they discern its signs and seek to express these signs sacramentally.

In order to do this, congregations bring together myriad elements of shared human life. Church members bring with them specific genetic inheritances, cultural idiosyncracies, traits of character, educational backgrounds, habits of language, economic involvements, family ties, occupational perspectives, and so on. Through their networks of relationship with others they represent still wider ranges of human experience. All these things are ingredients for the church community's construal or metaphorical construction of the world. A faith community cannot be adequately understood solely by consulting its formal polity. It can only be understood as a gathering of persons who bring with them all the kinds of life substance mentioned and more, a community which aims at configuring all this so as to represent the identity of Jesus Christ and thereby to articulate the shapes of God's presence in the world through the work of the Holy Spirit.

In practice, of course, it may be difficult if not impossible to find the Spirit's people-shaping work. The effort to discern and signify the reality of a people of God often finds the world of human action to be ambiguous, murky, or worse. Our best efforts may be short-circuited by misperception. Yet traces of a people-forming Spirit are sometimes discovered in seemingly unpromising situations of personal, economic, cultural or political life. This can happen when events are found to have some inherent reconciling power, or when participation in them, often entirely outside the bounds of the congregation, can be seen as an act of witness to the reign of God.

The churches' ties with the American civil rights movement during the 1960s are a case in point. The effort to achieve equality for Blacks was at first largely based in the Black churches, but it soon came to involve many other groups and social forces: unions, universities, the legal profession, and so on. White congregations were often indifferent or antagonistic, but white denominational leadership and the liberal wing of the white clergy not only rallied to the cause, but also found in it a sense, all but lost now for a generation or more, of God's active involvement in human life. One could readily understand the people of God to be those at any given time who worked together in the movement to be instruments of God's justice for humankind. Many congregations discerned here a larger people-forming work of the Spirit. None could identify themselves with this work; it was much larger than they. But some could and did find ways to manifest its deeper meaning sacramentally.

Thus it made sense for many Christian bodies to identify with and draw strength from the March on Washington of August 28, 1963. For many, the crowd in front of the Lincoln Memorial when Martin Luther King, Jr., delivered his "I have a dream" speech itself seemed itself to have "the soul of a church."[1] To this day those who were there remember not only the celebrated address, but also the sense of spiritual communion among the many political, social, and religious agendas represented in the crowd. Many commentators called attention to the power which lay in the convergence of these forces: civil rights organizations, labor unions, political action groups, veterans' groups, local synagogues and congregations, national denominations, government workers, delegations from overseas, and more. A strange courtesy and forbearance animated this throng through hours of waiting for the program to begin. Temporary and highly diverse "neighborhoods" coalesced on the sidewalks and lawns, companions breaking bread, conversing quietly, sharing expectations. Here was a threshold moment. A multitude of attitudes, agendas, cultural assumptions, economic and political interests, and forms of faith or unfaith were transformed for a few hours into vehicles for something more than the simple sum of what they were as they came. These forces were momentarily regrouped into a new pattern of meaning. Many churches identified themselves with that new meaning. They found in it the work of the Holy Spirit, and included the story of the day, at least for a while, in their own stories of faith.

I argue that this is a paradigm for ecclesiogenesis. The formation of churches always involves some sort of discernment of the Spirit's work in the world and an attempt to manifest that work in visible forms of life. With sufficient vision, the churches may come to see that the Spirit's people-forming work is larger and more inclusive than anything they can possibly represent with their own resources. Hence becoming the church does not mean making exclusive claims. It means prophetic decipherment on the one hand, and lived signification on the other. I maintain that this is essentially an exegetical or interpretative process which leads to the building and constant re-forming of the visible church in the midst of the world.

Such an interpretative process needs to be governed by a hermeneutic or pattern of principled reflection concerning its meaning. A "hermeneutic for ecclesiogenesis" is thus a coherently thought-through understanding of what is going on when believers form a community which interprets the world as the space of God's reign. Such a hermeneutic seeks to understand the process through which the congregation *itself* becomes a readable sign of the Spirit's work. The congregation reads the signs and symbols generated by the Spirit's energizing presence. It then appropriates these signs and symbols--makes them its own--so as to become itself a living sacrament or sign. But what makes the signs of the world "readable?" What happens when they are appropriated so as to form a church? And what is the proper method for studying these moves? Is it some hermeneutical form of the sociology of religion, or is it ecclesiology in the fully theological sense of the term?

A Phenomenology of Spirit

I have been using the word "spirit" (small "s"), as well as the related but distinct terms "Spirit" and "Holy Spirit," in descriptions of the way a world-involved people of God comes to be deciphered and made visible in particular faith communities. What justifies this terminology? How do these words function in my argument? Social reality is "readable" in the manner sketched above because it is an objectification of "spirit" (small "s") in the sense of shared human intention and meaning. Intention and meaning take concrete form in the structures of society and the achievements of culture, as well as in less permanent expressions. Given the right clues, these expressions, linguistic and otherwise, can be "read." I will argue that a reading of human "spirit" in the light of Christ can discern "Holy Spirit," and that a doctrinal construction of what is involved here can yield a concept: "*the* Holy Spirit."[2]

On the way to this worldly objectification of spirit is the unending dialogue among life possibilities which constitutes the realm of spirit as such. Spirit grows from consciousness to self-consciousness through encounter with others. It finds symbolic means of expression from the simplest to the most complex. It generates metaphor and language and narrative and history and philosophy. Spirit is not something ghostly or other-worldly or even idealistic. It is the substance of human life together seen as inherently, by its very nature, an expressive medium. By speaking of human being-in-time as "spirit" we are saying that it is alive, it is meaningful.

I am contending that congregations are lived readings of this human life process. I want to say more about human spirit now, leaving Holy Spirit for the next section of the chapter. Human spirit is lived sense in the social world. It is important for our analysis to have a vivid idea of how the different elements of human sociality participate in something that can be called by this term. How can the social world be understood as intrinsically a field of interacting intentions and meanings?

Let me now begin to draw a map of the conceptual field we are entering. The social world as space of enspirited interaction has both synchronic (meaning what is the case at any given moment) and diachronic (tracing the movement of persons and institutions over time) perspectives. At any given point in time, society exists as a vocabulary of possible shared significations. Sense-bearing gestures, symbols, metaphors, rules of syntax, parables, narratives, liturgies, conceptualities, the social order itself seen as text like, are all pre-given to potential social actors. These elements are ready to be set in motion as persons engage them in action or speech. The actual making of sense in the spirit and the gathering of human communities around resulting meanings is, then, a process of activity through time. In social interaction we selectively activate the possibilities of meaning at hand in the available sociocultural vocabulary, in the process creating new vocabulary for those who come after us. These two elements, the synchronic and the diachronic, are separable only in analysis. In actual life they go together. We will look at the ways in which human initiative and interaction engages works of spirit already existing and generates further configurations of sense or spirit in each succeeding moment of human consciousness.

What is the nature of the energy which powers this process? Many answers have been given. In interpreting Hegel's *Phenomenology of Spirit*, Alexandre Kojève identifies the force behind the dialectic as "desire."[3] Spinoza spoke of a life-force, the "conatus," which urges organisms to persevere in being.[4] Possibly the most persuasive contemporary formulation of how such energy works in social process can be found in the work of Paul Ricoeur. This philosopher has written what in its most basic intent is a spiritual phenomenology of the human will. Ricoeur speaks of our "effort to exist and desire to be,"[5] and of our "appropriation" of the signs and symbols we encounter or generate along the way.[6] We come to know our lives hermeneutically: that is, we read the sense-bearing products of those life efforts which express our existential desires. We will see that Ricoeur develops this position with special reference to narrative or story, a connection which will be helpful when we seek to show that living in faith is living a commonly held narrative. The appropriation of signs which Ricoeur sees in the life of the individual makes sense also for the life of congregations looking for signs of Holy Spirit in human spirit. At this point in the argument however, my focus is on spirit as human phenomenon. How does it come about that the social world is intrinsically a space for the outworking of spirit as the ensemble of enacted human intentions?

I will argue that our "effort to exist and desire to be" may be expressed as a lived dialectic between *power* and *imagination*. The shared assumptions, the symbolic forms, the social institutions, the classical texts resulting from this dialectic in turn mediate a kind of *presence*. They make present in the social order certain shared interpretations of what that order means, and of what interpretation of reality it therefore conveys.[7] These interpretations will generally include expressions or formulas of theological import, formulas which point to what the community believes to be the encompassing reality in which the social process is set. A community's total store of symbolic resources--expressed as custom and law, literature, architecture and all the rest--serve together to make present a sense of the ultimate conditions and goals of its shared discourse. In this analysis of spirit the three realities--power, imagination, and presence--interact. No one of them can be defined apart from each of the others.

By *power* I mean the capacity to direct my energies so as to influence the conditions of my own life or the lives of others. One must ask, of course, from where the impulse to bring energy to bear comes in the first place: to act rather than to remain inactive. Otherwise the origins and goals of human action as such remain a mystery. Why, we ask, does history move? This much we know: the effective application of energy always involves the use of imagination. I must rehearse in my mind how I may use my capacities effectively in relation to centers of initiative and resistance over against me. My ability to use energy effectively may be considerable, or it may be very small. To have power is to stand in a configuration of circumstances such that I have capacity and scope for some sort of effective, that is situation-altering, action. Power thus is not the same thing as force. Power is always defined in relation to some imaginative construal of the action world as a place for doing what I can do, however great or little that may be. Thus power is a felt capacity, and the felt capacity arises not only from an awareness of being endowed with resources, but from a certain reading of the situation as amenable to the organized use of these resources. A social actor with little command of raw force may exercise great power given the imaginative construal of the situation which makes the most of the capacities available. Power, in short, is the ordering of life energy within an understanding of the social world that invites meaningful action, within a way of seeing which portrays my situation as offering meaningful possibilities. Such meaningful action, in concert with or in opposition to other human beings, is an ingredient in the historical-cultural dialectic of spirit.

The nature of *imagination* comes to light as we mentally envision and rehearse possible ways of exercising power, or of dealing creatively with the fact that our literal capacity for action is limited. I imaginatively consider possible interventions in, or responses to, some situation in which I have a certain sense of my capacity, or lack of it, to bring influence to bear. Such deliberation generally proceeds with some symbolic or narrative construction of the action world. It begins with rudimentary hypotheses about the world and other selves. It reflects not only my sense of my physical surroundings, but also my construal of the capacities and intentions of my fellow human beings. I perceive others as beings who imaginatively construe me in return, and who have a greater or lesser power to act upon me or in response to me. Eventually such deliberation becomes an acted-out interpretation of society's panoply of symbol, metaphor, and narrative, of the signifying fabric which makes society what it is. This process of imagined and then enacted intervention is repeated many times over by individuals who depend on already existing social patterns and who, by their activities, help to create new ones. A society's stock of narrative literature--from epic poems to novels to newspaper accounts--is basically a storehouse of possibilities ready to be simply reenacted, or given imaginative variation, or continued into novel episodes or new chapters in response to situations utterly unforseen by earlier actors in the narrative.

The dialectic of power and imagination is the field of human spirit. On a large scale this dialectical process eventually precipitates certain more or less stable forms: a given civilization's worlds of business, politics, academic life, artistic endeavor, and so on. Taken together these worlds constitute a fabric consisting both of culture (art, music, literature, rituals, customs) and of the economic and political arrangements which make culture materially possible. In any given case society and culture objectify the supply of shared meanings which social actors draw as they seek each day to "make sense" to one another. It is as "objective spirit" that social reality is readable for congregations of believers who seek to discern, and then to signify, a more profound sense of God's configuring work in the historical process.

Meaning-Bearing Elements in the Social World

It will be useful now for purposes of analysis to disassemble these processes of the objectification of spirit into some of their meaning-bearing elements. As played out in actual events, the production of socially shared meanings is enormously complex. Its aspects intricately interact. But it is probably possible to distinguish, no doubt rather artificially, a series of levels of the power-imagination-presence dialectic from the dawn of consciousness itself to the generation and maintenance of the whole social organism. And at each level, as in the whole, ontogeny probably recapitulates phylogeny: the genesis of individual consciousness recapitulates the genesis of the social organism. One can look at the total socio-cultural process as an intricately articulated arena for the emergence of spirit, or shared sense, or intersubjectively maintained meaning.

Short of Hegel's phenomenology, there exists no "unified field theory" of the social genesis of spirit. I will not try to offer one here. There is no single route into the tangled underbrush of human social awareness. Instead, one chooses an approach corresponding to what one wishes to know. If one is interested in the origins of selfhood in society one may perhaps read George Herbert Mead. If one is interested in the roots of signification one reads Thomas Sebeok, Roland Barthes, or Umberto Eco. If the preoccupation is signs and the generation of knowledge in a community of interpreters, one goes to Charles Sanders Peirce. If one is concerned about the grammar of language games and their relation to "forms of life" one consults Ludwig Wittgenstein. If one needs help with the meaning of metaphor one engages Paul Ricoeur or the writings of George Lakoff and Mark Johnson. If the topic is texts and social phenomena as text-like, again the source is Paul Ricoeur.

These writers are my chief guides in the paragraphs that follow. From their works I lift up five ways into the dynamic phenomenon of human sociality as a field of spirit. These perspectives are arranged roughly in a series of levels or dimensions of increasing complexity. But they do not represent discrete provinces of meaning. Each dimension or perspective is present throughout the whole fabric of human interaction. Together they may come close to canvassing the elements which should be included in any "thick description"[8] of human social reality.

Gesture and the Social Self

The dialectic of spirit arises, as George Herbert Mead showed in *Mind, Self, and Society*[9], at the very threshold of consciousness. Mind emerges in an intersubjective process. One becomes a self through participation in social interchange: first rudimentary and then more complex. Before there can be selves in communication, we must account for the emergence of selves with meanings to communicate in the first place. The key term in Mead's account is "significant gesture." The self is given to itself, that is, it becomes self-conscious, through observation of the response other persons give to the self's gestures. I discover the meaning of my gesture by seeing what it means to another person. My initiative, say in pointing to or grasping something, taps into the patterns of imagination which already exist in society as I see how other people respond. I come to know what I "meant" in the symbolic currency of my society because I discover what the other self interpreted the gesture to mean. The self comes into being through communicative processes.

This begins to happen at the most primordial level. Each newborn re-experiences the genesis of social meanings. The infant's flailing of arms and legs, the child's cries, are exercises of innate capacity that explore the world by acquainting the infant with resisting objects and the responses of persons. This exploration leads to an initial construal of the world in the infant's imagination. Further initiatives encounter more reactions which build up for the child a fuller picture of the world. What begins as raw undifferentiated energy begins to be tagged with various sorts of inner meaning reflecting what the child observes in others. Innate capacity is refined through imagination to become a greater or lesser ability to exercise power.

In Mead's view, thought is the internal language of such exploratory and finally meaningful gestures. By the time gestures become consciously signifying, the objects which the gestures involve or to which they point have become signs. Inevitably, the reference of these signs becomes in part socially shared. The genesis of signification thus brings us to the next level or dimension of sociality as spirit.

Signification and Language

A symbolic-linguistic field now emerges in which elements and objects of the world take on meaning in relation to human intentions. The society establishes a pattern of broadly agreed sign values for such elements or objects. For grasping the meaning and implications of signification at this level I turn to the philosopher Charles Sanders Peirce. Peirce envisioned communities as conversations involving complex interchanges of signs. The formation of such a sign world is the first step toward what a community eventually takes to be "common sense," toward what it eventually understands as logic. Without the development of stable systems of signs, communities cannot exist.[10]

Signs refers to objects, or objects function as signs, in such a way that socially generated and maintained interpretations of the world are available to the community of interpreters. A sign may resemble the object designated (as in the case of a map); or it may have conventional meaning (a stop sign), or it may refer to a general category or class of things (words in a language). There may be signs which designate the relationships between other signs. The study of signs teaches us that all knowing is communal and inherently open-ended. What we know is tentative and fallible. Knowledge is refined in a communal give and take.

The French writer Roland Barthes has shown how far this conversion of the action world into a realm of signification can go. He has studied popular culture: clothing styles, posters, sporting events. He has also studied the semiotic conventions to be found in literary texts, and in urban settings of various kinds. The Parisian cityscape, in its details and as a whole, sends many messages that its inhabitants take for granted. Without these messages, the Parisians could hardly function as social beings.[11] A person who walks on a Parisian street wearing cowboy boots is then sending a message of his (or her) own.

Language is a special, privileged, and highly elaborated system of signs which have become conventional and shared. Language permits human beings to move beyond gestures and objects as elements of signification to expressions--sounds and words--exclusively dedicated to the signifying function. This step makes possible experimentation with combinations of signs and the development of signs which express the relationship between other signs. Above all, language is a sign system which enables us to express what is fictional, to signify what is in fact not the case but which can become the case in the world of imagination. And an imaginative world sustained only by language can sometimes literally come to power: a utopian vision may fuel a revolution and be tried out in the "real world." Again, we are speaking of one aspect of the genesis of spirit.

Grammar, Syntax, and Logic

Languages and cultures evolve customs for putting signs or signifying actions together. We call these customs rules of grammar or syntax. The combination of signs into messages, like the combination of words into sentences or physical movements into meaningful actions, requires certain implicit rules or codes which make possible the construction of complex messages. "Grammar" in this sense is not in the first instance to be found in grammar books. It is, as Ludwig Wittgenstein says, embedded in "usage," in the way signs or signifying actions customarily go together (*syn-taxis*) in a given human setting or situation.[12]

The native speakers of a language, the birthright members of a culture, are able to speak or act "correctly," usually without being able to articulate the "rules" their speech or actions embody. If the rules need to be stated, they have to be extracted by trained observers from a large number of instances. The native speaker or actor does not need such help. He or she can utter an infinite number of correct sentences with ever new content, or carry out an infinite number of socially understandable actions, all the time evincing the culture's rules for the combination of signs without being able to state what they are.

These rules of thought and action, spoken or unspoken, together constitute what Wittgenstein called "forms of life."[13] One cannot use language outside of the particular language game played within a given human setting. Language governed by such rules comes close to constituting what we mean by sociality. A given society has a linguistically sustained sense of reality itself. Subcultures within a larger society have their own versions of this reality sense. Forms of life, then, carry with them rules for thinking about the world as an arena for human action which, for participants in that world, quite simply represents the way things are. Yet such visions of the world are enormously varied in different cultural settings. What seems immutable to a French *philosophe* in 1789 may not seem so to a German romantic poet in 1821. What is logical to a captain of industry in 1890 may not follow for a union leader in 1947. And the differences named lie within the context of Western society. The differences are greater between the West and the East, between the "first world" and the "third." Logic itself, some say, is a notation for describing the socially maintained syntax of signs and expressions, and therefore the form of world coherence that obtains in a given human community at a particular time or place. Again, I am describing an aspect of objective spirit.

Metaphor, Concept, and Symbol

Very soon certain signs begin to take on special importance because they violate these syntactical codes, or do interesting and unexpected things with them. Fresh combinations of signs enable the confrontation of otherwise disparate realms of discourse to create new meanings. Juxtapositions which bear such creative power we call metaphors. Language acquires a metaphorical structure that eventually gives rise to concepts, which in turn are represented by symbols. Paul Ricoeur, in *The Rule of Metaphor*, argues that our sense of reality itself is based upon the juxtaposition of disparate signs to generate new kinds of meaning.[14]   Ricoeur's theory of metaphor is important to an unpacking of the process of objective spirit. This philosopher has helped us see that metaphor is more than a trope consisting of deviant naming ("the moon was a ghostly galleon..."). It is, in fact, a form of "impertinent predication," a form of *discourse* which says something that could not have been said before. Metaphor is a kind of "seeing as" which suggests a new way of relating imagination to power, a new way of orienting oneself to the world.

Once this is understood, it begins to be clear that a metaphorical process has been at work through all the levels of signification discussed here, from the origins of language and action in significant gesture to the most advanced achievements of culture. Signification itself can be understood as a metaphorical process. To say "jazz is a blind drummer" is to be present at an origin of meaning which incorporates and extends the reach of all the gestures and signs that hover about the primordial power of imaginative expression which the jazz idiom represents.

The power of metaphor in ordinary language, once fully understood, is striking. George Lakoff and Mark Johnson show in *Metaphors We Live By* how metaphors dominate basic concepts in our language and hence in our life world, where they control the ways in which power and disempowerment are imaginatively construed.[15] Examples make the point. It is clear, for example that in English and many other Western languages "argument" is metaphorically understood as a kind of warfare. "Your claims are indefensible," we say. Or, "He attacked every weak point in my argument." Or, "His criticisms were right on target." Or consider the reach in Western imagination of the metaphor of the marketplace. From barter in the village square to world economic order to the notion of a "marketplace of ideas," this trope occupies a dominant position in our contemporary social imagination.

One receives a hint of the extent of this dominance by trying to imagine the metaphorical structure of our world view as other than it is. Suppose, Lakoff and Johnson suggest, we lived in a society in which argument is not a form of warfare but a kind of dance. Participants then would not be combatants but performers. Their goal would be not to wipe each other out but to interact in an aesthetically pleasing way. In such a society, the military metaphor for argument would not be available; it would not be part of the stock of metaphorical possibilities. With just this one change, our life world would become radically different. Or suppose that the world of human interaction were not thought of as a marketplace, but as a context for the exchange of gifts, a realm of mutual generosity. Again, certain meanings common to our civilization would not be available, while others would come into play.

A very wide range of expressions belonging to specific semiotic domains or provinces of meaning show their rootage in metaphors, primitive at first yet eventually enormously ramified. Even the most abstract concepts, including notions both scientific and theological, are ultimately metaphorically based. Take, for example, the physical sense of "mass." It is grounded in the sense of bulk or weight, but has reached a very abstract and precise meaning through mathematical and, therefore, symbolic refinement that could not have taken place in the way it has were it not for the metaphorical ground. The same could be said of the concept "spirit." It goes back to a metaphorical identification of life with "wind" or "breath," but has been elaborated to refer to the form of God's presence in the historical process which we call Spirit or Holy Spirit. Without the metaphorical work underlying them, certain thoughts could not be thought at all, much less brought to such conceptual elaboration.

Texts

Using all the just-analyzed elements of expression, each society and culture constructs and maintains its characteristic texts. These often take narrative form. The stories or epics or poetry or liturgies of a culture are intelligible because they are expressed not only in grammatically correct sentences but also represent a recognizable grammar of actions and ideas which exemplify the culture's metaphorical construction of reality These texts are most varied in literary genre and social function. Only some achieve classical status: that is, only a few are recognized by the society or culture in question as in some respect normative or disclosive of the culture's highest values or transcendental grounds. Thus in ancient Greece the Iliad of Homer apparently had this status, in Judaism the Hebrew Scriptures; in Christianity the New Testament; in German romanticism Goethe; in America the Bible, the Declaration of Independence, the Constitution, or the works of Mark Twain.

But a given society also produces a rich profusion of texts which are constitutive but not classical. Memoranda, shopping lists, reports, brochures, and the like help to constitute the society as a realm of discourse. Some of these documents will hark back in one way or another to the culture's classics, although in modern times such references and echoes grow fainter and less frequent. The important point is that there is bound to be some relationship between the society as realm of discourse and the styles of activity that the society regards as meaningful, understandable, or sane. Indeed some philosophers, following Paul Ricoeur, are now saying that societies *themselves* may be understood "on the model of the text."[16] That is, they are text-like in that they consist of interconnected networks of signifying elements and actions. Societies, in short, are tapestries which follow rules of grammar and exemplify metaphorical constructs. Hence, as patterns of human interaction, they can be read.

We now begin to see how the study of culture can be a "hermeneutical" science. If what the human scientist studies is, in effect, a "text," or if it is for heuristic purposes text-like, then human science cannot be content with functional or structuralist or material approaches to culture. The student of society and culture needs to decode what any given tract of human expression and action is saying. The meaning of action goes beyond what social actors intend or have in mind in what they say or do. The panoply of action is like the combination of sentences in a poem or in a novel. Action--analyzed in terms of the gestures, signs, grammatical codes, ruling metaphors, and now the rules of syntax involved in text construction--takes on a meaning in its own right which can be ascertained. A culture text is neither simply what the original actors had in mind nor what the observer reads into it. It is what it is. It is this fact, Paul Ricoeur thinks, that gives the human sciences their "objectivity." They interpret the meanings which social realities convey by existing as text-like realities in the world.

Synthesis: Making Sense

Taken together, these levels of analysis can function to constitute what Clifford Geertz calls "thick description," the notion that the actual fabric of social reality is drenched with sense, or as we could also say, is a realm of spirit. In this thickly described realm of socially maintained sense, the activities of persons and institutions generate meanings that both turn the social world into what Jürgen Habermas calls a realm of "communicative action," and also add to the stock of sense available to social actors yet unborn.

We have also come as close as we can to what Hegel meant by objective spirit. "Objective" because it exists in tangible social and cultural forms; "spirit" because it consists of embodied forms of sense which can be read and interpreted. And yet here lies the danger of which Ricoeur warns: that objective spirit becomes embodied in political "totalizations" that represent forms of imagination which have definitively come to power. However laudable such a system's claim to foster of reason and freedom may be, it may also become a principality or power menacing to human well-being. The great instruments of such totalization, Ricoeur says, are the state and the institutional church.[17]   Hence the need for the prophetic or critical spirit, and the requirement that institutions be open to reform.

It is important, thus, to link objective spirit to what I have called "presence." The power of a given metaphorical-social system to represent what we take as "reality" is related to the accuracy of its underlying observations and the persuasiveness of its arguments. It also is tied to forms of imagination that have come to power in a given social context. Presence is a form of socially enacted power which has won a definitive victory in the human perspective of a given time or place. Presence is something like the total life vision of ancient Rome at the height of its influence, or the combined vision of the American "founding fathers," or the view of the world from the higher reaches of the Vatican curia. It is an interpretation of the world so seemingly obvious and close at hand as to be entirely unproblematic for those who live within it. Here lies a reality of which the churches must be critically aware as they try to understand themselves in their socio-cultural settings.

Churches in the World of Social Meanings

What happens when churches arise within this meaning-making process? Churches are subcultures within the larger social process. In simplest terms, they exist by selectively appropriating signifying elements from the cultures that surround them. Just as an individual appropriates the signs generated by his or her passage through the social world in an "effort to exist and desire to be" (Ricoeur), so a congregation, living a story which embodies its own identity, takes on certain signifying elements of the society and culture around it. Forms of governance, works of art and architecture, perspectives related to class race and gender, newspaper stories used as sermon illustrations: these are the sorts of things that are appropriated into the fabric of ecclesial existence. Such elements of sociality in turn will be composed of ingredients of the kind analyzed in the preceding pages. They will be texts or text-like combinations of primordial gesture, sign, syntax, and metaphor, parable, narrative. They will be elements of society and culture.

By being appropriated, these elements will inevitably be in some degree transformed in meaning. If a particular denomination or congregation is only "the Republican Party at prayer," the change will be slight. If another Christian body is radically critical of society to the point of subversion, the change will be much greater. But in either case the faith community involved is living in society and appropriating elements of it which signify the *sense* of its passage through it. The sense acted out in that passage will naturally reflect the congregation's or denomination's understanding of the biblical story and its idea of how and where that story is being continued in the social world. The story may be understood as confined to the religious community concerned. Or it may, as this essay argues, be discerned to be going on in the larger human world, wherever configurations of human spirit are momentarily identifiable as the work of Holy Spirit establishing the conditions of God's reign.

When these things happen, appropriated social meanings are trans-signified. They are organized around new *foci* of meaning. They are thereby enabled to convey the identity of Jesus Christ. The church bodies in which such trans-significations take place *themselves* become signs or parables within the social orders they inhabit. They join their societies' stock of meaning-bearing elements, to be respected or mocked, comprehended or misunderstood, as the case may be.

Something like this must be the meaning of the famous sentence of *Lumen Gentium*: "By her relationship with Christ, the Church is a kind of sacrament or sign of intimate union with God, and of the unity of all humankind." What is true of the sacraments is thus true of the worshipping, witnessing, gathering itself. Ordinary social substance is taken up "from a common to a sacred use" without ceasing to look and feel--and in fact be--what it has been before. Trans-signification occurs in the forms of human life together without making these forms unrecognizable.

The most obvious example of such trans-signification of culture is the parable, which combines elements of common life into new configurations that now perform metaphorically. They enable the hearer, as Paul Ricoeur says, to see the possibility of a different way of being, of living in a "world in front of the text,"[18] without leaving this present world. John Dominic Crossan adds that parables function not only metaphorically but subversively. Over against the tendency of socially maintained meanings to turn into myths which portray the world as a realm of opposites--clean versus unclean, civilized versus savage, raw versus cooked, we versus they--parables subvert the myths imposed on us by powerful establishments, break their power over our lives.[19] They also open us to the possibilities of the life in the Spirit.

Above all, the parables see through the constellations of power (in Paul's words, "principalities and powers") which maintain certain imaginative constructions of life in being. So it is with the story of Jesus, a parable writ large. And so it is with each congregation or base community: each is called to be a kind of lived parable, a kind of metaphorical transformation of the social world in which it lives. It makes present a representation of the world as the realm of God's ruling. It thereby enacts within the world something that is ultimately true about the world but not evident without the word of faith as hermeneutical key.[20]

The most powerful instruments of this transformation of worldly meanings are no doubt the biblical narratives which communities of faith bring interactively into their situations. Every congregation continues the biblical story through its own stories. These contemporary extensions of the biblical style and plot in the congregation's own history become the carriers of the faith community's identity. Such continuations of the biblical story highlight significant events which have had a certain transforming and binding power for those who participated in them. The congregation's constitutive narrative inscribes a sequence of meaning through the field of signs, usage codes, root metaphors, and texts of a given culture. It is the genre of lived text among all the others which comprehends the phenomenon of change over time, accounting for the perception that this individual, this congregation, this ethnic group, this nation, though it may change in important respects, maintains its essential identity.

Above all, such narratives recount stories of faith. While faith as personal existential disposition is not wholly accessible to language, faith may be represented in stories which, in effect, describe dramatic trials of truth, which embody the question of ultimate loyalty, ultimate concern. The litany of acts of faith described in the eleventh chapter of the Epistle to the Hebrews is a case in point. By faith Abraham...., by faith Isaac..., by faith Moses..., by faith Rahab..., to the point that we are "surrounded by a cloud of witnesses." Such narratives represent struggles with the claims of final Power--the ultimate Power with which we have to deal--as these claims are conceived to be present in the human action field. They are community-constituting answers to the question "Who is God?"

We need to pursue these insights still further. We must ask what it means in practice to "decipher" configurations of human spirit christologically, and thereby to approach them as points of meeting, however fragmentary, between Holy Spirit and human experience. Just as Paul Ricoeur sought to understand not merely philosophical formulas but also "the fullness of language," so we must find ways of grasping the many forms of grace-filled reality which Holy Spirit generates in its encounter with human spirit. Sociality is the medium in which the gift is given. It is therefore a primary datum for theological reflection, not just a consequence of practical reasoning. "The holy catholic church" is not merely a gathering of like-minded people. It is one of the gifts of the Spirit which, according to the creeds, we "believe in."[21] No mere principle, no mere invisible idealization or theological surmise is confessed here, but an actual historical reality. How is such a historical reality possible? How does the holy catholic church of the creeds "subsist" in the institutions we know? How is the gift of grace in the form of sociality to be discerned there?

Decision-Making in the Congregation: Practical Reasoning

One answer is that the gift is to be discerned in the actual decision-making processes by which a community of faith conducts its affairs so as to maintain its identity as sacrament and sign of the Kingdom. At the close of his book *Christ and Culture*,[22] H. Richard Niebuhr wrote an epilogue, "A Concluding Unscientific Postscript," in which he made clear that no amount of doctrinal or cultural analysis, however insightful, can foresee the actual decisions by which a faith community is carried forward through time. The lives of individuals and their communities are lived in an historical process in which every decision is made in the midst of culture's relativities, in objective uncertainty about their true motives and about the outcome. There is no direct way to move from the community's story up to a given moment to certainty about the actual decisions it must make if it is to continue authentically to exist. The continuation of the story always rests on the lonely acts of faith of individuals whose decisions nevertheless need to take the existence of others into account and whose moves in concert with others make the faith community what it will be.

> We raise our existential questions individually, doubtless, and we do not forget our personal, individual selves. But the existentialist question is not individualistic; it arises in its most passionate form not in our solitariness but in our

fellowship. It is the existential question of social men who
have no selfhood apart from their relation to other human
selves.[23]

The church arises and continues in existence as faithful persons make
the choices which determine their relationships to all the other human
beings they meet. It may be, of course, that looking back on these
decisions we will find a pattern. They may look like the latest pages in
the story of Calvinism, or Lutheranism. There may be evident what
Jonathan Edwards,[24] and after him Edward Farley,[25] called a
habitus, a theologically reflective disposition to shape life in faith in a
certain way. But such is the existential, risky, character of decision in
a field of relative values that one can never, in advance, simply
translate one's confessional tradition into clear directions for action.
One never knows enough. One never knows what will happen in the
next day, or hour, or minute. One may know something about
Calvinism, but one never knows what the next episode in the history of
Calvinism will be or whether, by one's choices, one will be part of it.

Still, there are reasoning processes involved in such decision-making
and acting. A congregation faced with issues needing resolution will
engage in a process of deliberation or practical consideration. At some
point, a decision will emerge: whether by vote, by "sense of the
meeting," or in some other way. It is not always self-evident how
groups move from an initial shared "interpretation of the situation" to
a shared conclusion. At a certain point a decision seems to take form.
All or most of the relevant factors are perceived by a majority to be in
place. The conclusion appears as a precipitate of the deliberative
process. Suddenly it is there, needing only a formal action to catch it
in words. This does not mean that existential uncertainty disappears.
It is only that a certain decision seems right *for now*. For this moment,
the deed is done.

Clearly, this process is not a purely logical or syllogistic one.
Presuppositions, images, symbols, and feelings all play large roles.
Above all, as we have seen, a given community is likely to share a
certain pattern of social imagination within which there is an
interpretation of power. The group tacitly understands where power is
located, what assumptions motivate its use, and how it is likely be
exercised. Such understanding forms within a certain parabolic,
narrative, or other construal of the life world. This process of practical
reasoning is well worth study, and indeed has attracted the attention of

philosophers over the centuries. Aristotle believed that the wisdom of the scholar is built upon the *phronesis* or practical reasoning of the wise person, or of the community exercising practical wisdom. In order to devote him or herself to theoretical matters, the sage must possess, or presuppose, "practical knowledge."[26] This insight also goes back to the ancient Roman concept of the *sensus communis*: which Hans-Georg Gadamer defines as "the sense of the right and general good that is to be found in all men, moreover, a sense that is acquired through living in the community and is determined by its structures and aims."[27]

Interestingly enough, the notion of *phronesis* is plainly visible in the rhetoric of Paul. Many of Paul's references to a collective "mind" employ the Greek noun *nous* as in references to "the mind of the Spirit" (Rom. 8:27), "the mind of the Lord" (Rom. 11:34), and "the mind of Christ" (1 Cor. 2:16), but one especially important instance employs a verb related to the noun *phronesis*. This occurs at Phil. 2:5: "Have this mind among yourselves which you have in Christ Jesus." The Greek is *touto phroneite*. The context has to do with shared decision-making in the Philippian church. Paul ties this *phronesis* to the christological hymn of Phil. 2:5-11. The Philippian congregation is implored to conform its practical reasoning to this particular interpretation of Jesus' ministry. Yet the existential element of radical uncertainty is not absent. Paul also advises the Philippians that in his absence they are on their own. "Work out your own salvation with fear and trembling" (2:12b). This is not, as subsequent commentators have sometimes feared, a lapse into what later became Pelagianism. The "working out" of salvation is precisely *phronesis*, practical reasoning in the community of faith.

The patterns which in fact emerge from any particular case of communal deliberation call for explanation. *Some* tradition of interpretation, whether that of Phil. 2:5-11 or otherwise, generally lies embedded in the systems of signs and symbols that make up a congregation's social life world. Interpretations of the meaning of Christian faith are implicit in the way congregations or base communities put their worlds together. These interpretations may or may not correspond to any of the great confessional traditions.

If they do, they represent those aspects of these traditions which have found their way into the taken-for-granted systems of meaning that make the world of action coherent for the people concerned. In any process of discussion or deliberation, whether in a congregational meeting or in an individual soul, some courses of action will unaccountably recommend themselves more than others. Some possibilities will "make sense." People will be able to envision themselves more easily doing this rather than doing that. Because the symbolic shape of the life world is largely below the level of conscious awareness, and especially if the tradition embedded in that unobtrusive symbolic shape tends to reinforce risk-taking and personal responsibility, decisions will still be existential acts of faith, not risk-free processes of inference from conscious premises to conscious conclusions. Those who make such decisions act in the hope that, when the results are in, their life worlds, and with them their communal and personal identities, will still be intact.

Narratives of faith capture in retrospect, and make available for purposes of interpreting the world, events which in the actual experience were often deeply ambiguous, uncertain, and risky. Yet the social worlds in which these acts of faith took place, the traditioned communities that lay behind the faithful actors, already predisposed them to make some choices more readily than others. So it is today. Never do socially embedded predispositions eliminate risk. Never do they make it inevitable that the next chapter in the story of faith will be this rather than that. But the socially projected patterns of faithful behavior enable the character of faith to be objectively read. If one wishes to talk *about* faith, the only authentic way to do so is to tell the community-forming and communion-maintaining *story*. If one wishes to be *in* faith, the only way is to join those who riskily try to write the next chapters in the story themselves.

This position has important implications. I am saying that although faith decisions are made in existential uncertainty, the meaning of faith does not lie in my inward and inaccessible feelings or dispositions. The meaning of faith lies in certain traditions of shared understandings. These may run from Abraham to Exodus to resurrection and beyond. Faith's meaning also resides in some continuing tradition of shared behavior arrived at in the practical reasoning process. Theological concepts, indeed, depend for their intelligibility on their anchorage in a public historical tradition, such as the life of Israel or the experience of the church. These histories, with the narratives and parables in which they are told, become part of the "grammar" of each theological idea.[28]

I think of the churches' trans-signification of social reality as creating a heightened version of what I have already called presence. This is meant as a challenge to deconstructionists for whom nothing is made present by human expression in any of its forms. The activities of believers may come to constitute more or less stable communities in the world which deserve more than sociological analysis, more, even, than sociological analysis informed by a "hermeneutic of everyday life." I have already related the word *presence* to interpretations of reality so sustained, stable, and pervasive that for those who participate in them they *are* reality pure and simple. But the notion of presence is also a way into understanding what the Christian tradition has meant by *parousia* (the word "presence" in Greek), or the coming to power anew in our social imagination of a messianic vision of reality referred to traditionally as the "second coming of Christ." It is also a way into what has been meant by "real presence" in the sacramental sense. The churches mediate a presence in the midst of the social world which has its own coherence as the portrayal of a Person. This presence is composed of the symbolic materials of the world around it reconfigured and thereby transformed--like the many-colored pebbles in a mosaic--in such a way as recognizably to represent Jesus of Nazareth as the Messiah. Human spirit taken into this Messianic reconfiguration tells a new story, that of a people of God as the worldly instrument or expression of Holy Spirit.

Notes

1. My account of the August 28, 1963, "March on Washington" is based on personal experience.

2. The reference to Hegel is obvious, but our dependence on this philosopher should be kept within limits. The distinguished historian of ideas, John Herman Randall, once said that Hegel's great contribution to Western thought is this notion that spirit can become "objective." By "objective spirit" Hegel meant the historic monuments and classics of human civilization seen as products of the process by which consciousness dialectically evolves in a dance of intersubjectivity which generates self-knowledge, the means of expressing it, shared symbols, a social will, and finally the society's enduring cultural expressions of its self-understanding: literature, art, music, architecture, the state. Hegel seeks to portray a realm of law or *Recht* in which freedom and reason are upheld by established social arrangements. Spirit has become objective. The most lucid exposition I know of Hegel's understanding of "spirit" and objective spirit is in J. N. Findlay, *The Philosophy of Hegel: An Introduction and Re-examination* (New York: Collier Books, 1958), especially

313ff. My purpose here is not to expound Hegel's views as such. The philosopher might or might not recognize himself in these paragraphs. My point is only to give credit for a basic idea where credit is due, and then to adapt the material for my own purposes. Hegel can plausibly be seen as the inventor both of pragmatism and the sociology of knowledge. His notion of the human realm as essentially and intrinsically a spiritual dialectic of life-possibilities gives us something suggestive and useful. His way of seeing Christian faith as saying ritually and symbolically what the philosopher seeks to grasp conceptually is also highly suggestive. As the sequel will show, I have also learned from Peter Hodgson's portrayal of Hegel's notion of *Gestalt*, or life-configuration, as developed in the *Phenomenology of Spirit*, trans. A. V. Miller, (Oxford: Clarendon Press, 1977), 104-107, 264-65, 410-16. References in Peter C. Hodgson, *God in History: Shapes of Freedom* (Nashville: Abingdon Press, 1989), 274.

    3. Alexandre Kojève, *Introduction to the Reading of Hegel*, ed. Allan Bloom, trans. James H. Nichols, Jr., (New York: Basic Books, 1969), 3ff., *et passim*.

    4. Benedict (Baruch) de Spinoza, *Ethics* (London: Oxford University Press, 1923), Pt. III, Prop. VII, 144. See also the discussion in Stuart Hampshire, *Spinoza* (Harmondsworth, England: Penguin Books, 1951), 76ff.

    5. Paul Ricoeur's "effort to exist and desire to be," unlike the formulations of existentialists driven by despair, or suffering the dread and anguish of existence, stems from a fundamental affirmation of life as the gift of grace. He identifies his passion to exist with faith in the meaningfulness of existence. I owe this helpful formulation of what many have said less well to Kevin J. Vanhoozer, *Biblical Narrative in the Philosophy of Paul Ricoeur: A Study in Hermeneutics and Theology* (New York: Cambridge University Press, 1990),

    6. For the phrase itself, see Ricoeur, *Freud and Philosophy* (New Haven: Yale University Press, 1970), 46.

    7. In the classical philosophical tradition, what is *present* denotes what really exists, as opposed to that which is merely imagined. In Plato, for example, imagination brings to mind absent or non-existent things. A similar position is found in Jean-Paul Sartre. My use of the term "presence" implies that symbolizations of reality held in being by forms of the imagination which are in power, arbitrary though they may be, are to be taken as interpretative manifestations of being, as recreations by the creative imagination of what is. Such interpretations of reality powerfully influence our behavior and self-understanding. They make something "present" in a sense different from that envisioned in Plato. In this, as in other ways, I take my departure from the thought of Paul Ricoeur, for whom the imagination both "invents" and "discovers" something about reality itself. Again, my formulation follows that of Kevin J. Vanhoozer, *Biblical Narrative*, 9-10. This process of invention and discovery becomes more experientially, if not metaphysically, real when certain

works of the imagination play dominating roles in some social or cultural synthesis. A helpful discussion of theological meanings of "presence" can be found in Peter Hodgson, *Jesus--Word and Presence: An Essay in Christology* (Philadelphia: Fortress Press, 1971). Hodgson writes in the context of the "absence of God" theologies of the sixties and of the earlier work of Jürgen Moltmann and Wolfhart Pannenberg, theologians of hope and of the presence of the future God. For Hodgson, God is present, if at all, by means of word. "If God's presence is to be experienced afresh, then what is required is a rebirth of language" (p. 23). The word "God" in fact means "the promise of presence:" this on the strength of von Rad's translation of Exod. 3:14 as "I will be there." Hodgson's 1971 book, of course, predates deconstructionism's assault on the tie between language and being, an attack which demands the kind of comprehensive reply found in George Steiner's *Real Presences*. Hodgson's book, read today, cries out for a treatment of human spirit and Holy Spirit of the sort supplied in his more recent work *God in History*.

8. The term "thick description" (originated, it seems, by Gilbert Ryle) has been taken over by the anthropologist Clifford Geertz, who means by it a focus on the richness and intricacy of human signification in the world of action. Geertz describes Moroccan sheep thefts, Balinese cockfights, a Javanese funeral, so as to expose the whole range of layers of meaning involved in these activities. He writes, "Whatever, or whenever, symbol systems 'in their own terms' may be, we gain empirical access to them by inspecting events, not by arranging abstracted entities into unified patterns." See Geertz, "Thick Description: Toward an Interpretive Theory of Culture," in *The Interpretation of Cultures* (New York: Basic Books, 1973), 17.

9. George Herbert Mead, *Mind, Self, and Society* (Chicago: University of Chicago Press, 1934), 13ff., 51ff., 363ff. I am indebted to a discussion of Mead in Gibson Winter, *Elements for a Social Ethic* (New York: Macmillan, 1966), 17ff., 85ff.

10. See Robert S. Corrington, *The Community of Interpreters* (Macon, Ga.: Mercer University Press, 1987), 1-29.

11. Roland Barthes, *Systeme de la Mode* (Paris: Editions du Seuil, 1967) and *Mythologiques* (Paris: Editions du Seuil, 1957).

12. Ludwig Wittgenstein, *Philosophical Investigations* (Oxford: Blackwell, 1956), sects. 248, 373, 664, *et passim*. I owe these references to Anthony Thiselton, *The Two Horizons: New Testament Hermeneutics and Philosophical Description with Special Reference to Heidegger, Bultmann, Gadamer, and Wittgenstein* (Grand Rapids, Mich.: William B. Eerdmans, 1980), 386-87.

13. Ibid., sect. 23.

14. Paul Ricoeur, *The Rule of Metaphor* (Toronto: University of Toronto Press, 1977), especially 65ff.

15. George Lakoff and Mark Johnson, *Metaphors We Live By* (Chicago: University of Chicago Press, 1980), especially 3-9.

16. Paul Ricoeur, "The Model of the Text: Meaningful Action Considered as a Text," in John B. Thompson, ed., *Paul Ricoeur: Hermeneutics and the Human Sciences* (Cambridge: Cambridge University Press, 1981), 197ff. I am aware that Ricoeur's proposal to conceive human action on a textual model has received significant criticism. See, for example, John B. Thompson, *Critical Hermeneutics: A Study in the Thought of Paul Ricoeur and Jürgen Habermas* (Cambridge: Cambridge University Press, 1981), 125ff. Thompson believes that Ricoeur, like Peter Winch, is guilty of "illegitimate generalization from the linguistic sphere." Social circumstances and institutional contexts, Thompson thinks, have a reality of their own which resists reduction to a purely linguistic model.

17. "The true malice of man appears," Ricoeur writes, "only in the state and in the church, as institutions of gathering together, or recapitulation, of totalization." "Freedom in the Light of Hope" in *The Conflict of Interpretations* (Evanston: Northwestern University Press, 1974), 423.

18. John Dominic Crossan, ed., "Paul Ricoeur on Biblical Hermeneutics," Semeia 4 (Missoula: Scholars Press, 1975), 82, 104.

19. John Dominic Crossan, *In Parables: The Challenge of the Historical Jesus* (San Francisco: Harper and Row, 1985).

20. Two recent works which draw significantly on human science insights serve to illustrate the approach to faith-community formation we have in mind. In *Congregation: Stories and Structures* (Philadelphia: Fortress Press, 1987), James Hopewell recommends an approach to local ecclesial gatherings which resembles that of the cultural anthropologist who comes upon a previously unknown tribe and who seeks to discern the nature of that tribe's coherence and self-understanding. Hopewell, along with many others today, forswears structural-functional approaches to try to discern how the congregation gathers around and embodies the unique significations inherent in its stories, its relationships, its architectural and neighborhood-discerning mapping of meanings. Hopewell's approach is an extension of the science of ethnography. It is ethnographic in the sense that it studies the sense-making elements in the life of the *ethnos*, the "people." Hopewell tries to read the messages embodied in the tales church members tell and in the ways they conduct their common life. Robert Schreiter's equally important book, *Constructing Local Theologies* (Maryknoll, N.Y.: Orbis Books, 1985), does something similar with its emphasis on signification: the "semiotic" study of the way in which the world with its objects becomes a field of "signs" whose usages come to be controlled by "codes" which are in turn gathered around significant metaphors and finally incorporated in characteristic narratives. Schreiter is less interested in the study of actual ecclesial gatherings and more concerned to ask how theology can actually be pursued in the local or congregational mode. But he produces a result compatible with Hopewell's, if in a somewhat different vocabulary. Schreiter takes his inspiration from theorists like Roland Barthes and Umberto

Eco. The world and its objects are not just there: they signify. Human life in society is a journey through a realm of meanings ready to be activated by our touch.

21. As one might expect, the words "I believe in" with reference to "the holy catholic church" have been controversial. The phrase is not found in the Nicene Creed of 325 or in the Niceno-Constantinopolitan Creed of 381. In the Apostles' Creed the "in" is not repeated before "holy catholic church." The earliest texts of the Apostles' Creed, in fact, do not mention the church at all. Peter Hodgson, in his note on this subject in *Revisioning the Church: Ecclesial Freedom in the New Paradigm* (Philadelphia: Fortress Press, 1988), 113, writes, "It appears, then, that when reference to the church was added to the creeds, the church was first viewed as an instrumentality of belief, the place where the Spirit is at work; then it was to be 'believed'. . . but not 'believed in' the sense that God is to be 'believed in.'"

22. H. Richard Niebuhr, *Christ and Culture* (New York: Harper Torchbooks, 1951).

23. Ibid., 244.

24. Cf. Sang Hyun Lee, *The Philosophical Theology of Jonathan Edwards* (Princeton: Princeton University Press, 1988).

25. Edward Farley, *Theologia* (Philadelphia: Fortress Press, 1983), 31, 35-36, 55.

26. For references to Aristotle, see Hans-Georg Gadamer, *Truth and Method* (London: Sheed and Ward, 1975), 19-29. See also Gadamer, "The Power of Reason," *Man and World*, III, 1970, 5-15. References in Thistleton, *Two Horizons*, 294ff.

27. Gadamer is discussing the Italian philosopher Vico, who argued the case for the importance of practical reasoning, especially attacking Descartes for his mathematization of reality and lack of a sense of history. See *Truth and Method*, 22-23.

28. This view is derived from points made by Wittgenstein in *Philosophical Investigations*. I owe this reference and this application of Wittgenstein's views to theological language to Thiselton, *Two Horizons*, 381ff.

IV

Civil Society

9

Faith, Ethics, and Civil Society

My assigned topic for this consultation on church and civil society is "faith and ethics." Right away, I want to say that we are heirs to a long and rich tradition of theological reflection on just this topic. Is it not rash to suppose that we have something new to say? We must certainly reiterate certain basic convictions at the outset. Faith always has moral implications. To be in faith is to be part of a community whose story has public consequences. We must act accordingly. As Paul Lehmann used to put it, for the Christian there is really only one question: "What am I, as a believer in Jesus Christ and a member of his Church, *to do*?" Yet we must not collapse the faith/ethics distinction by making some particular ethical or utopian vision the *object* of our faith. Christian social activists have sometimes come close to doing this. We must insist up front that the One whom we *worship* is God alone.

But it is increasingly clear to us that faith in God and wrestling with ethical issues concerning the integrity of human life do belong intimately together in an emerging, comprehensive, ecclesio-social vision. Somewhere in this vision lies a "new paradigm." One way to state it is that "church" and "world" are ultimately bound up in a "household of life" which represents God's reign within history as well as beyond. In this perspective faith and ethics are two aspects of a reality ultimately one: the beloved community, the holy city come down from heaven like a bride (Revelation 21:3), in which God dwells among, and thereby constitutes the very being of, God's people.

In the meantime, the Church of Jesus Christ is called to be a community of faith-full moral discourse and practice, a space of solidarity-in-faith with humanity in anticipation of this fulfillment. Seen in this perspective, faith and ethics are like two *foci* of an ellipse. Each can only be adequately understood in relation to the other within the all-embracing circumference of God's promise to humankind.[1] Faith and ethics must continue to be discrete categories in the present penultimate time because the whole reality they represent together will otherwise be misunderstood. We are victims of the dichotomous thinking built into our modern sensibility, separating object from subject, theory from practice, inner history from outer history, and so forth. Such thinking requires us to form dialectical concepts. Faith and ethics together are a single spiritual reality which cannot be adequately expressed by either of these two terms taken alone. In the end we are talking about an entire theonomous pattern of life--the whole fabric of justified, reconciled human existence--which the gospel calls into being in the world.

Such a comprehensive perspective should be the starting point for any attempt to rethink the character of Christian commitment in and for our time. What faith is concretely, the kind of lived substance it has in the world, is the heart of the matter. Thus faith is *not* in the first instance a series of propositions to be believed, any more than ethics is a set of rules to be obeyed. Together they are a form of life to be lived: what early Christians called "the way." This lived form of life has its faith language and its moral precepts, but it is not to be *reduced* to its language or its precepts. It is rather to be seen as a mode of shared being-in-the-world which makes a difference: in the best sense a *political* difference.[2]

This paper seeks briefly to defend these theological convictions. I have divided it into five parts. The first seeks to set the stage by tracking the "faith and ethics" theme in current ecumenical discussion, showing that the different sides of this debate correspond to different theological views of the current human situation: our judgment of what is happening to us, our view of the eschatology in play. The second looks at the role "civil society" as a concept has taken on in secular appraisals of our current moment in history. Is the glass half empty or half full? The third asks what potential there may be in the attempt to engage this question theologically. What are our expectations? Can the "civil society" theme deliver? The fourth considers the terms of theological engagement with several different secular civil society discourses representing different political philosophies. The last section considers different possible outcomes of such engagement and suggests a paradigm of faith's interaction with politics drawing on recent experience in East Germany and South Africa and leading to a brief commentary on Revelation 21:3.

Faith and Ethics in Recent Ecumenical Debate

The "faith and ethics" theme has had two ranges of meaning in recent ecumenical dialogue. It has had to do first with the whole trajectory of ecumenical *understanding* from historic faith confessions to common witness in a world seen as God's household, or God's metropolis. It has secondly concerned *practical strategies* for the behavior of people of faith seeking the common good in this pluralistic world.

The trajectory of ecumenical understanding is well-known to us. How can we move from our confessional commitments--loyalties to primary communities of faith which still sustain us and which we want to maintain--toward enactments of our unity in Jesus Christ which bear witness among the struggles of the world for a just, peaceful global society capable of maintaining the integrity of creation? We know that enacting the unity given us in Jesus Christ is only possible if we simultaneously urge the churches to grasp the pain and the possibilities of the human world about them. Yet this trajectory of concern is beset by numerous misunderstandings and difficulties. The historic tension between Faith and Order and Life and Work has played itself out down the years and is still plainly visible in the divergent emphases of different WCC departments. The WCC staff and committees perpetually seem far out ahead of the member churches. The Ronde (Aarhus) Consultation in 1993, jointly sponsored by Unit I (Unity and Renewal) and Unit III (Justice, Peace, and Creation), made a major effort to bridge this gap in understanding, producing a text titled *Costly Unity*, subsequently transmitted to the Faith and Order World Conference at Santiago de Compostela in August of that year. It is not clear that most delegates to that meeting fully grasped the point. The "new paradigm" is present but not prominent in the Santiago documents. In short, despite several generations of ecumenical effort, we have not yet convinced the majority of Christians that faith *does* lead to the kind of worldly ethical responsibility the notion of "civil society" seems to require.

And even if we do grasp adequately the relation between faith and a vision of ecumenical moral community, the question of strategy for local and particular situations remains unclear. We need to ask how people of faith who are also citizens of various civil polities can in fact think and act so as to foster, enable and enact their faith in serious civic intercourse. I suspect that at least some of the resistance we meet comes from our not having made clear at the level of congregational life what a strategy for life in the household of God would look like. This question pinpoints the constant struggle of the "layperson" in the church to make sense of the faith in the modern world. Many persons of faith simply do not recognize the kind of ethical concern we have in mind as a vocation for themselves. Many of the most effective Christians in the world's struggles have difficulty relating their moral and political convictions to the faith they are being taught in Church. Our preoccupation with large ecumenical ideas may well divert us from the "parish pump" responsibility of making sense of all this on the ground.

These are not simply debates between traditionalists and progressives, although they are partly that. Behind our ecumenical encounters at both the global and local levels lies a difference in the way we see God at work in the world, and ultimately a difference in eschatology. Is the Reign of God something to be worked for in political terms within the context of human history as we know it, or does the Bible teach, and our practical observations reinforce, the view that God's rule is at least partly to be expected beyond history? And what, exactly, does this "beyond history" mean in relation to the world of our experience?

Is the "civil society" discussion to be seen as an extension of the relatively optimistic Ronde dialogue, and hence of the affirmative eschatology which has run through ecumenical documents ever since the end of World War II? This eschatology is an expression of confidence that God's work intersects political reality here and now, and above all, that God's purposes make some kind of historical progress of which there are signs to be seen all around us. Yet there are also notes of caution, dismay, and outright warning in the Ronde materials not to be overlooked.[3]

The "Civil Society" Theme at this Moment
in World History

The ecumenical "civil society" discussion parallels both the affirmations and the hesitations of the extensive secular wrestling with this subject over the past few years. This secular discussion represents *both* a continuing concern about the fate of democratic institutions in the West dating at least from the late seventies, *and* an optimistic surge of confidence that began to take off in 1989 with the fall of the Berlin Wall. It received further impetus with the adoption of a new constitution and the election of Nelson Mandela in South Africa. In 1991, Robert Bellah was quoting Walter Lippmann's world-historical pronouncements made seventy years ago. With the coming of interdependence and technological abundance, Lippmann wrote, "the vista was opened at the end of which men could see the possibility of the good society on this earth." At long last, he continued, "the ancient schism between the world and the spirit, between self-interest and disinterest, was potentially closed, and a wholly new orientation of the human race became theoretically conceivable and, in fact, necessary."[4] And here is Bellah's own summary:

> ...the world democratic revolution that began in the seventeenth and eighteenth century in Europe and America, having suffered severe setbacks earlier in the twentieth century, has entered a new stage of intensity in many parts of the world: in Eastern Europe, the Soviet Union, South Africa and elsewhere.[5]

And three years later Ernest Gellner was taking a still longer and equally optimistic view.

> A new idea was born, or reborn, in recent decades: Civil Society. Previously, a person interested in the notion of Civil Society could be assumed to be a historian of ideas, concerned, perhaps, with Locke or Hegel. But the phrase itself had no living resonance or evocativeness. Rather, it seemed distinctly covered with dust. And now, all of a sudden, it has been taken out and thoroughly dusted, and has become a shining emblem.[6]

Jean Cohen and Andrew Arato, in their magisterial *Civil Society and*

Political Theory, have put it most succinctly of all. "We are on the threshold of yet another great transformation of the self-understanding of modern societies."[7]

In my own country many have simply sat back to observe and celebrate what they see as the victory of capitalism in the cold war. Meanwhile such a deterioration in democratic institutions and in the quality of dialogue in the public world has occurred that the U.S.A. is scarcely an example to anybody else on this globe. As everyone knows, we are seeing the rise of hatred, fear, violence, and all the rest. As an American I have little but cautionary tales to offer to the rest of the world.[8]   As I write, our radio "talk show" hosts are violently denouncing Mr. Clinton for calling for a reduction in violence, thereby showing what he is talking about. If anything, fresh inspiration for the rejuvenation of our own democratic traditions may need to come to us from South Africa, Eastern Europe, and elsewhere. And even in these places the gloss is off many of the new democratic experiments. The need now is to sustain these initiatives in the midst of contrary tendencies of various kinds.

Thus I cannot speak of civil society without giving expression to the fear that the window of opportunity which gave rise to the renewal of discussion of this topic may be closing as rapidly as it opened. The "triumph of capitalism" in the West has never been what some trumpeted it to be. We live in an age threatened by a wholesale return to sectarian strife, born, ironically, of the ways people are led to interpret their traditions of faith. Samuel P. Huntington of Harvard has recently argued that future wars and global tensions will no longer be primarily based on conflicts between nation-states but on clashing civilizations defined by history, language, ethnicity, and above all, religion.[9]   In fact, we could be headed back to a pre-Enlightenment age: to something like the era of the Thirty Years' War.[10]

Robert D. Kaplan has carried these themes further. The twenty-first century, he thinks, will see radical environmental degradation and tribal violence in an effort by communities and cultures to survive in an increasingly anarchic human situation. The distinction between state-sponsored warfare and gang-type violence by members of religious and ethnic groups will virtually disappear. Hordes of refugees will pour over the borders of the privileged nations. The legal and economic structures of our world will break down once again into a war of all against all.[11]   If, as some say, the Enlightenment is dead, religionists should not be dancing on its grave. *Post*-modern separatism and anarchism in our thinking may well be accompanied by *pre-modern* political consequences.

Perhaps such insights give us even greater reason to be talking about civil society, but certainly a sobering sense that renewal of it will not be easy and that we may have to pass through some difficult times on the way. On the one hand, the glass is half-full, and on the other the glass is half-empty. The question of democracy, its creation and its maintenance over time receives focal attention. Yet, simultaneously, others see the beginning of a shut-down of our global life-support systems, physical and spiritual, which presage a new dark ages. Which picture are we to credit? The answer we give makes all the difference in choosing practical strategies for the Christian community of faith.

I will not choose between short-term readings of the situation. Both the optimistic and pessimistic views can be defended with ample evidence. The essential question is: What do we believe about human history in the long term? This could be a question for which immediate evidence is almost irrelevant. How long is the "long term" we have in mind? The democratic revolutions we have seen beginning may themselves signal, despite setbacks, a long-term mutation in human affairs. We are being pushed by circumstances toward being an interconnected planetary whole which desperately needs to find some spiritual dimension beyond the massive economic, communications, and military dimensions it has today.

Ironically, this is also a time in which many are reaffirming ancient faiths: Islam, Judaism, Buddhism and Christianity among them. The recovery of specific spiritual identities--vital to human survival as such re-traditioning may well be--will misfire unless they are accompanied by an appropriate new ways of seeing the broader human horizon. Our two-hundred-year-old notions of the reasoning powers and rights we share as human beings--all that the Enlightenment asserted and bequeathed to such contemporary statements as the Universal Declaration of Human Rights--no longer serve this purpose, and especially not for thinkers of the post-modern type. People need a sense of community and identity, and they also need a larger context of common human assumptions that keeps the negative consequences of particularism in check. What is to be put in place of the assumptions both about religion and the larger community which have kept the needed balance in the West for two hundred years but now seem deeply threatened in our fragmented world?

What Can We Expect This Inquiry to Accomplish?

Given that the civil society discussion has emerged in the midst of these opportunities and threats, does it promise to address them usefully? Does analysis of the theme of civil society simply pick up an optimistic, worldly eschatology and thus become one more stage in a series of ecumenical discussions tied to that perspective? Or does it give us scope for more sophisticated, dialectical approach? Is there room for human sin in this discussion? Can current considerations of this topic-- inside the churches and beyond--play a focusing, clarifying role in our ecumenical "pilgrims progress?" I believe the answer to the latter three questions is "yes." But we must clearly understand the kind of discussion to which we are committed by saying this "yes." I see four broad reasons for entering the "civil society" dialogue at this moment in ecumenical history.

First, the "civil society" debate is a focusing mechanism for dealing with what otherwise is a bewildering array of threatening social issues, both in the North Atlantic world and across the globe.[12] Some of these matters have already been mentioned. There are many more. The attempt even to list our discrete (yet no doubt interconnected) problems tends to reduce our sense of their seriousness: the catalogue is so long as to need a kind of rueful gallows humor in the telling! By concentrating on the "civil society" issue we get at what is certainly one of the underlying conditions of breakdown in our common life: our loss of the means of civil (as opposed to suspicious, angry, accusatory) communication across great gulfs of culture, interest, and power, race, class and gender. The "civil society" discussion certainly doesn't get at everything, but it helps organize a good deal of it.

Second, attention to the question of "civil society" helps theologians and ethicists to join forces with sociologists and political philosophers in a recognizable, ongoing, socially located, and reasonably well defined set of questions for dialogue. These questions are "in play" among political philosophers at the moment and promise to remain so for some time. Yet, despite its active character, this discussion is not right now moving toward any recognizable conclusions or closure. The field is very open, very tentative. The openness in question is exacerbated by the breakdown of the very Enlightenment-derived categories which until recently have dominated the field. Whether or not this means theologically oriented participants are more welcome than they otherwise would be, whether or not there is any recognizable place at the table for the likes of us, there is nonetheless great opportunity for the representatives of religiously traditioned communities to make contributions that can merit a hearing by their quality and invite attention by their pertinence.

Third, the notion of "civil society," despite uncertainty about its deeper intellectual foundations, has clear cross-cultural relevance. "Civil society" refers to a kind of coherence in civil discourse and social interaction that is everywhere a *precondition* for the development of democratic institutions, while in turn it needs such institutions for its continued well-being. The condition of social civility can undergird and accompany a great variety of specific *forms* of democracy. It can even co-exist with (and challenge from within) many forms of political tyranny. Basically, "civil society" means a realization-in-practice of public human interactions which prepares and enables the "people" to rule: through whatever particular political institutions they find possible in their situation. This broadens the discussion. Civil society is not tied to any one particular political persuasion. It is not socialist doctrine, nor is it necessarily tied to capitalism. There is room at the table for very conservative persons and for very radical ones. There is room for those who see in recent events a great change, a great opportunity (it is they who have sparked the interest), but also for those who think democracy proceeds much more slowly, that we cannot do the job in a generation. This gives the "civil society" discussion its inter-institutional, inter-cultural, international reach. One can speak of European, American, Latin American, African, Asian forms of civil society despite the differing (and perhaps structurally incompatible) political institutions to be found in these different parts of the world. This means, among other things, that civil society is a concept highly useful for understanding the new political movements, the different "transitions to democracy" emerging by fits and starts in these and other parts of the world. There are those who would like to turn these many political initiatives into a "common normative project."[13]

Fourth, there is a quality in this discussion which we sorely need. We look today for something beyond confrontation and fragmentation, beyond contests between saints and devils. We have been driven, in the name of differing visions of righteousness passionately held, to denounce one another both in the public world and in the churches. "Liberation theology" has sometimes taken this direction, as have the forces of the radical right. Despite the need to name and confront the evils we see, many of us are beginning to realize that today such conduct may contradict the principles we so passionately hold. Many of us begin to feel we have been too self-certain, if not self-righteous. Now, as many societies enter post-revolutionary situations in which the priority is on reconciliation and nation-building, we need to ask what the churches stand for in positive political terms and how they can help themselves and their fellow human beings attain it.[14] We can learn from the example of Nelson Mandela rather than from his wife Winnie! If there ever was a time for humility, the quiet voice, this is it.

And finally, there is a specifically theological opportunity, already mentioned at the start of this essay. It is to begin to construct a new "theology of the public world." In our present pluralism and social fragmentation, our "post-Westphalian" world in which nation states cease to be the peace-making instruments of Enlightenment reasonableness (if they ever really were) over against religious sectarianism, we need to think of the churches' worldly role anew. In this "civil society" dialogue we can begin to talk in secularly understandable terms about what we know theologically as the appearing of a People of God, the "Beloved Community," in history. There is room here for theologians of many different persuasions: for those inclined to identify certain political developments as signs of God's reign, and for those reluctant to do so.

Having aroused such great expectations, does the "civil society" theme live up to its billing? If we try to grasp all these opportunities, where does the discussion lead? As a historical concept, the notion of civil society has a distinctive form given it by John Locke, the New England Puritans, the philosophers of the Scottish Enlightenment, and a few others. In all these cases the relation between faith and ethics is *organic*. There seems general agreement, however, that the original philosophical and religious notions will not serve without some sort of radical reframing. Not only are the original religious motivations atrophied and the Enlightenment assumptions dubious, but the roots of the idea still left in our psyches now shrivel in an acid soil of multicultural conflict and mutual distrust.

We need some new working definition of civil society as idea and as social reality. That may be hard to achieve. With Hannah Arendt, I like to speak of civil society in spacial metaphors. I think of it as a social space, a certain kind of "sphere," a "region of interaction," or as something needing "room to exist." Civil society is a social space held in being by the existence of a certain kind of discursive interaction characteristic of citizenship. It exists when human beings freely contend with one another about the conditions and purposes of their common life. Such talk occupies a region of interaction beyond what we call "the private sphere," but sensitive to private concerns and values: personhood, home, and family. This sort of conversation also marks out a social space distinguishable from what some call "the system"[15] --the economic and political worlds with their power structures--but nevertheless in a position to influence what goes on these regions of macro-management and instrumental reasoning.

But it's important not to take the metaphor of "space" too literally, and especially not to use it to say too quickly who is "in" and who is "out." The history of the subject, especially among philosophers of the "social contract," shows many different mappings of the field. One mythical model shows the sons of a patriarch murdering their father in order to make a pact among themselves for managing their affairs corporately, including the access to women taken as possessed objects rather than equal participants. Sometimes civil society really consists only of rich landowners and highly educated urban elites who declare independence and make constitutions. Or it is thought to consist of workers whose consciousness has been raised: the industrial proletariat led by middle-class political theorists. Today "the people" who think they determine their own political destinies are often victims of a system which manipulates instead of liberating them.

Thus it doesn't really work to say that civil society is a specific group of people: say those who aren't involved with the government or with large-scale economic structures. It seems better to say that civil society can be a dimension of *everyone's* existence, a state of participation in the forming of the world's population *as* a people. In this sense, the "space" of civil society is not a describable location. Rather, it is a discursive territory held open by the exercise of the distinctive responsibilities of citizenship: responsibilities for fostering a free exchange of views in the common pursuit of social goods under conditions of distributive justice. Such a free exchange of views leading to moments of decision actually gives society its dynamic nature and form.

It is important to see that this dynamic reality has been given room to exist, traditions to enact, and continuity over time by certain political *institutions*, from the Athenian *Agora* to modern schools, churches, and town meetings. Robert Bellah has written of these institutions and their importance in *The Good Society*. They are not identical with the civil realm. They are necessary instruments of it. If these institutions do not work, then civil society is *literally* nowhere at all. Perhaps civil society then becomes largely a regulative idea for detecting scattered remnants of a former reality in new institutional forms that are taking over from the old. In some cases we may be able to identify civil discourse--even if it is sometimes uncivil in tone--emerging in unexpected places such as new social movements, the European "green" parties, the environmental movements, and so on. Civil society even happens after a fashion on radio talk shows, in letters to the editor, on e-mail and sometimes even in political TV commercials. But such civic conversation--if it is that--is generally too occasional and incoherent, and often too manipulated and politicized, to stand out as something worth defining and protecting. Yet it is better to seek out the real possibilities in such things as these than to ignore them in nostalgia for eighteenth-century New England town meetings which, despite useful modern parallels, will never return as they once were.

If it is to survive, the notion of "civil society" needs to find some new philosophico-religious basis: a conceptuality drawing on the past, certainly, but also looking toward a very different human future. A spate of recent writing has recently been devoted to finding such a new basis: rearticulating civil society as an idea, and weighing the prospects for its practical realization in some fresh form.[16] Some of this writing uses "civil society" terminology explicitly. Some does not, but deals with issues in political philosophy which are foundational to the idea. Can theologians representing the Christian communities of faith become usefully involved in such discussions? If so, what is involved?

Theological Engagement in Secular Political Discourses

The issue of faith's relationship to ethics becomes concrete and highly pragmatic when Christian faith communities and their thinkers try to become involved in essentially secular discourses which have the promotion of social civility as their object. Such engagement brings lived stories of faith into relationship with the many contemporary attempts to conceive and live out "post-conventional" moral visions.

Do Christian faith-communities exist which are capable of doing this effectively? Not many do. This is a question for another occasion. But obviously we need realizations of *koinonia* in faith--congregations, religious orders, theologically focused groups--which can prepare and sustain dialogers in the civil society arena. What such dialogers often find is that secular groups which have identified serious moral issues may be more focused and devoted than they are. A real sort of secular *koinonia* forms around deep moral concerns, such as the environment, combatting racism, ending warfare, and so on. Such groups often outstrip churches in pointed concern, focus, devotion, willingness for self-sacrifice.[17] The discourses of such groups often involve one or another concept of the unity of humankind as those *for* whom the issue in question is focused. Formulating the concern on a global level-- however practical and specific the terms of reference--will imply a notion of humanity's unity as a solidarity capable of collective decision which comes to consciousness in the particular group in question. The more all-embracing the secular vision, the more morally challenged the people of faith involved are likely to feel.

Much of the time the involvements I have in mind lead directly to one or another kind of political action. This is as it should be. But, for analytical purposes, I want to step back and consider these secular civil society groups as engaging in distinct sorts of political *discourse*. By this term I refer to the *sets* of philosophical assumptions, language usages, habits of association, and the like, which make up the imaginative and conceptual *worlds* different civil society groups occupy: worlds within which practical political initiatives take form. These worlds are very diverse. It makes a difference which world of discourse one gets into. Not only do different discourses have different assumptions about the roles people of faith ought to play. They also construe or map the space of political action in different ways, and have different visions of humankind as the ultimate community in whose name all this is being done.

One useful way to get clear about the discourses one is dealing with is to study their representative political philosophers: those who speak to and speak for the civil society discourses in question. But why study philosophers? Why not people closer to the action? Would it not be

better to try to characterize a range of actual social-cultural
circumstances: say Eastern Europe, South Africa, Latin America, North
America and the like? Is it not too abstract simply to be arguing with
social theorists?

Moreover, do contemporary social philosophers not tend to squeeze
the life out of integrative moral visions by refusing the working wisdom
of the people, (not to speak of "moral sources", many religious in
origin, of our cultures) and trying to rethink ethical issues in strictly
logical, "post-conventional" ways? As Charles Taylor says, the way
some philosophers talk of the possibility of a public good, the way they
confine the issues within the narrow boundaries of this or that secular
horizon or academic method, gives the very idea of goodness a bad
name.

In many ways secular social theories are merely constructions
produced in this or that scholar's study. But in another way, these
visions are, as Hegel said of his own philosophy, our own times
captured in the medium of constructive thought. I have picked out
particular writers who have "captured" our age in this way or that,
whose works are characteristic of certain kinds of civil society
discourse. These works are always more coherent and ordered than the
actual language spoken on the streets on in political party gatherings.
By being so, they bring to the surface the upstream assumptions which
more results-oriented kinds of language imply. They make important
connections between ideas that otherwise might be overlooked.

What kinds of civil society discourse are out there? Should they be
categorized by cultural or political location, or by subject matter?
Instead of a right-left spectrum[18], I offer five quite *different*, yet
probably not incommensurable, discourses. There is no agreement
among the philosophers about how the civil society question should be
framed, no agreement about terminology, no accord on basic
principles.[19] And are these writers actually involved in serious
political discourses themselves? Perhaps not as much as we would like.
John Rawls has been criticized as not political enough, i.e. not realistic
enough. But Karl Marx sat in the British Museum thinking on behalf
of the political discourses of proletarian risings far away. Are these the
highly conceptualized and reflective tips of the icebergs of political
movements: the abstractions by which all the muddy detail is refined
out, the geometrical curves which *approximate* the shotgun array of
actual data? I think we are dealing, in Max Weber's sense, with "ideal

types. " I am not sure these correlate neatly with different regions of the world or even with particular political situations.[20] The relation between the ideal-typical categories of today's political philosophy and actual situations "on the ground" is rather like the relation between the "salvation anxiety" reasoning sketched out in Max Weber's *The Protestant Ethic and the Spirit of Capitalism* and the actual Puritan discourses (political in the fullest sense) of seventeenth-century England, as recorded--mostly from sermons, public broadsheets and the like--by Michael Walzer in *The Revolution of the Saints*. There is a certain, but limited, "fit" between the two. Weber's theory gives Walzer something to falsify in the light of detailed study of the sources. But it is useful just for that reason. One has to start with *some* hypothesis.

On what terms can theologians be involved in these discussions? As we will see, few of the social philosophers of our time offer any constitutive role for religious traditions in reconstructing the civil realm. All mention religion in one way or another, even occasionally with appreciation. Most think it possible for religious groups to cooperate in essentially secular social visions, provided these groups behave "reasonably," keep their stranger views to themselves, and translate what they have to say into publicly acceptable terms. A few social philosophers, without having any personal sympathy for religious belief or practice as such, recognize that a restoration of civility cannot do without the active support of religionists and are prepared to court such support by being at least friendly.

On the other hand, at least a few theologians have sought to make use of social philosophy in their work: often in ways which at least bemuse, and often astound, the philosophers in question. Jürgen Habermas is probably the best example. A number of theologically-oriented books have been written about him.[21] Yet, in his closing remarks at a symposium centered on his work at the University of Chicago Divinity School, he expresses amazement and incomprehension that theologians should find his work so interesting, an interest he does not in any obvious way reciprocate.

We proceed to discuss five current types of social theory informing civil society discourse. We ask in each case about the role assigned to religious communities on the one hand, and on the other the possibility that theologians of those communities might exploit the patterns of thought concerned in ways the social theorists might not expect. We will ask whether the social placement of religion on the one hand, and the theological exploitation of social theory on the other produce a coherent, even illuminating, pattern. I believe that this type of dialogue is indispensable if we are to see faith as lived in religious community in relation to the moral struggles of a public world in which we also live. Without such dialogue there is no serious, reflective entry into that public world. [22]

The five types of theory to be explored are most easily identified by their best-known proponents, as follows: reasonable political liberalism (John Rawls), communitarian particularism (Alasdair MacIntyre), communicative action (Jürgen Habermas and Seyla Benhabib), modest pragmatism (Richard Rorty and Jeffrey Stout), and resourced authenticity (Charles Taylor). [23] In each case we are viewing the witness of faith in relation to one or another secular attempt to define a "post-conventional" public ethic of civility.

The Witness of Faith in the Discourse of "Reasonable Liberalism"

Christian faith is seen as potentially one among a number of "reasonable comprehensive doctrines" whose active expressions overlap in a cultural matrix which helps sustain a public ethic of "fairness." This is the characteristic individualistic, "rights"-oriented, civil society discourse of Western liberalism. We formulate it in the terms used by the Harvard philosopher John Rawls. Rawls argues that we need a universal, and therefore limited or "thin" public agreement about what *justice* is, leaving all other questions of social value, e.g. the pursuit of the *good*, to private individuals and groups. People will commit themselves, in a profusion of ways, to much more than this thin notion of justice which unites society as a whole. They will adhere to various "comprehensive doctrines" concerning the total meaning of life in which notions of the good can be set forth. But they will be prevented from imposing their comprehensive doctrines on others. Instead, comprehensive doctrines will be urged to be "reasonable," i.e. contributing in a civil manner to the resolution of public issues. (Some doctrines, of course, will never be reasonable in this sense and will always need to restrained.) The reasonable doctrines, Rawls opines, will "overlap" with others in their practical effects to constitute a common culture supportive of the thin universal notion of justice as fairness, but not definitive of it or able significantly to modify it.

Religious groups are in effect invited join with others to play this supportive role, influencing the content of the "overlap" to the extent that they can.

The Witness of Faith in the Discourse of Communitarian Particularism

Christian faith is understood as commitment to a specific traditional and narrative community which defines and sustains virtues relevant to public practice but largely lost or ignored in our present society. Here we consider the role of faith in the characteristic civil society discourse of those who wish, for the *general* good, to recover *particular* shared forms of life based upon religious and other traditions. This perspective is articulated by the philosopher Alasdair MacIntyre. MacIntyre thinks that in this age of pluralism no post-conventional philosophical justification for public morality, such as Rawls's conception of justice, is possible. Philosophers have tried, and they cannot agree. The real choice is between something like Nietzsche's nihilism and adherence to a long and deep moral tradition such as that of Aristotle. In this perspective, Enlightenment liberalism is just one tradition among others, and a notably thin one at that. Real traditions generate deeply resourced and nuanced understandings of life. The Aristotelian tradition (including its extensions and modifications in Augustine, Aquinas and various forms of neo-Thomism) articulates "virtues" which make for the good life by expressing the ends or *teloi* of human beings. These Aristotelian and Christian virtues can be translated, even today, into contemporary social practices. If they were remembered, they could make sense for lawyers, physicians, professors, assembly line workers and city managers, despite the fact that they cannot be defended in post-traditional, universal, philosophical terms. Hence it is the calling of religious communities to gather in small groups to keep these virtues alive in a society which otherwise will forget them. Religious groups must concentrate on learning and transmitting their traditions, keeping their particular communities as vital as possible: hopefully for the sake of contemporaries, but if necessary for the preservation of such virtues through what could be a new Dark Ages.

The Witness of Faith in the Discourse of Communicative Action

Christian faith is seen as enabler and sustainer of the moral attitudes required for a public "ethics of discourse." This is the civil society discourse of "critical social theory," as articulated by the German philosopher Jürgen Habermas. Habermas tries to keep the Enlightenment alive as a universal human perspective, substituting the notion of "communicative rationality" for the "instrumental rationality" that imprisoned humanity in an "iron cage" (Max Weber). Society is envisioned as a community of symbolic interaction in which everyone capable of rational communication is potentially in the conversation. Conditions which limit participation by certain social groups, as sexist language does for women, are to be removed. For Habermas, the presuppositions of such a universal discourse are derived, not from tradition of any kind, but from the practical logic of discourse as such, presumed to be present wherever and however human beings communicate with one another. In such a free field of discursive exchange, "the better argument" will eventually triumph. From this notion of "communicative action" Habermas derives the idea of a "discourse ethic" in which proposals are tested by the principle that all participants must give their free, unconstrained, consent. But among the preconditions of all discourse whatever are sincerity, truthfulness, trust in the process. Habermas thinks these are part of the pure logic of the matter. Traditioned groups may argue that such attitudes are grounded in assumptions ultimately religious in character. Habermas does not agree. Yet, of all the discourses of civil society, his has been subject to the most involvement and commentary by theologians.

The Witness of Faith in the Discourse of Modest Pragmatism

Christian faith is seen as one source of perspectives or practices (spare parts) useful in constructing a public ethic of provisional expediencies based on generally agreed platitudes. Here we consider the role of faith in the characteristic civil society discourse of practical politicians, as articulated in the thinking of Richard Rorty and Jeffrey Stout. These two philosophers think it impossible to build public moral principles on the basis of generally held "truths." They deny the very notion of coherent conceptual schemes: i.e. they deny that moral ideas can only make sense in relation to other such ideas in fully articulated contexts of reasoning. Thinking of every kind, they claim, including moral reasoning, proceeds by way of *bricolage*, the lashing and nailing together of disparate elements drawn from a variety of sources into something that works well enough for the time being. We construct our social ethics out of "platitudes," things everybody more or less believes. There are more of these around than we think, and we should make the most of them. There are also moral ideas and ethical arguments from various sources, including religious sources, which lie ready at hand to be put together into workable, if temporary, structures of reasoning. Because conceptual schemes (even those of great philosophers) have *always* been put together his way, and because there is no *necessary* coherence in them, it does no harm for us to take what we can use and leave the rest. Hence it is perfectly all right to detach Aristotle's virtues from his "biological metaphysics" and use those virtues in ways which help define and shore up the many "practices" characteristic of an urban-industrial society. Religious groups can offer what they have.[24]. Yet, for Rorty and Stout their role is ambiguous. Where they support the platitudinous pragmatism that makes modern societies work, that fact is appreciated. Yet it would be nice if they could put their further claims in ways that made more sense to pragmatists. The pragmatists are looking for something here which they cannot define. The texture of a pragmatist society is open for theological initiatives, provided they have understandable practical consequences that tend to fit the needs of the moment.

The Witness of Faith in a Discourse of Moral Retrieval

Faith communities are seen as sponsors or instigators of the recovery of "moral sources" needed for recognition of authentic forms of selfhood. These are the terms of faith's entry in a civil society discourse for members of a dominant culture who seek to deploy historic resources both to deepen their own sense of selfhood and to recognize the authenticity of others who represent the culture in variant or minority ways. Our political philosopher is the Roman Catholic scholar Charles Taylor, formerly of Oxford and now teaching at McGill. If MacIntyre argues for a sectarian communitarianism, Taylor (like Robert Bellah) has a communitarian vision for the whole society. Rather than lamenting the shallowness and fragmentation of the West-- its individualism and instrumental rationality, the dominance of markets and bureaucracies--Taylor seeks the historic "sources" of its forms of life, confident that the richness of its life can be restored, and with that, the capacity to "recognize" minority groups. A central category here is "authenticity." Taylor means not what the existentialists have intended but something closer to life lived within frameworks of strong moral valuation: frameworks which have largely disappeared from contemporary culture. By recovering such frameworks, we will be enabled to grasp, for example, that valuing the person need not mean support for brittle, selfish, individualism. We will also be able to extend that valuing to others, whose cultures, perhaps, have analogous resources to offer. One senses that for Taylor a dominant culture may be oppressive when its values are forgotten or poorly understood, but creative and generous when those values are restored. Thus, for example, South African blacks are drawn into a democratic tradition of European origin which finally discovered the "better angels of its nature," and have, in turn, transformed that tradition for their own purposes. Taylor sketches no particular role for religious communities. But he would have no objection to their sponsoring or instigating the recovery of culture-enriching sources, some of which figure importantly in their own histories.

Where May Such Engagements Lead?

What happens when the theologian, who speaks in and for the community of faith, enters any one of these discourses? There are two possibilities. On the one hand, there is the risk of becoming no more than an accessory to the secular moral construct involved. On the other, there is the possibility of taking the secular story into the biblical narrative and thereby transforming it into a stage on the way to the City of God. Let us look at each possibility.

Traditions of faith anxious to be socially relevant run the risk of letting themselves be located or placed in the scheme of things, if not actually defined against their will, by the regnant political philosophy and its concepts of "religion." In spite of themselves, faith communities tend to accommodate themselves to the possibilities for thought and action afforded by the political ideology of their own time and place. The temptation to accede in such placement is subtle, yet its blandishments are well-nigh irresistible. In a world in which religious communities are marginalized, especially by secular media,[25] to the point of being pushed almost off the map, it feels empowering to be given any place on the map at all. But Stanley Hauerwas warns us: the price the churches pay for aligning themselves even with very good things--justice, democratic freedoms and the like--is to be taken over, limited to a particular place, forced to adopt the self-definitions the secular world wishes upon them.[26]

But the opposite possibility is also present. New forms of social theory almost ask to be taken up into something more than themselves. The substance of modern secularity *enters* the faith community in its membership and in its basic assumptions, its views of the world. If these concrete persons are to be caught up into a metanarrative they are taken like blocks of a mosaic of different shapes and colors: here is an insurance salesman, here is a professor, here a doctor, here an assembly-line worker. These people come to the community of faith *with* their genetic qualities, their habits, their employment, their views of the world. In Milbank's view, and Hauerwas's, they are somehow asked to form a community of *practice* which lives out the Christian metanarrative. They are, in a highly disciplined way, to take secular stories into the biblical story. What does this taking-into really mean? Maybe this is the true meaning of *bricolage*: one unavoidable in gathering any congregation. You build the faith community out of what you've got. Can this be done in such a way that the assumptions and orientations of people are shorn of their ultimacy, so that they become mere practices without the reality-assumptions, the implicit metaphysics or foundational beliefs that are attached to such things in the world out there? Or, to put it differently, can the Christian metanarrative take up and take away the anxieties and attachments involved in worldly life, exorcise all these penultimate concerns, and turn a motley group into a biblically-formed people in the world? Does *ekklesia* finally triumph? Is the distinction between religious faith and public ethics to be finally overcome?

We can only approach this ultimate question from the penultimate knowledge we have at this historical moment. Obviously, churches need to be communities whose practice embodies the trusting relationships, the rejection of violence, the devotion to justice, which characterize the biblical vision. They need to be communities of moral discourse. But, paradoxically, they *therefore* need first to be communities of articulate faith. And thus they need some conceptual restatement and reinterpretation of the biblical narrative. They need theology which leads to ethics, not a reduction of theology *to* ethics, or to sociology either for that matter.

Let me come at this from the point of view of the Church's being and doing in the world. I argue that the Church functions above all as *place-holder* in the world, what Bonhoeffer called *Stellvertreter*, for the possibility that human society can overcome its violent origins, its continuing resentment and mistrust, and come to realize its true calling to become the beloved community envisioned in the biblical metanarrative. The churches exist to *hold open* a social space in which society's existing structures and practices can be seen for what they are and in which human community can be articulated in a new way, a space in which the metaphors of our common life can be exposed to their transcendental ground. The community of faith can thereby declare a critical solidarity with social movements and visions which pragmatically accord with the gospel, refusing to credit underlying ideological assumptions which do not so accord.[27]

Can the theologian, bearing the biblical narrative and the history of its interpretation, enter any one of these discourses in such a way as to *deconstruct* its claims to be autonomous? Can theological participation provide space for a re-construction of secular moral discourse by giving it a language for ceasing to be tongue-tied about its ultimate concerns? Can the theologian speak persuasively about the grounds for a trust in one's fellow human beings that is required for the workability of the discourse itself? The theologian may well find in all these discourses elements of the gospel in forms alienated from means of explicit expression. By providing a kind of dialogical space in the midst of the civil society argument in any of its forms, the theologian of Christian community may help the secular discourse to come to itself. In that event, it may cease to be alienated. Faith and ethics come closer to one another than before.

The essence of the space held open resides not in doctrinal orthodoxy but in a certain kind of *practice*. By coming within, or even near, that realm of practice, human beings are led to extend the meanings of their own ordinary-life activities to fulfill the potential that exists in them without the limitations imposed by ideological, positivist or merely pragmatic understandings of what such occupations mean. Brought into a social space kept open to transcendence because it permits the articulation and sharing of basic trust or faith, the virtues connected with ordinary human practices both deepen and ramify to become what they were meant to be.

Duncan Forrester illustrates this point by showing how the virtue of justice deepens and extends itself to become *generosity*.[28] One could likewise say that the virtue of *prudence* deepens and extends itself to become *wisdom*. Legal correctness becomes the *righteousness* which flows down from heaven "like a mighty stream." Paul Ricoeur catches this note of metaphorical deepening and broadening in a famous sermon titled "How Much More." If an earthly father provides for his children, "how much more will our heavenly father provide?" These transformations of finite, worldly virtues into qualities of character which exceed all reasonable expectation happen when human beings are drawn into a space of discourse in which language mediates the reality of "grace."

The presence of communities bearing the biblical metanarrative thus creates metaphorical space in which the human world can come closer to realization of the nature for which it was created. The lived language of traditional faith makes room for the language of this world to become a new, post-traditional secular language of faith. The new language of faith sustains practices of wisdom, generosity, and righteousness in which the outlines of the beloved community can begin to appear. The new language can do this without having to repeat the technical, constructed, theological language which opens the way for it.

Are there examples of such transformation? In my own experience, people who actually had the faith (mostly traditional in form) to go on "freedom rides" through the American South in the late fifties and early sixties opened space for many with less courage or more secular bent to expand their horizons and hence engage in new political practices which moved the cause of civil rights forward across the nation. Or consider a more recent example. Among the many roles played by the churches of East Germany before the Wall came down, and of South Africa before apartheid was abolished, was to keep open sanctuaries, both literal and metaphorical, in which these two democratic revolutions began to take form strategically in the minds of their founders. It is said by critics that the churches merely provided legally extraterritorial places for secular agents of change to meet. But I think that the churches also offered the protection of certain kinds of public rhetoric which provided moral space for the politicians to dream in. The theological utterances of Desmond Tutu, for example, offered a kind of rhetorical room for the secular political vision of Nelson Mandela. A certain imaginative, resourceful, boldness becomes possible when one stands in space maintained by a theological vision, even when one cannot accept the traditional language in which the vision is expressed.[29]

This paper has argued that civil society, however defined penultimately by political philosophers, is the enactment in space and time of the vision of the Holy City, the household in which God "dwells," found in Revelation 21. What are the implications of this imaginative picture of the end-time? The striking fact is that in this representation of the Beloved Community all the usual penultimate distinctions are transcended: between the natural and the supernatural, between the religious and the secular, between the clerical and the lay, between theological language and other language. We are told of "a new heaven *and* a new earth." The two have apparently become one. We have here the fulfillment of the original divine purpose sketched in Genesis 3: the creation of humankind in God's "image." The *imago Dei* turns out not to refer--as theologians have speculated for centuries--to some particular characteristic of the human which separates us from other living things. It is not the ability to think and reflect. It is not the power of speech. It is not the "immortal soul." Rather the entire human *community* is here called to make God's "glory", in Hebrew the *kabodh* or *shekinah*, God's luminous presence, present to the universe. Instead of the Ark of the Covenant, the Holy City becomes the *locus* of this presence, this glory: the place where God *dwells* (Greek *skenosei*, literally "tents"[30]) in the midst of God's people, to be their God. This fulfillment of the *imago Dei* is thus the living presence of God, Godself, who gathers and constitutes the community of the end-time, lived reality and symbolic expression of itself simultaneously. In the final event (not merely in this text *describing* the final event) the form of the "image of God" ceases to be a mere sign which substitutes for, refers to, something absent. This "image of God" *is* that to which it points, rendering God present by being the actual *locus* of the Reality of God in question. The Holy City thereby becomes sacramental in the fullest sense of "real presence."[31]

The distinctively theological language worthy of our confidence as a medium for expressing the basic trust connected with our origin and ending will in the end cease to be distinguishable from the moral language of the heavenly city where God dwells with God's people. In the consummatory vision of Revelation 21, there is no longer any theological language separate from the discourse which constitutes the beloved community itself. The language of faith and the language of ethics become one. Life in the metanarrative of faith is simultaneously life in the heavenly city where the historically constructed and mutually alienated categories of "secular" and "religious" no longer designate separate realms.

On the way to that end, the biblical images play a helping, but not ultimately constitutive, role. Church and theology fulfil their function by keeping space open in the human community for the seeds of this fulfillment--those hidden in the community's own inherent nature under God--to take root and grow. When the end is attained, the special functions of theology and church have also been fulfilled, and as such they disappear. In the penultimate time, any confusion between faith in God and even the most purely theologically grounded ethical position as actually lived out in the world runs the risk of idolatry. In the Heavenly City, the distinction between faith and ethics becomes inconceivable. There, God is all in all.

Notes

1. I do not mean to take on everything that Albrecht Ritschl built into his *Rechtfertigung and Versöhnung*, but the interplay he saw between "justification" and "reconciliation" is clearly an instance of our problematic.

2. I do not believe everything Stanley Hauerwas says, but on this topic he is right. He writes in *After Christendom* (Nashville: Abingdon Press, 1991), "Our beliefs, or rather our convictions, only make sense as they are embodied in a political community we call church" (p. 26). And, further, "...questions of the truth or falsity of Christian convictions cannot be separated from how the church understands its social and political stance" (p. 16).

3. See, for example, the address given by Lukas Vischer, "Koinonia in a Time of Threats to Life," who argues that we are approaching a qualitatively new and highly threatening period of human history with the ecumenical methods and assumptions of an earlier time. He writes, "But above all, *how do we cope with the evidence of an increasing degradation in history*? Do we not have to admit that the historical future is radically hidden from our eyes? We must always be prepared for life *and* death." (*Costly Unity*, p. 72f. Vischer's italics.)

4. Walter Lippmann, *The Good Society* (Boston: Little, Brown, 1937), 194, quoted in Bellah, Ibid., 8.

5. Robert Bellah, *The Good Society* (New York, Knopf, 1991), 3.

6. Ernest Gellner, *Conditions of Liberty: Civil Society and its Rivals* (New York: Viking Penguin, 1994), 1.

7. Cambridge, MA: MIT Press, 1.

8. Any attempt even to list the social ills which burden the United States would be likely to go on for pages. I have made an enumeration of more than thirty discrete social and political problems which afflict us at the moment. There is no need to repeat it here.

9. *Foreign Affairs*, Summer, 1993. Huntington's article is summarized by Peter Steinfels, "Beliefs," *The New York Times*, April 16, 1994.

10. The "Thirty Years War" is cited by certain intellectual historians as the final demonstration of Christianity's inability to unite Europe around a decent civil order, a demonstration which energized the Enlightenment attempt to privatize religious convictions in the face of a universal human reason supporting democratic principles to be carried forward by a new political invention, the modern nation-state. Robert Bellah has written that we may now be moving into a "post-Wesphalian era," although we do not yet live in a post-Westphalian world. See his essay "How to Understand the Church in an Individualistic Society," in *Christianity and Civil Society*, ed. Rodney L. Petersen (Maryknoll, NY: Orbis Books, 1995), 4. Bellah credits this idea to a conversation with Bryan Hehir.

11. Robert D. Kaplan, "The Coming Anarchy," *The Atlantic*, February, 1994. And see Anthony Lewis's reaction to this piece, "A Bleak Vision," Op-Ed page, the *New York Times*, March 7, 1994.

12. I have thought for some time that one of the factors differentiating life in the two-thirds world from that in rich northern hemisphere countries is that for the former societies there is liable to be one or another problem that stands out in its immediacy and seriousness to the point of simply overpowering all others. Poverty, or disease, or political oppression, or violence will tend to preempt consideration of most other matters, which tend to merge into the background. This, (as someone has said of the approach of one's death) tends "to focus the mind wonderfully." In the industrial societies of the northern hemisphere, by contrast, the problems are so numerous and their relative priority so difficult to determine that we hardly know where to begin. This leads to "single issue politics" in which groups of people solve the priority problem by letting themselves become fixated, seemingly arbitrarily, on something like abortion, or euthanasia, or saving endangered species, or the like. The specially focused concerns, and others like them, are unquestionably worthy of attention but become distorted by receiving exclusive attention.

13. See Jean L. Cohen and Andrew Arato, *Civil Society and Political Theory* (Cambridge, MA: MIT Press, 1992) 2ff. These writers are carrying forward an essentially post-Marxist project in political philosophy. They want to locate civil society within "the universalistic horizon of critical theory rather than within the relativistic one of deconstruction." They write: "At issue is not only an arbitrary theoretical choice. We are truly impressed by the importance in East Europe and Latin America, as well as in the advanced capitalist democracies, of the struggle for rights and their expansion, of the establishment

of grass roots associations and initiatives and the ever renewed construction of institutions and forums of critical publics. No interpretation can do these aspirations justice without recognizing both common orientations that transcend geography and even social political systems and a common normative fabric linking rights, associations and publics together. We believe that civil society, in fact the major category of many of the relevant actors and their advocates from Russia to Chile, and from France to Poland, is the best hermeneutic key to these two complexes of commonality."

14. Defining "pre-revolutionary" and "post-revolutionary" situations is admittedly complex. The "post-revolutionary" eventually becomes the "pre-revolutionary" again. Just as Thomas Jefferson said, it's good for democratic societies to have rebellions from time to time. Still, in many parts of the world, the priority right now is nation-*building*, which requires atonement for, and reconciliation of, estrangements caused by past injustices, rather than the attempt to throw off oppression. Yet the struggle against oppression is never far away. Some think that the society most likely to become "pre-revolutionary" in the near future is the United States. We are hearing talk of Civil War I (1861-65) *and* Civil War II (dates as yet unknown).

15. "The system," of course, is Habermas's term for the combined operation of macroeconomic and political forces which "colonize" the human "lifeworld."

16. The religious and religio-philosophical origins of the idea of civil society have been carefully traced by Adam Seligman in *The Idea of Civil Society* (New York: The Free Press, 1992). See also Alan Wolfe, *Whose Keeper? Social Science and Moral Obligation* (Berkeley: University of California Press, 1989), a book which argues that the social sciences must now take up the historic roles of moral philosophy, and Jean L. Cohen and Andrew Arato, *Civil Society and Political Theory* (Cambridge: MIT Press, 1992), a work which seeks to reconstitute civil society along the lines of Habermasian critical social theory.

17. Bert Hoedemaker has made this point graphically in his essay "Introductory Reflections on JPIC and Koinonia" in *Costly Unity*, 1ff.

18. I have tried to show elsewhere that the *principled* right and left, at least in the United States, are breaking down into something far more elemental, in fact into two kinds of anger at the center. That has always been there. But now it takes the form of desire to remove taboos, to break through the excluding, categorizing, hierarchy-maintaining forms of "old-think," on the one hand, and a desire to protect traditional values, including values once fought for on the revolutionary battle fronts on the other. How do you explain the fact that conservatives are life affirming on abortion and life-denying on capital punishment?

19. This fact in itself leads Alasdair MacIntyre and others to reject the whole post-conventional attempt to formulate ethical principles to deal with fundamental issues of what we believe human life to be, in favor of a

repristination of Aristotle and the latter's massive influence in the discourse of catholic Christianity. Similarly, one can say that Rawls produces an ideal-typical version of the discourse of classical Western liberalism, trying to explore its inherent logic as clearly as possible. Habermas does the same thing, works out an idealization of the discourse of post-Marxist, neo-Enlightenment, European social democrats. This is not to say that politically engaged people in either camp take their language out of Habermas. They may or the may not. But we can read Habermas as a typifying abstraction of the essence of a certain kind of political argument.

20. The inquiry into specific circumstances is of course indispensable, and is being done by excellent scholars, e.g. John de Gruchy in his about-to-appear work (Cambridge University Press, 1995) comparing churches' civil society concerns in the former East Germany with similar patterns in pre-liberation South Africa. The present work may support such more empirical efforts by outlining patterns of reasoning to be tested for their analytical or illuminative power in relation to situations on the ground. Its value will only be tested in the doing.

21. See, for example, Paul Lakeland, *Theology and Critical Theory* (Nashville: Abingdon Press, 1990) and Charles Davis, *Theology and Political Society* (New York: Cambridge University Press, 1980).

22. This, of course, is not the first time such dialogue has been attempted. The history of Christian faith's relationships with the societies in which faith has grown up evinces many patterns of interaction made explicit in thought. Ernst Troeltsch's *The Social Teachings of the Christian Churches and Groups* distinguished "church-type," "sect type," and "mystical (i.e. individualistic) type." In his *Christ and Culture*, H. Richard Niebuhr, with a slightly different method, distinguished five. The five types to be laid out in the pages ahead represent a largely new typology of possibilities for contemporary church and society. While these types may in places resemble those of Niebuhr, I have deliberately refrained from explicitly connecting them with his famous five. Our situation is new. We must explore what is there, rather than what we think *should* be there.

23. What follow are merely notes which cannot possibly do justice to the positions involved. In a forthcoming book these notes, *deo volente*, will be expanded into chapter-length analyses. The brief paragraphs supplied here only indicate the direction in which these analyses will tend.

24. I think, for example, that William Werpehowski's notion of an "*ad hoc* apologetic," in which Christians offer moral concepts out of their tradition which fit the public need for ideas that work in particular situations, corresponds to the notion of moral *bricolage* in modest pragmatism. See Werpehowski, "*Ad Hoc* Apologetics," *The Journal of Religion*, 66 (July 1986), 282ff.

25. See Stephen Carter, *The Culture of Disbelief: How American Law and*

Politics Trivialize Religious Devotion (New York: HarperCollins, 1993.

26. See Stanley Hauerwas, *After Christendom: How the Church is to Behave if Freedom, Justice, and a Christian Nation are Bad Ideas* (Nashville: Abingdon Press, 1991). Hauerwas insists that the attempt to play a role in the upholding even the best features of any established political order results in capture by the presuppositions of that way of life. He writes, "We...live in a time where Christians in the name of being socially responsible try to save appearances by supplying epistemological and moral justifications for societal arrangements that made and continue to make the church politically irrelevant." (27) Hauerwas observes further that "...the religion we have is one that has been domesticated on the presumption that only a domesticated religion is safe to be free in America."(88)

27. I am indebted to a paper by John de Gruchy, "Dietrich Bonhoeffer and the Transition to Democracy in the German Democratic Republic and South Africa," presented at the Chicago meeting of the American Academy of Religion in November, 1994.

28. Duncan Forrester, in a paper presented to the 1993 meeting of the International Society for Practical Theology in Princeton, New Jersey.

29. Lest we become too romantic about these "transitions to democracy," it is important to note that democratic revolutions can be sidetracked and that the role of the church in a post-revolutionary period can become far more complex and difficult than it was when the only issue was ridding a nation of oppression. Speaking of Germany, John de Gruchy writes, "The revolution of 1989 only led to the 'incomplete liberation' (quoting Huber, in Witte, *Christianity and Democracy*) of the GDR. With the reunification of Germany the revolution was in a sense hi-jacked by the architects of liberal, capitalist democracy who, in many ways, proceeded to strip the country of its assets and undermine some of its achievements." (De Gruchy, "Bonhoeffer, etc." AAR, Chicago, 1994)

30. An allusion to the Tabernacle in the wilderness is of course intended. The verb here is *skenosei* instead of the expected *oikodomeo*. Why is the dwelling envisioned in this eschatological vision still represented as impermanent? Is it because the writer knows that his rich metaphorical *language* is impermanent: that it does not literally describe the end, but only occupies the space of the end in our imaginations until the end itself comes?

31. See my discussion of "real presence" in *The Sense of a People*, ch 4.

10

Traditioned Communities and the Good Society
The Search for a Public Philosophy

Is something like a civil society possible in the world we know today? This question increasingly exercises political scientists and philosophers, not to speak of religious scholars who offer theological appropriations of social theory as settings for the theoretical rearticulation of faith traditions.[1] It does seem that the civic virtues until recently taken for granted in the democratic West are today deeply threatened. A spate of writing on the subject is appearing; works such as Robert Bellah's *The Good Society*,[2] Adam Seligman's *The Idea of Civil Society*[3] and Alan Wolff's *Whose Keeper?*[4] If civility and the sense of a public good are to survive in the twenty-first century, the democratic idea itself may have to be reconstituted with a philosophical basis departing substantially from its former grounding in an Enlightenment individualism combined with one or another form of New England Calvinism or Jeffersonian Deism.

My essay is an attempt to address this bundle of issues programmatically: that is to map out the territory and identify what needs to be done. I will seek to relate critical social theory to themes from the biblical tradition, with background assumptions drawn from the field of hermeneutics. My own most recent book, *The Sense of a People*,[5] begins to get at the question of civility in this way, particularly in its last chapter titled "Churches in the Human Conversation." But now I want to wrestle not only with churches but with traditioned communities in general[6] and their possible roles in the search for a good society."[7] I will ask what such a differentiated yet covenantal social reality might come to mean if many distinctive traditions of life's meaning could join an honest dialogue about human solidarity and human flourishing.

Beyond the scope of this essay, of course, lie all the practical questions of how such a civil order could be realized in the world, not only in North America but in culturally appropriate ways across the globe. I will not take up the politics or the diplomacy, as it were, of making a multi-cultural "good society" actually come to be. The task of conceptualizing it is difficult enough.[8]

But our thinking does need to be done with awareness of what has been happening over the past few years. Events in Eastern Europe, the collapse of the Soviet empire, the apparent deterioration of political discourse in the United States: all these things conspire to raise the question whether civil society as we have known it in the West since the Enlightenment *can* live on into a post-modern age. It is plain that what has happened in the former Eastern bloc nations does not give careful observers much to hope for. The notion that these events will make way for the establishment of some form of liberal democracy is held today only by American conservatives who have ideological and political reasons involved with claiming credit for the "defeat of Communism." In fact Mr. Seligman argues that these nations, far from establishing liberal democracy, are reverting to their old, pre-revolutionary habits, modified only by the fact that the Czar is no more and seventy years of technological innovation have passed by. What we see is better described as "privatization and a sort of anarcho-capitalism à la Mafia."[9] This pattern is being repeated in lesser degree throughout much of the rest of the post-Communist world, "with the possible exception of the Baltic states and the Czech lands of Bohemia and Moravia."[10] As for the United States, the widely noted deterioration of the public world into a cacophony of attack ads, sound bites, obfuscation, and transparent attempts to mislead and distract the public suggests that liberal democracy, if more successful here than in Eastern Europe, is nonetheless in serious trouble.

The Eclipse of "Public Philosophy"

Must intellectuals shoulder some of the blame for these difficulties? Perhaps. Robert Bellah has noted the loss of a significant tradition of writing about the philosophical foundations of democracy.[11]   In America, at least, there seem to be few, if any, contemporary counterparts to such figures as John Dewey, Walter Lippmann, John

Courtney Murray, and Reinhold Niebuhr, who dealt with the question of "public philosophy" (Lippmann's phrase originally) in a way both philosophically profound and accessible enough to influence public debate. Such writers have been supplanted by scholars of narrower scope studying discrete social problems (health care, social security, welfare, etc.), compiling statistics, advising on the particulars of government policy. The new thinkers are academics, but seldom in the true sense public intellectuals. Few are asking the large questions for which there used to be generally understood vocabularies: questions about the common good, freedom, justice, and the like. Concerns such as these are virtually incomprehensible to those engaged in the "squalid scrimmage of appetitive impulses" which characterizes our social world.[12]

Political philosophy today has become both highly technical and seriously fragmented into many frames of reference and schools of thought. Whether these phenomena reflect the failure of these philosophers and others to develop a secular basis for public morality is hard to say. It may be, instead, that the failure of the professors reflects events in the society. At any rate, we have seen that the long-standing efforts of secular moralists to construct a universal basis for moral reasoning, what John Dewey called "a common faith," has apparently foundered. Secular rationalism has been unable to produce a compelling, self-justifying, moral code. This fact is the more remarkable in an age that has produced such documents as the *Universal Declaration of Human Rights* and organizations such as Amnesty International. There clearly *seem* to be standards of conduct recognized as valid cross-culturally, yet we are experiencing a loss of confidence that there are coherent underpinnings to any such consensus.[13] Philosophical reasoning in this area is in disarray in the face of relativisms and tribalisms sponsored by "post-modern" and other attacks on Enlightenment styles of reasoning. And with this collapse of rational coherence, the whole enterprise of secular humanism begins to lose its intellectual legitimacy. Major philosophical as well as cultural trends have for some time now been repudiating Enlightenment-style rationalism in favor of various "post-modern" styles of relativism or nihilism.

In fact, the traditional meaning of "civility" as civil righteousness eludes us, as the term deteriorates toward the sense of mere politeness. We thus also lose the very idea of a public philosophy which articulates such righteousness. The idea of "civil society," such as it is for us, takes on different meanings in different societies and cultures.[14] Seligman asks whether today there is any stable core of meaning to the idea. Do we have anything coherent to work with?[15] If in the West the modernist creeds of the Enlightenment that form the philosophical foundation for civil society are decreasingly credible, in the post-Communist world such claims are increasingly subordinated to those of ethnicity. In both cases, the roots of allegiance to civil society are weakened, by skepticism and anomie in the West, and by neo-tribalism in the post-Communist east.[16] The radical question we must face is whether the "individual"--a notion theorized in Western accounts of civil society as a sort of abstract, universal, entity, a distillation of generic humanity--is not, in the end, an illusion. Perhaps civil societies depend for the allegiance of their citizens upon specific cultural traditions, rather than upon an Enlightenment-based humanism making universal claims. Of societies claiming a purely rational basis for their public order we must say, with Mr. Seligman, that "it is their fate to weaken" precisely those cultural traditions on which they in fact depend.[17]

Seligman argues that the lack of a concept of "revelation" (he uses the word metaphorically), or of reference to the "transcendental," leaves current attempts to reconstitute civil society truncated and deprived of staying power.[18] We will not likely restore a dependence on revelation in the theological sense to the self-understanding of the public world. For that unpromising strategy we must substitute an attempt to redefine the social role of traditioned communities for whom "revelation," however esoterically defined, means a form of symbolic representation of the final order of things peculiar to the group in question so formulated as to be relevant to its conception of the *polis*. Yet, ironically, in our fragmented, multicultural world, specific religious traditions often have little depth for the persons who claim most vociferously to be defined by them. The clash of cultures and interest groups in today's democracies often involves persons with minimal grasp of the traditions they represent, but with strong desire to exploit their claimed identities for political or economic gain. This adds another layer of complexity to our problem. The weakening of traditions to which Seligman refers, the "homogenization" of Western cultures lamented by Charles Taylor:[19] all this has already gone a long way. Society may well need to help its competing, feuding, cultural groups to recover a deeper sense of their own histories, rituals and symbols, the better to generate sustenance for civic virtues to be celebrated in common.

These pages, then, begin to explore the relations between such specific cultural traditions--with the institutions that maintain, protect, or tend to dissipate them--and the search for a civil order that could deserve to be called a "good society."

A Frame of Reference: "Communicative Action"

We need some frame of reference in which to work. I will choose the "theory of communicative action" set forth by the German social philosopher Jürgen Habermas as a point of departure for this inquiry. Why Habermas?[20] For many he is not "postmodern" enough: indeed he seems to be carrying the torch for a version of Enlightenment reason. Making reasoning "communicative" instead of "instrumental" does not, for many, fully answer the criticisms of Enlightenment thought set out so long ago by Horkheimer and Adorno,[21] let alone the deconstructive work of Foucault, Derrida, and their admirers. Yet I believe that we let go too easily of the conviction that human beings, however culturally diverse, can be in touch with one anothers' meanings, that they must, as Isaiah says of the people of Israel in relation to YHWH, "reason together." The new appreciation of diversity, of the value of specifically traditioned communities,[22] does not relieve us of the obligation to seek out regions of pragmatic agreement in the construction of just societies. And I will argue that Habermas, neo-Enlightenment figure that he is, is also expressing in philosophical terms something very close to what the prophet Jeremiah meant when he wrote of a new covenant law "written on our hearts."

But to realize such values from Habermas's theories, we must set them in the context of hermeneutical discourse out of which they arose and with which they are still in dialogue.[23] After all, Habermas owes much to his teacher Hans Georg Gadamer, and indeed stands with him in a tradition which stretches from Kant through Hegel to Husserl and Heidegger. The debate between Habermas and Gadamer,[24] so much a fixture of German academic life a half-generation ago, has tended to obscure the essential continuity between the work of the two men. Both Gadamer and Habermas are interested in emancipatory social programs.

Both are interested in the growth of freedom and human flourishing. Although Gadamer in *Wahrheit und Methode* speaks largely of works of literature and art, in his writings since, no doubt under the influence of the debate with Habermas, his interest in social and political matters has grown.

Moreover, the two philosophers are saying very much the same thing in different vocabularies. In fact they illustrate in their *own* failures to understand each other many of the problems of communication between different generations and political-cultural traditions. As Richard Bernstein puts it, "...we can employ Gadamer's analysis of what constitutes hermeneutical understanding, which includes the moments of interpretation and application, to get a clearer grasp of what Habermas is actually *doing* (as distinguished from what he sometimes says he is doing)..."[25] And further,

> If one were to translate Habermas's project into Gadamerian terms, it might be put like this: Gadamer, you yourself have argued that all understanding involves application, and furthermore that our hermeneutical horizon is limited but not closed. Indeed, you emphasize the very openness of language that is the condition for all understanding. So the question becomes, what is it about the linguistic medium within which we participate that allows for such appropriation and understanding? How are we to account for the fact that we can in principle always understand that which strikes us as alien or strange? What is it about the very character of language and rationality that enables us to grasp the possibility of the type of dialogue, conversation, and questioning that you yourself have so penetratingly elucidated?[26]

The central question in all such concerns can only be this: how is the inter-subjective, inter-cultural, understanding needed for the building of a good society *possible*? What is required? On the one hand, we have an emphasis on the functioning of diverse human traditions in practical reasoning or *phronesis*.[27] On the other, an analysis of "communicative reason" as general human possibility. The first seems to leave out the critical element, the other seems to rule out participation by persons who speak out of their traditions directly, who make kerygmatic proclamations unintelligible to others. But, as I will try to show in this essay, we are seeing two poles within a common field of discourse.

Habermas's project in itself has strong ethical overtones. The "theory of communicative action" is intended as a theory of social justice, even if it does not reach to the issue of the good society as such. Our sense of the latter, Habermas sees, is bound to be culturally variable. But a search for justice is the indispensable ground floor of the moral project. Habermas pursues this search by means of an inquiry into the logic of human communication as such. Moving in the Kantian frame of reference which prescribes the logical universalizability of one's maxims of conduct as the primary criterion of moral behavior, Habermas asks what universal conditions we presuppose in the very act of communicating with others. These fundamental conditions of communication become the basis for a universal, if "thin," ethic for the modern world.

Briefly stated, Habermas posits a "speech-act immanent obligation" in every act of communication whereby the communicator takes on, and expects from others, an accountability for justifying what has been said. Such a view of communication in turn presupposes an "ideal speech situation" in which all can participate free of restraint or any sort of ideological disadvantage, and the assumption that one's own communications are unconstrained, candid and truthful. But it is Habermas's assumption that the resulting ethic is incompatible with all forms of "traditional ethics," that is, "with any ethical system which keeps 'a dogmatized core of basic convictions' away from the demand for justification."[28] I agree, furthermore, with Stephen White,[29] that such an ethic is rather minimal in the sense that it does not provide much basis for "sorting out types of ethical positions as more or less rationally justifiable," and that it is based not on a universally applicable concept of communicative action, but only on a distinctively *modern* notion of argumentation shared by only a portion of the human beings alive today.[30]

Habermas writes as if all qualified participants in the human dialogue will in the long run recognize "the better argument." What does this assertion really mean? I think it is a way of saying, with Hegel, that ultimately "the real is the rational and the rational is the real," even if we cannot prove, except by way of a kind of pragmatic "as if," that it is so. Habermas is building an interpretation of what Hegel called "objective spirit," as it were, from below.[31] The fact that he does so procedurally, rather than ontologically, does not blind us to what is, in

Kantian terms, "postulated" by the very fact of entering a moral argument in a field of communicative action. Needed to complete the logic of this field of discourse is something like a notion that all human beings, given sufficiently extended conversation, will find themselves within a single field of rationality in which "the better argument" will be evident to all discussants.[32]

If Habermas is right, we need some sense of what "the better argument" would be like. Recent attempts to understand the nature of practical moral reasoning do not reassure us that agreement will come at the end of a dialogical process, even if that is envisioned as indefinitely prolonged. The current field of debate has settled into an argument between the "objectivists" on the one hand and the "relativists" or "tribalists," on the other. In the first camp, there is the position of Rawls, who is an anti-traditionalist, neo-Enlightenment figure, who seeks to eliminate the element of personal interest in argumentation by postulating the formation of moral principles behind a "veil of ignorance." Rawls illustrates one option: try to grasp principles which lie beyond all particular cultural locations, all special interests. But it has become clear since *A Theory of Justice* that these principles are not as universal as Rawls once thought. They represent only what seems right for educated women and men of the West in the late twentieth century.[33]

In the opposite camp there is Alasdair MacIntyre, who is trying to repristinate a clear *tradition* of moral argument (the Aristotelian) in terms which would make it communicable in the contemporary intellectual marketplace. MacIntyre illustrates the other option: take a particular tradition of discourse and find a way to state its essence in terms that can be widely shared in the modern world. But it is not clear that this attempt succeeds either. Richard Bernstein's critique of MacIntyre suggests not only that the moral tradition of the Aristotelian virtues is less coherent than the Catholic scholar alleges, but also that his derivation of basic virtues from the practical needs of realms of "practice" involves a *non sequitur*.[34] Can one translate the pragmatic essence of a moral tradition into language that will pass muster in a world of "communicative action" without also defending the "biological metaphysics" or other fundamental assertions of the tradition's classical texts? Can such a defense possibly succeed in the public world with which we are concerned?

One way to evade the clash of objectivists and relativists may be by recourse to two of Gadamer's central convictions: that the meaning of interpretation lies in application of our inherited meanings to pragmatic concerns and that such application leads us to a process of practical reasoning or *phronesis*.[35] A contemporary definition of the latter term runs as follows: "Phronesis is the historically implicated, communally nurtured ability to make good sense of relatively singular contexts in ways appropriate to their relative singularity."[36] This is as good a description of the actual character of reasoning in the public sphere as any I know. It says that, quite apart from the theories of either "objectivists" or "tribalists," we settle public questions by piecemeal argument in ways appropriate to the kind of question we are dealing with and the specific situation we have to face. Political, legal, economic, educational and other kinds of questions need attention in the vocabularies and conceptualities native to those disciplines. But they are translated into the public realm in highly practical ways, on the basis of some sort of minimal general agreement among people about what "makes sense." While special interests and ideologies always enter the debate, in the end we are very pragmatic about what we do. If we want broad support, we have to confine ourselves to a sense-making which is communicable at press conferences and on the evening news.

When Habermas speaks of the ultimate victory of "the better argument" it is in this sort of sense-making arena that his claims must be tested. On what grounds can his confidence in the victory of "better argument" be based? I will argue, with Karl-Otto Apel, that this confidence is necessarily grounded in assumptions about the way human selves meet and understand one another. Apel constructs his argument that such understanding is possible as a "transcendental-pragmatic hermeneutic of human intersubjectivity." And I will further claim that this transcendental argument, if pushed far enough, will turn out to be based on convictions about the *final* reality which is manifest in such selfhood formed in intersubjectivity, i.e. convictions metaphysical in nature. Yet I will also say that neither the transcendental nor the metaphysical grounds for communicative action can be *formulated* apart from particular traditions of human community which supply the symbols which "give rise" to the needed thought.[37] Hence, in the end, it is not the necessary presuppositions of universal discourse as such which provide the grounds for believing that "the better argument" will prevail, but rather symbolically formed perspectives on selfhood and the human community as a whole found *within the many communal, cultural, and religious traditions of those who keep the discourse going.*

After all, is it not a salient flaw in Habermas's logic of communicative action that he has nothing to say to the person (or group) who simply opts out, who refuses to communicate and hence refuses the logic of communication?[38] The reasons for, the energy behind, social responsibility in the first place are not contained in communicative action logic as such. They come from elsewhere, from overlapping but independent religious and cultural visions which the good society cannot afford to ignore or be without.

The poignancy of Mr. Seligman's diagnosis of the ailments of our "civil society" becomes still clearer. The contemporary world's civility, such as it is, depends on the presence of specific cultural traditions: yet it is the fate of this world that its nature systematically weakens the traditions on which it depends.

How is Communicative Action Possible?

I will argue that there is a serious philosophical question how "communicative action" leading to the "cognitive redemption of validity claims" is possible. This despite the claims of Rorty and others that instead of tackling such questions we should "just change the subject." On the contrary, we will not understand communicative action, or the role of religious communities in relation to it, unless we grasp the conditions which successful instances of such shared dialogue and practical reasoning presuppose. In short, we must ask about the need of such dialogical reasoning for a transcendental basis.

For this purpose, I will follow, with certain critical adjustments and departures from his line of argument, the reasoning employed by Karl-Otto Apel in several recent works.[39] To ask about the conditions of possibility for communicative action is, in fact, to ask about the *a priori* character of rational subjectivity as such.[40] For Apel, transcendental reflection means "reflection upon the presuppositions of any instance or act of valid cognition or understanding--or, since all understanding claims to be valid, of human cognition as such."[41] Hence these presuppositions may be called transcendental conditions of subjectivity, and Apel also calls them "the transcendental subject" or "transcendental subjectivity."[42] Apel transforms Kant's project in the *Critique of Practical Reason* by showing that subjectivity as such is intersubjective.[43] Kant's notion of practical reasoning presupposed a solitary reasoner: one who could test whether the maxim implied in a possible action could be universalized without inherent contradiction. But for Apel, the transcendental subject is constituted by relations to others.[44] The very notion of truth makes sense only if there exists the possibility of reaching consensus in an unrestricted communication community.

It follows that all thinking, even unexpressed, is implicit *assertion*. It involves an implicit public claim. To think is to presuppose that our thought can if necessary be justified to an indefinite community of communicators. Subjectivity itself *is* implicitly an offer to communicate.[45] Apel uses the word "pragmatic" to refer to this performative or communicative character of thought. It is "an offer to communicate the thought to other subjects for their confirmation,"[46] "made in principle to any and all other subjects,"[47] with "expectation of agreement from an indefinite communication community."[48]

We infer, then, that cognition cannot be independent of language. The offer to communicate presupposes prior communication and projects a field of unlimited ideal communication. There is no nonlinguistic or prelinguistic understanding of reality. This is a "transcendental pragmatics of language." We cannot validate our claims by comparing them with some prelinguistic reality-apprehension. We can do so but only by argument, that is, by appeal to the assent of a communication community which is unlimited and indeterminable in its extent.

But *can* all others understand? Post-modern awareness recognizes the philosophical importance of realizing that there are cultures radically different from our own. Thus comes our awareness of the possibility of "incommensurability." For Apel, however, to acknowledge an ultimate hermeneutical incommensurability is to assert an ultimate epistemological relativism. Some writers indeed reject transcendental philosophy because they believe epistemological relativism is true. For Apel this position is not only false but pernicious. Far from being a formula for toleration, "*it is a refusal to recognize other subjects as persons who could contest one's validity claims.*"[49]

At this point one cannot help but notice the moral, and perhaps religious, element which has entered the argument. What leads us to "recognize other subjects as persons?" What is the moral force behind this demand? We can, for example, follow the line of Peukert, who speaks of *willing* the integrity of the other; something beyond our human power to confer. Peukert writes:

> The practical recognition of the freedom of the other in communicative action, which means the willing of his or her genesis as a subject, aims, however, at the future realization of possibilities of freedom which, in part, can only be disclosed in mutual activity. This recognition affirms in an unconditioned way a developing, yet still presumed integrity of the other which does not lie within the power of the one initiating the communication. This mode of communicative action that sets out from the freedom and the integrity of the other trusts in more than what it could achieve by itself."[50]

Hence the integrity of the other, like our own, must be something like a work of grace in which we must have deep confidence before the possibility of communication, and therefore cognition itself, can be understood.

A similar notion can be found in H. Richard Niebuhr's *The Responsible Self*, a work to which Bellah refers with appreciation in *The Good Society*. According to Niebuhr, we are called upon to be responsive and accountable within a web of interaction in which we interpret the meanings of others' actions and respond appropriately. This network is grounded in the possibility of *trust*: trust in the integrity of others, trust in the final reality of Being with which we have to do. That trust is a gift of grace, not something we generate ourselves.[51]

In the Christian tradition, then, there are *religious reasons* for presupposing the integrity of the other as presupposition of genuine communication. The other exists in a grace-founded integrity of which I must take account. The notion of total incommensurability between persons and cultures is inconsistent with the Christian belief that human beings owe their deepest dimensions of selfhood, and therefore what they ultimately have to *say, to a divine gift which is intelligible on grounds of revelation.* Consider the Johannine notion of Christ as *logos*. The Word is come to *all flesh.* Christianity is radically "logocentric" at least in this sense of the term. Transcendental reasoning about the possibility of communicative action discloses the need for *some* such regulative idea about the world of self and others, together with the possibility of cognition which rests upon it, which can only be symbolically, and thereby conceptually, funded by some appropriate religious or cultural tradition.

Communicative action, then, is not finally self-justified within the bounds of publicly available forms of reasoning about it. It is justified by the cultural and religious presuppositions or regulative principles which participants in the conversation bring to it. It follows that each cultural or religious tradition today needs to examine and lift up the commitments in the tradition concerned which tend to fund the attitudes needed to be fully part of the human dialogue. No greater contribution can each tradition make to the well-being of humankind, and hence to its own relevance and possibility of flourishing in the contemporary world.[52]

What Reality Does Communicative Action Disclose?

Traditioned communities not only provide morally persuasive perspectives or regulative principles which lead us to attend to others and will their integrity, their right to be heard. Many such communities also interpret the social nexus as a place where a moral *substance* of humanity comes to expression, where a certain kind of direction, or *telos*, is concretely disclosed. The latter perspective is one in which the "symbol gives rise" to a kind of thought that is ontological or metaphysical: that enables us to articulate a final reality underlying all appearances, including those of the social nexus in which we live.

Gamwell's *Divine Good* seeks to set out this final reality in Whiteheadian terms as these are interpreted by Charles Hartshorne. I will instead follow Charles Taylor in seeking help in Hegel's notion of "objective spirit." But I will point to Hegel's thought not as a position which could today be established in the academy by force of argument alone, but rather in the way Alan M. Olsen understands it as *a metaphysic derived from the language and symbolism of a specific religious tradition.*[53] Olsen argues that Hegel's category of *Geist*, in effect, rises from Luther's understanding of the Holy Spirit. Something like this, indeed, is what we might expect. Metaphysical realities, "things in themselves" Kant called them, are not open to us on the basis of reflective or argumentative treatment of empirical data. We cannot know on the basis of reflection alone that "the real is the rational and the rational the real." But once the human world is "seen" in a certain way from the standpoint of a religious or cultural tradition, the philosopher can render conceptually "the movements and actions of the believing soul."[54]

Charles Taylor has attacked the Habermasian position as merely "proceduralist,"[55] saying that it offers no place for "constitutive" or substantive moral visions of the self. I am arguing that such sub-stance, or reality-affirmation, can only be supplied by construals of the human world built upon the narratives and rituals of traditioned communities. How is the world of "communicative action" open to such tradition-based constitutive interpretation? Certain features of the action world *lend* themselves to such "seeing as." But to see these features for what they are, we need philosophical insights which mediate a certain cultural and religious framing or focus. This, I take it, is what Charles Taylor is doing in his applications of Hegelian insights to contemporary political and social reality. Taylor does not think, and I agree, that Hegel's metaphysics can serve us as a self-standing, arguable on its merits, phenomenology and logic of human consciousness. But Hegel's philosophy nonetheless can function as a lens through which we see things about the social and political worlds we would not otherwise discern: things which, once pointed out, can be seen to be true independently of the religious tradition whose language brought them to our attention.[56]

Among these insights is the perception that different configurations of social life, what Bellah calls "institutions" in the larger sense of the term,[57] are *expressive* in character. The kind of *polis* in which we live can *mean* something in addition to providing the material conditions for our "appetitive scrimmage." The intersubjective world can be seen as consisting of what Hegel called *Gestalten* or world-historically expressive shapes,[58] in such a way that in the time dimension it can be interpreted as a "phenomenology of spirit."[59] Charles Taylor richly develops these Hegelian perspectives both in his magisterial book on the philosopher[60] and in his more recent *Sources of the Self*.[61] The starting point is a preoccupation with the social world in all its concrete detail as a fabric of human interaction.[62] This is precisely the realm of the unfolding of objective Spirit, or *Geist*, surely Hegel's central ontological category. *Geist* is a barren abstraction unless it is concretely embodied. Because the fabric of common life is objective spirit, it is expressive, or meaningful. What has gone wrong with our society is that there is a poor fit between "what we take ourselves to be" and the meanings which our public institutions express by being what they are.[63]

The pattern of meaning and implicit demand for allegiance that we find in our public institutions is expressed in the peculiar Hegelian usage of the German noun *Sittlichkeit*, whose routine but inadequate translation is "morality." Hegel's meaning, expounded by Taylor, reminds us strongly of Bellah's focus on the character of social "institutions,"[64] by which he means not only specific institutions (e.g. the Roman Catholic Church, the Federal Reserve Bank) but also institutionalized practices (e.g. the "institution" of marriage, or the Western university, or common law, etc.). Taylor tells us that *Sittlichkeit* is "the set of obligations which we have to further and sustain a society founded on the Idea."[65]

This Hegelian conception not only permits us to see something that is true of human community. It suggests that this community, through its institutional forms, manifests a reality. What does it mean to say that the unity of the Greek *polis* is "expressive?" How can persons see "the collective life of their city as the essence and meaning of their own lives?" Taylor again. "The structure of the Hegelian state was to be understood and valued for what it expressed or embodied, the Idea, not for its consequences or achievements. The rationality of the Hegelian state was something quite other than the rationalization of bureaucratic structures."[66] The issue is not what various aspects of the social order *do*, but what is it that they *say* by being what they are.[67]

What contemporary society says today is alienating for its citizens. Taylor puts it memorably. "Modern society, we might say, is Romantic in its private and imaginative life and utilitarian in its public, effective, life. What is of ultimate importance in shaping the latter is not what its structures express but what they get done."[68] Critics from Tocqueville and J.S. Mill to Sorel and Nietzsche, Taylor tells us, "castigate modern society as expressively dead, as stifling expressive fulfillment through the power of conformity, or through the all-pervasive demands of utility, of producing a world in which all acts, objects and institutions have a use, but none express what men are or could be."[69]

This lack of expressiveness opens the way for the coming of what has been called mass society. "The modern ideology of equality and total participation leads toward a homogenization of society. This shakes men loose from their traditional communities, but cannot replace them as a focus of identity. Or rather, it can only replace them as such a focus under the impetus of militant nationalism or some totalitarian ideology which would depreciate or even crush diversity and individuality."[70]

We need to move both toward a renewal of specific traditions, and also toward a new appreciation of human universality. Taylor again: "Hegel's answer, as we saw it, is to give social and political differentiation a meaning by seeing them as expressive of a cosmic order, but he conceives this order as the final and complete fulfillment of the modern aspiration to autonomy. It is an order founded on reason alone, and hence is the ultimate object of the free will."[71]

But this notion that society's expressiveness is founded on a cosmic order, that it is indeed objective spirit as the expression of absolute spirit, will not work for us. Taylor concludes:

> We cannot accept Hegel's solution today. But the dilemma it was meant to solve remains. It was the dilemma Tocqueville tried to grapple with in different terms, when he saw the immense importance to a democratic polity of vigorous constituent communities in a decentralized structure of power, while at the same time the pull of equality tended to take modern society towards uniformity, and perhaps also submission under an omnipotent government.... But whether we take it in Hegel's reading or in de Tocqueville's, one of the great needs of modern democratic polity is to recover a sense of significant differentiation, so that its partial communities, be they geographical, or cultural, or occupational, can again become important centres of concern and activity for their members in a way which connects them to the whole.[72]

It follows that human beings have the right to live in primary communities which form them as persons-in-relationship. But our North American society is a scene of radical fragmentation: few of us live in such communities of depth, and we must find some way to recover them. This means that we must once again rejuvenate or generate institutions that can be carriers of meaning, institutions that can express something which connects human beings in their many smaller communities to a sense of the meaning of the whole.

But no sense of the meaning of the whole is available to us unless the communicative action nexus is interpreted as, *seen as*, expressive of a larger reality in the terms provided by religious or other communal traditions. We have seen how Hegel provides such an interpretation of the social world with a philosophy which Olsen claims is grounded in Protestant Christianity. There exist many other interpretations of the nexus of human interaction grounded in other contexts of meaning. These visions of the human world variously supply encompassing meanings for the communicative action nexus itself and also meet on the common terrain of human debate about practical questions. Rather than arguing imperialistically for a particular idea of cosmic unity in "absolute spirit," perhaps we can live it in our variously interpreted practice of meaningful communication itself, in "communicative action" among persons living in different cultural and religious traditions which give them a sense of identity in the midst of the larger human dialogue.

Faith-Traditions in a Common Social World

We can now harvest the yield of this discussion. Religious and cultural traditions, with the philosophical visions of the human world that flow from them,[73] permit us to see the realm of communicative action in particular ways. We have taken the Christian case as an example. Christians may see the communicative action world transcendentally as a realm of intersubjective responsibility for mutual understanding shaped by a regulative construal of the human community as kingdom of ends or household of God through which we *will* what we cannot bring about by our own powers: the grace-founded integrity of the other human being. They may see that world metaphysically, with a line of argumentation conceptually elaborating a religious vision, as a space for the expression or signification of Holy Spirit brooding over the face of the deep, shaping the form of reality itself. Without such sorts of *seeing as*, translated into moral behavior, the modern secular social order cannot maintain itself. But the secular form of life tends to erode the traditions, the special ways of seeing, on which it must rely for participatory energy and communal substance. We are back to Mr. Seligman's point: contemporary Western societies tend systematically to undercut the religious and philosophical visions on which they depend. What then?

We need a philosophical description of communicative action in which the contributions of traditioned groups to maintaining the moral coherence of society as a whole are recognized and acted out responsibly both in society at large and among the adherents of the cultural or religious traditions concerned. Habermas does not provide such a description. He seems not to recognize the possibility that specific traditions of understanding--other than those compatible with Enlightenment rationalism--can as such be part of the dialogue of humankind. Our reflections on tradition-based readings of the communicative action field--whether transcendental or metaphysical in character--should help us state more satisfactorily the relation between the discourse shared by all members of the human community and the visions of particular cultural and religious communities.

Traditioned groups interpret the field of public practical reasoning *as* this or that kind of action arena. They may see it as a field of honor, as a trading pit for acquisitive struggle, as a universe to be scientifically understood, as a realm to be technologically managed, or merely as a place to survive. Each such seeing-as turns the social world into a particular kind of game. The rules for playing the game in question, as Gadamer thought, come from some appropriate tradition of understanding. Those who play the game can interpret the human playing field this way or that because the field *itself* is a signifying, potentially expressive, medium. It can be *read*.

But traditioned communities do more than confer meanings on the worlds in which their members live. They also appropriate the structures of these larger social worlds, so interpreted, into their own forms of organization or polity. In doing so they act out certain meanings of which the expressive materials of the common world are capable, but which are not otherwise actualized. Thus a Presbyterian General Assembly makes something special of the broader institution of representative government, the New York Stock Exchange makes something special of the perennial activity of buying and selling and a football team makes something special of the possibilities inherent in "agitating a bag of air." Each of these traditioned activities or games acts out a possibility of which the common social world is capable because of its inherently expressive character. And the influence may go the other way. A particular traditioned community, interpreting the metaphors of the common world in particular ways, may in turn provide that larger social world with metaphors it can use for quite unforeseen purposes. Military castes from time immemorial, for example, have formalized the methods of conflict and given us metaphors based on the arts of war, which seem, ominously enough, to underlie much of our language in Western culture about academic argumentation![74]

To the extent that different interpretations of the life-world's expressive possibilities coincide or overlap there may be a great deal of socially shared content, including moral content. The problem, already noted, is that we have no commonly accepted way of articulating and grounding that content philosophically. We may have a greater or lesser degree of overlapping practical moral agreement, but a hundred different "upstream" reasons for participating in the life-world that agreement defines.

Each tradition of life coherent enough for the task needs social philosophers to bring out what that tradition's interpretative responsibility for society as a whole yields in practical moral terms. Each tradition needs to set forth a self-conscious interpretation of the entire human communicative action nexus as a field of understanding which leads to certain patterns of action. I have already argued that such interpretations will tend to bring out, raise to conceptual salience, characteristics of the social world which are already there, which, once highlighted, can be seen by others.[75]

The common field of human discourse is always more than merely a projection of the logic of communication as such. The social world as a whole, at any time or place, will always have certain meanings held in common precisely because of the interpretative activity described. Despite our social fragmentation, we of the West have much in common, much overlap of interpretation. Think of the standards of honesty inculcated in the upbringing of children, or of the content enshrined in civil law and civil procedure, or of the simple fabric of what, in many places, is just "done."[76]

I think that Habermas is trying to get at this in his appropriation of the Husserlian-Schutzian concept of the "lifeworld." We have seen that the notion of communicative action as such does not tell us much about the validity of particular kinds of moral argument. It only shows that the logical conditions of communication establish a kind of moral minimum or thinly descriptive ethics to be filled in by arguments suited to the specific situation and matter at hand. The understanding of specific situations, that to which *phronesis* refers, "must take place against the 'horizon of a lifeworld' constituted by 'more or less diffuse,...unproblematic background convictions.' From the viewpoint of understanding-oriented action, the lifeworld, 'stores the interpretive work of preceding generations...'"[77] What is picked up for discussion in any instance of communicative action always comes out of this unproblematic background which defines, for the culture in question, what is the case and what ought to be done.[78] I would argue that, in somewhat Hegelian fashion, communicative action brings the unrationalized lifeworld, our *Sittlichkeit*, to a form of expression which shows its rational potential. If the entire lifeworld is capable of being brought to active reflection in this way, and if "the better argument" in the end wins, then are we not saying that in society at least "the real is the rational and the rational is the real?"

But such a philosophical high-wire act is diversionary. The character of our existing *Sittlichkeit*, limited or incoherent as our initial understanding of it may be, deserves careful analysis in its own right: perhaps of the sort Bellah and his colleagues have provided in *Habits of the Heart* and *The Good Society*. It is neither the product of a claim to rational moral universality of the earlier Rawlsian type, nor is it a projection of a particular philosophical and religious tradition of the virtues such as MacIntyre might wish. It is best approached, I think, in the spirit of "thick description," much as Michael Walzer has done in his *Spheres of Justice*[79] and other works. What is seen as "just" depends on the sector of the human life-world concerned. The world of commerce generates different standards from the world of education. The total human world, especially in the contemporary West, is a complex set of overlapping "spheres" of moral meaning.

One wonders, then, how far it is useful to abstract from all this detail in search of a "communicative ethics" based on the "thin" characteristics of discourse as such. In fact, I believe that Habermas's thin, purely logical, description of communication is itself not as tradition-free as it claims to be. The theory of communicative action actually has a particular moral nexus underlying it: notably the Enlightenment-based "sphere of justice" found among contemporary northern European intellectuals and those they influence. And one finds something else in Habermas as well. What do we make of the fact that this philosopher is really stating philosophically and accessibly much that is present in the Biblical covenant idea?[80]

The whole Habermasian argument about the presuppositions of communicative reason indeed reminds one of Jeremiah's "new covenant" prophecy in 31:31ff., whose principles are described as intrinsic to the consciousness of the Israelite people: i.e. written "within them" and "upon their hearts." Compare Habermas's statement that the principles of communicative action are "intuitive knowledge."[81] Can such a covenantal tradition be carried over into philosophical terms without reference to its theological presuppositions? We have here what Ricoeur would call a "philosophical reenactment"[82] of Jeremiah's vision. Once again, the philosopher "adopts provisionally the motivations and actions of the believing soul."[83] In simplest terms, communicative action has to do with promise-keeping and truth-telling. But these virtues, for virtues they are, cannot be articulated and maintained by the sheer logic of communicative action as such. They must come from somewhere.

But can traditions of interpretation of the life-world actually meet in argumentative encounter? Can communicative action come to include conversation about our ultimate warrants for acting as we do? One can see here the possibility of the kind of tradition-based advocacy which William Werpehowski calls "*ad hoc* apologetics."[84] Thinking from a Christian standpoint, Werpehowski writes,

> The Christian apologist...seeks to establish common ground with the non-Christian as creature with reference to a particular context of action or a particular contested question of belief. That Christian identity is sustained thereby is what makes the apologetic *theological*. At the same time, the common ground sought and supportive of Christian identity also must be seen really to sustain and nurture the non-Christian in some particular area of belief or practice.[85]

Such an apologetic "moves from a set of shared commitments toward a deeper agreement that crucially reflects, on one side, coherence with background warrants in Christian belief and, on the other, coherence with non-Christian projects and purposes."[86] The problem of incommensurability between different interpretative schemes is thus dealt with not only in concrete practical encounter leading to the formation of public policy, but also in argument about the reasons or warrants for the policy adopted.

Obviously, of course, public dialogue among religious or cultural groups often leads to no agreed policy at all, but only to seemingly intractable conflict. One need only think of issues involving entitlement programs, abortion or homosexuality. Yet if the contending parties can agree on *something*, however minimal, they can go on "to assess contrasting analyses and prescriptions for their explanatory value."[87] It could turn out, according to Werpehowski, that "the better argument" for justifying any achieved accord would be found *within* some particular tradition of understanding, or in a public philosophical restatement of that tradition, rather than in the thin presuppositions of communicative action as such. It might be shown, say, that the world depicted in Hebrew Scripture includes, and most profoundly illuminates, certain standards and values present in the way we agree, despite differences, to live together.

Showing that this was so in a manner not alienating or oppressive to others would constitute an "*ad hoc* apologetic" in Werpehowski's terms. Presumably the Christian participant in such an apologetic dialogue would be prepared to hear, and perhaps accept, arguments that the achieved common ground actually presupposed still deeper warrants of Jewish, Buddhist, Moslem or other origin. In any case, we would have a dialogue of warrants centered upon the already-existing moral content of a shared social world. I believe that such a dialogue would, if properly carried out, increase both the range and the depth of pragmatic agreement held in common among us.

The warrants religious communities might bring to bear on regions of shared moral judgment could well come from the sorts of transcendental and metaphysical insight described earlier in this paper.[88] Suppose, for example, that the issue was the character of the personal relationship between doctors and patients. Suppose that our society were to reach an agreement that some sort of human compact between doctor and patient, some mutual sharing of the burdens and mysteries of life and death, rather than an approach coldly technical to the last gasp, was greatly to be desired. Could Christians and Jews not then argue, ultimately on traditional religious grounds, for a transcendental philosophy of communicative action, in which selfhood grows in intersubjectivity and intersubjectivity rests on *willing* something we cannot in our own power provide: the integrity of the other as she or he stands before the God of "lovingkindness" or grace?

Or suppose that the issue was the citizen's sense of dignity or equal worth in society. Suppose it began to be understood, ironically, that a particular society threatened to devalue its citizens in the very task of achieving the security needed to defend their worth and dignity against "enemies foreign and domestic?" Suppose we were to agree that we needed some kind of "politics of recognition" (Charles Taylor) in the context of the practical arrangements need for social stability. Suppose that we could say, again with Charles Taylor, that the issue here is "situated freedom," the ongoing affirmation of the individual in his or her autonomy, carried on without contradiction in a social fabric or *Sittlichkeit* capable in practical terms of indefinitely sustaining such freedom for all. What warrants might religious discussants bring forward? Christians and Jews might say that society, however it is organized, must in its nature express something that is not alienating to persons, and that such expression is ultimately a mediation of God's presence religiously symbolized as *ruach* or *pneuma*, and philosophically conceptualized as *Geist*.

These thoughts offer one way, at least, of grasping what might be involved for traditioned groups to promote the good society as they critically explore their own heritages of faith and understanding. Society at large needs to value more the resource it has in human beings who still live in deeply coherent and communal forms of life. And those who live these ways need to discover the potential they have for strengthening the whole body politic, and, with that, their own freedom.

Notes

1. I am thinking of Paul Lakeland, Helmut Peukert, Francis Schussler Fiorenza, J. B. Metz, and others.
2. New York: Alfred A. Knopf, 1991
3. New York: The Free Press, 1992.
4. Berkeley: The University of California Press, 1995.
5. Philadelphia: Trinity Press International, 1992.
6. My use of the term "traditioned communities" includes a wide range of phenomena. I refer to any more or less institutionalized social configuration through which persons gather around a reasonably stable store of literature, folklore, legislation or custom which distinguishes them from members of the general public. Orthodox Judaism represents a traditioned community. But so do neighborhoods of Polish Catholics, the United Auto Workers, the American Association of University Professors, and organized baseball. Traditioned communities vary greatly in the nature of their heritages, their degrees of coherence, and their capacities for persistence in homogenizing societies and cultures.
7. I approach this term, at least at the outset, much as Bellah does. He

writes: "It is central to our very notion of a good society that it is an open quest, actively involving all its members. As Dennis McCann has put it, the common good is the pursuit of the good in common." Bellah goes on to summarize ideas found in Dewey and Lippmann. He writes of "a widening of democratic participation and the accountability of institutions; an interdependent prosperity that counteracts predatory relations among individuals and groups an enables everyone to participate in the goods of society; a peaceful world, without which the search for a good society is surely illusory." And, of course, freedom is "an essential ingredient." "Freedom must exist within and be guaranteed by institutions, and must include the right to participate in the economic and political decisions that affect our lives. Indeed the great classic criteria of a good society--peace, prosperity, freedom, justice--all depend today on a new experiment in democracy, a newly extended and enhanced set of democratic institutions, within which citizens can better discern what we really want and what we ought to want to sustain a good life on this planet for ourselves and the generations to come." (Bellah, et al., op. cit. 9)

8. I am aware that in saying this I disagree with Richard Rorty's position in "The Priority of Democracy Over Philosophy," in Merrill D. Peterson and Richard Vaughan, eds., *The Virginia Statute for Religious Freedom* (New York: Cambridge University Press. 1988) 257-82. Rorty argues that the achievement of a democratic social order is prior to philosophizing about the nature of a good society: i.e. that you won't philosophize adequately about it until you have it. I believe on the contrary that it is meaningful to consider "various conceptions of the human good within the moral pluralism of American culture prior to our democratic politics and essential to supporting such politics." (Bellah, *Good Society*, 319-20 n.6)

9. John Gray, "Authority's Ghost", a review of Seligman. *The Idea of Civil Society*, New York Times Book Review, September 13, 1992.

10. Gray, Ibid.

11. See Bellah, et al., *The Good Society* (New York: Alfred A. Knopf, 1991). Bellah speaks of "a tradition of public philosophy which has been attenuated if not lost in recent years" (272 *et passim*). Many would say that this noble tradition has been renewed for our own time by Bellah himself and his colleagues Richard Madsen, William M. Sullivan, Ann Swidler, and Steven M. Tipton.

12. Robert M. Adams, "The Beast in the Jungle," *New York Review of Books, 35*, (November 18, 1988) 4.

13. See the discussion by Gene Outka and John P. Reeder in the Introduction to *Prospects for a Common Morality* (Princeton: Princeton University Press, 1993), 3ff. *et passim*.

14. It "meant one thing in Hungary in the late 1980's, another in the United States at the same time. Its political deployment may be conservative or radical, depending on circumstances." (Gray, Ibid.)

15. Seligman argues that civil society does indeed have a historic meaning deriving from John Locke's transformations of medieval ideas of natural law into a social vision based on 17th-century Christian individualism. John Gray observes: "This dependency of the Lockean conception of civil society--of a form of life in which individuals are related to one another, not as members of specific groups or holders of particular statuses, but as carriers of universal human capacities, equal under a rule of law--on Christian presuppositions is also its weakness in an age when the certainties of revelation can no longer be taken for granted." (Gray, Ibid.)

16. Gray, op. cit.

17. Gray, op. cit.

18. Seligman, *Civil Society*, 6, 8.

19. See Taylor, *Hegel* (Cambridge: Cambridge University Press, 1975), 414-416.

20. Robert Bellah and his colleagues, in *Habits of the Heart*, make use of Habermas both explicitly and in their background assumptions. They speak of "constant reference" to Habermas's work: "Our substantive debt to him is great." (*Habits*, 291) The "notion of economic and political 'systems' invading and colonizing the 'life-world' significantly influenced us. In the end, we decided not to use his terminology, which seemed to imply a sharper dichotomy between systems and life-world than we intended. In particular, Habermas's language made it difficult for us to argue for the institutional humanization of the economy and the administrative state, even though we know he shares our hope for that possibility." The "constant reference" to Habermas is easily seen in Bellah's concept of "paying attention," which implies being in the nexus of "communicative action," being tuned in to the messages by which the meanings of living in our particular society are constantly expressed.

21. See Horkheimer and Adorno, *Dialectic of Enlightenment* (New York: Herder and Herder, 1972).

22. I am thinking of the many writers who find in post-modern relativism a context for reaffirming particular communities with their particular traditions. Stanley Hauerwas is a prime example.

23. The role of the hermeneutical tradition in Habermas's work is complex. Robert C. Holub disentangles the subject in *Jürgen Habermas: Critic in the Public Sphere* (London and New York: Routledge, 1991). Holub shows (page 49) that, in his debate with positivism, Habermas uses hermeneutical insights, in a manner that distinguishes him from Adorno, "as a counterweight to empirico-analytical methods." Yet the term in these contexts has a wide range of meanings. It can refer to "understanding" as opposed to "explanation," to unthematized structures of "pre-understanding," or to the Husserlian-Schützian conception of the "lifeworld." It is only in the debate with Gadamer, however, that Habermas considers "how he sees hermeneutics fitting into a tradition of

critical science with an emancipatory interest" (page 49).

24. The issues in the Gadamer-Habermas debate cannot be rehearsed here except to say that Habermas challenges Gadamer's attempt to give hermeneutics a universal status, to conceive it, with Heidegger, as the "essence of our being-in-the-world" (Holub, *Habermas*, 54). Still, Habermas "wants to recruit hermeneutics for the methodology of the human sciences" (Holub, 65). But against Gadamer, he wants to find a point of reflection outside the nexus of tradition interpretation, which can overcome tradition's potentially oppressive and distorting qualities. We can, he says, "discern a prelinguistic basis for purposive-rational action" (Holub 69). If meaning can be retrieved in a way not dependent on hermeneutical presuppositions, a way specifiable in methodological terms, "then hermeneutics must forfeit its claim to universality" (Holub 70).

25. Richard Bernstein, "Gadamer, Habermas, and Rorty," in *Philosophical Profiles* (Philadelphia, University of Pennsylvania Press, 1986), 78.

26. Bernstein, *Profiles*, 70-71.

27. I will say more about this Aristotelian term later on.

28. See Stephen K. White, *The Recent Work of Jürgen Habermas: Reason, Justice, and Modernity* (Cambridge: Cambridge University Press, 1988), 54.

29. Ibid., 55 *et passim*.

30. It is worth noting, as well, that Habermas heavily depends on the psychological theory of moral development worked out by Piaget and Kohlberg, and specifically on the assumption that Kohlberg's sixth level of moral development, the "universal ethical principle orientation," is implicit in the idea of communicative action and exhibits the moral potential of the modern world at its best. See Lawrence Kohlberg, "From Is to Ought," in Theodore Mischel, ed., *Cognitive Development and Epistemology*, (New York: Academic Press, 1971).

31. I do not **mean that Habermas** self-consciously bases his thinking on Hegel, but only that **here, as in** so many other places in German thought, the legacy of Hegel's formulations lies just beneath the surface. Compare Holub's remark about Gadamer: "The fusing of horizons actually takes place, Gadamer maintains, but it means that the historical horizon is projected and then canceled or eliminated as a separate entity. In an almost Hegelian manner it seems that understanding is historical consciousness becoming aware of itself" (Holub, *Habermas*, 59). Is not the theory of communicative action also an instance of "historical consciousness becoming aware of itself"? Is it not itself a form of rationalizing reflection upon the fusion of horizons?

32. It is important to grasp what is at stake here. Habermas's emphasis on rational consensus is only another version, as Rorty has observed, of the assumption "that all contributions to a given discourse are commensurable." For Rorty, "hermeneutics" (as he uses this expression) is "largely a struggle against this assumption." Rorty, *Philosophy and the Mirror of Nature*,

(Princeton: Princeton University Press, 1979), 316, quoted in Bernstein, *Philosophical Profiles*, 79-80.

33. See Rawls's own comments in "Kantian Constructivism in Moral Theory," *The Journal of Philosophy*, 77 (Sept. 1980). He modifies the universalistic claims of *A Theory of Justice*, remarking that his theory is directly applicable only to a "a democratic society under modern circumstances" (p. 518).

34. See Bernstein, *Philosophical Profiles* (Philadelphia: University of Pennsylvania Press, 1986), 124.

35. See Gadamer, *Truth and Method* (New York: Seabury, 1975), 20ff., 278ff., 376ff., 490. Gadamer connects practical reasoning with the *sensus communis* or sense that founds human community. *Phronesis* is knowledge that "is directed toward the concrete situation" (p. 21) It is "a determination of moral being which cannot exist without the totality of the 'ethical virtues', which in turn cannot exist without it" (p. 22).

36. Charles W. Allen, "The Primacy of *Phronesis*, A Proposal for Avoiding Frustrating Tendencies in our Conceptions of Rationality," *The Journal of Religion* 69 (July 1989), 359ff.

37. I am of course referring to Ricoeur's famous formulation in *The Symbolism of Evil* (Boston: Beacon Press, 1967), 19. The philosopher "adopts provisionally the motivations and actions of the believing soul."

38. Stephen K. White argues, "If there is any obligation flowing from engaging in communicative action, then it is an obligation one *chooses* to take on; one could just as easily choose to avoid communicative action altogether...and orient oneself exclusively toward strategic action, thereby avoiding any normative obligation. This choice to renounce systematically *all* communicative action could be defended by the skeptic and opted for by actors whose behavior falls into categories such as the first-person dictator or systematic free rider" (*Habermas*, 51-52).

39. See "The Problem of Philosophical Fundamental-Grounding in Light of a Transcendental Pragmatic of Language," *Man and World* 8 (1975): 239-75; "The Common Presuppositions of Hermeneutics and Ethics: Types of Rationality Beyond Science and Technology," *Research in Phenomenology* 9 (1979): 35-53; "The Conflicts of our Time and the Problem of Political Ethics," *From Conflict to Community*, ed. Fred K. Dallmayr (New York: Marcel Dekker, 1978), 81-102; *Toward a Transformation of Philosophy* (London: Routledge and Kegan Paul, 1980); *Understanding and Explanation: A Transcendental-Pragmatic Perspective* (Cambridge MA: the M.I.T. Press, 1984). I am much indebted to Franklin I. Gamwell's *The Divine Good: Modern Moral Theory and the Necessity of God* (San Francisco: Harper and Row, 1990) for his interpretation of Apel's work, which I follow in several particulars, as indicated, in these pages.

40. Gamwell, *Divine Good*, 85. I am aware, of course, that several

contemporary philosophers deny the need for transcendental thought, or even its possibility. Alasdair MacIntyre is one, Rorty is another. On the contrary, I will argue, with Gamwell, that our beliefs about the transcendental conditions (whether metaphysical or not) of moral behavior make a difference which Gamwell states as the "difference...between integrity and duplicity in our coping with the world." (p. 118) And I agree with Gamwell that, apart from this consequence for our integrity, the "denial of *a priori* conditions of practical reason is itself an *a priori* claim." (p. 122) "The pragmatic importance of arguing against amoralism consists in making explicit the transcendental conditions of our practice and thereby having whatever measure of full conviction we may have regarding the ground of the moral enterprise." (p. 124) Here is an answer to those who say they know intuitively that the practices of Naziism were wrong, but yet would not know how to answer a philosophically sophisticated Nazi.

41. Ibid., 85.

42. Gamwell, *Divine Good*, 128.

43. This transformation results in what Apel describes as "transcendental-pragmatic philosophy." (Gamwell, 128) This insight enables us ultimately to justify a "material" moral norm something like Kant's second formulation of the categorical imperative: treat each person, including oneself, as an end rather than as a means. This is a *telos*, which Apel argues is independent of metaphysics, i.e. not dependent on assertions about the final nature of reality as such.

44. See Gamwell, *Divine Good*, 135.

45. "Self-reflection is then self-expression in which a subject seeks to communicate his or her thought to others." (Gamwell, *Divine Good*, 131).

46. Gamwell, Ibid., 131.

47. Ibid, 132.

48. Ibid., 132.

49. Such an attempt to understand the nature of argumentative discourse as such is a kind of transcendental philosophy which implies, as Gadamer argued, that hermeneutical rationality underlies both scientific and practical reason. "Hermeneutical rationality is the capacity to understand the validity claims and arguments for them offered by others, that is to understand the thought of other subjects." (Gamwell, *Divine Good*, 135) Apel's attempt to identify the conditions of subjectivity as such is, then, a *transcendental hermeneutics*.

50. Peukert, "Enlightenment and Theology as Unfinished Projects", in Browning and Fiorenza, eds., *Habermas*, 59.)

51. Robert Bellah makes much of Niebuhr's thinking in *The Good Society*. He quotes Niebuhr as follows: "The idea or pattern of responsibility, then, may summarily and abstractly be defined as the idea of an agent's action as response to an action upon him in accordance with his interpretation of the latter action and with his expectation of response to his response; and all of this in a

continuing community of agents." (*The Responsible Self*, New York: Harper and Row, 1978, 65, quoted in Bellah, 283.)

52. I have tried in *The Sense of a People* to suggest ways in which the Christian and Jewish traditions can make such positive contributions to civil society.

53. See Alan M. Olsen, *Hegel and the Spirit: Philosophy as Pneumatology* (Princeton: Princeton University Press, 1992). Olsen explores the meaning of Hegel's *Geist* as a speculative pneumatology which completes what Adolf van Harnack called the "orphan doctrine" of Christian theology, the doctrine of the Holy Spirit. For Olsen, Hegel's development originates in a deep appreciation of Luther's dialectical understanding of Spirit and thus is deeply interfused with the values of Württemberg pietism. Hegel's *Enzyklopädie* is thus the post-Enlightenment philosophical equivalent of a *Trinitätslehre*, and his *Rechtsphilosophie* is an ecclesiology. Olsen remarks that his book demonstrates the truth in Karl Barth's observation that Hegel is the potential Aquinas of Protestantism. Robert Bellah, in a private communication recommending Taylor's *Sources of the Self*, has made the same point.

54. Ricoeur's phrase again. See *Symbolism of Evil*, 19.

55. Charles Taylor, *Sources of the Self: The Making of the Modern Identity*, (Cambridge: Harvard University Press, 1989), 512.

56. Dr. Johnson is reported to have said that universality of "sin" is the only empirically verifiable Christian doctrine. That, of course, is not strictly true, but true enough to make the point. Much is lost when the idea of "sin" is abstracted from its context in the doctrine of salvation, but enough remains to be able to say that the Christian language, even if not believed as doctrine, can alert us to something true of human beings as such.

57. See Robert Bellah, et al., *The Good Society*, (New York: Alfred A. Knopf, 1991), 3ff. Not only is there a parallel in Bellah to Hegel's notion of *Sittlichkeit*, which I will shortly expound, but Bellah and his colleagues have used an open-ended method of interview which comes as close as empirical human science can to catching society's expressive, sense-making character.

58. For a contemporary development, by way of Troeltsch, of Hegel's concept of *Gestalten* or configurations of historical-social factors, see Peter C. Hodgson, *God in History: Shapes of Freedom*, (Nashville: Abingdon Press, 1989).

59. In *The Sense of a People* I have described a "phenomenology of spirit" which seeks to set forth the expressive or "text-like" character of the social world and the sequences of human interaction that go on in it. This description begins with a conception of primordial "gesture" (Mead), moves to the origins of signification and language (Pierce, Barthes) and from there to grammar and syntax (Wittgenstein), to symbol and metaphor (Ricoeur, Lakoff and Johnson), and finally to the world of action seen "on the analogy of the text" (Ricoeur), until we see that the social world itself "says" something by what it *is*.

60. *Hegel* (Cambridge: Cambridge University Press, 1975).

61. *Sources of the Self: The Making of the Modern Identity* (Cambridge: Harvard University Press, 1989). I am indebted to my daughter-in-law Ingrid Creppell for calling my attention to this book, and to Robert Bellah who gave me the same advice in a letter received the next day!

62. In Richard Bernstein's words, "Few philosophers have equalled Hegel in the passion with which he argued that the character and dynamics of human action must be understood within the context of intersubjective interactions....For if there are intersubjective rules and practices that are constitutive of human actions, then it becomes essential to gain some understanding of how such practices emerge, what sustains them, and how they pass away. These are the very issues that are in the foreground of Hegel's philosophy." Bernstein, "Why Hegel Now? in *Philosophical Profiles: Essays in a Pragmatic Mode* (Philadelphia: University of Pennsylvania Press, 1986), 156.

63. Bernstein, again expounding Taylor's *Hegel*, describes the philosopher's notion of what has gone wrong in the body politic. Alienation occurs when the norms, as expressed in public practices, cease to hold our allegiance, when there is a growing sense of the disparity of what we take ourselves to be and the forms of public life in which we find ourselves. This recurring experience of loss of a sense of identity and attempts to find a new form of cultural identity in the community is the story of objective spirit--a story which promises a possibility of a successful identification between the individual and the community." And again, "...the mode of interpretation that [Taylor] adopts in dealing with Hegel's understanding of social and political reality is one where Taylor is clearly interested in showing how Hegel still 'speaks to us,' that there is a way of understanding what he has to say about 'objective spirit' and *Sittlichkeit* that provides a richer orientation and set of categories for coming to grips with our own attempts to understand and interpret present social and political reality." Bernstein, *Profiles*, 175.

64. The importance for democracy of institutions in both senses of the term (i.e. specific institutions such as the Roman Catholic Church and institutionalized forms of life such as marriage, higher education, etc.) is the central message of Bellah, et al., *The Good Society* (New York: Alfred Knopf, 1991).

65. Taylor goes on: "This has been variously translated in English as 'ethical life,' 'objective ethics,' 'concrete ethics,' but no translation can capture the sense of this term of art, and I propose to use the original here. *Sittlichkeit* is the usual German term for 'ethics,' with the same kind of etymological origin, in the term *Sitten* which we might translate 'customs.' But Hegel gives it a special sense, in contrast to *Moralität* (despite the etymological origin of this word in the Latin *mores*, which brings it close in sense to *Sittlichkeit).* *Sittlichkeit* refers to the moral obligations I have to an ongoing community of

which I am a part." And again, "Hegel's notion of *Sittlichkeit* is in part a rendering of that expressive unity which his whole generation saw in the Greek *polis*, where--it was believed--men had seen the collective life of their city as the essence and meaning of their own lives." (Taylor, *Hegel*, 378.)

66. Taylor, *Hegel*, 542.

67. Some of these insights are present explicitly or by implication in my 1992 book, *The Sense of a People: Toward a Church for the Human Future*. I argue there for the use of a hermeneutically conceived, semiotically formulated, form of social inquiry in thinking about the church as social institution. I seek to formulate a new sense of the nature of the people of God to whom the different specific institutions of the church belong. This people is the trans-institutional gathering of what Josiah Royce meant by "beloved community" and Philip Hallie called "a community of ethical belief." I argue that the "sense" or regulative idea of such a "people" whose lives give hope to humankind by representing God's purposes for humanity, needs to function *in* ecclesiological thinking as a regulative idea, the notion of a whole which completes or makes coherent sense of a field of discourse. The idea of a "kingdom of God" functions this way, but it is not enough: it is too monarchical and patriarchal, and conveys too much the sense of a political power field. I seek rather to express the notion of God's active presence in human affairs as gathering a trans-institutional, multi-faith, mostly invisible human solidarity, which comes into view, when one has eyes to see, at certain times and places, in fragments and partly discernible configurations. I learned much in writing this from *Lumen Gentium* and also from Peter Hodgson's *God in History*. The churches are, as I see it, called to be "signs, sacraments and instruments" of this solidarity of humanity in the power of the Spirit.

68. Taylor, *Hegel*, 541.

69. Ibid., 545.

70. Ibid., 414.

71. Ibid., 415.

72. Ibid., 415-416.

73. The position outlined here could lead to a renewal of the notion that philosophical positions can, and indeed should, be identified as Jewish, Moslem, Buddhist, Christian, or otherwise. Of course, one can use such an expression as "Christian philosophy" simply to refer to a body of philosophical literature associated with the tradition in question without opening the question whether philosophy in principle is the sort of inquiry that *should* be tied to a specific cultural or religious tradition. My own view is that only by being located in one or another specific communal context can philosophy persuasively restore the status of metaphysics: seeing that inquiry now as the rational articulation of a particular belief-full vision of reality.

74. See on this last point George Lakoff and Mark Johnson, *Metaphors We Live By* (Chicago: University of Chicago Press, 1980). Many metaphors derive

from tradition-shaped activities which interpret the common social world as a particular sort of action-field (football field, field of battle, etc.). These metaphors thus carry over easily to other activities in that same social world. The use of metaphors derived from warfare to speak of various kinds of argumentative debate is particularly striking. It tells us something about the culture in which we live.

75. This seems to have been true, for example, of St. Augustine's doctrines of the Golden Rule, and of lying, in their illuminative power for the surrounding society. In the first case, Gene Outka comments that "for Augustine...the Golden Rule is commonly knowable prior to or apart from the moral law the Decalogue specifies" (Outka, "Augustinianism and Common Morality" in *Prospects for a Common Morality*, Princeton, Princeton University Press, 1993, 118). As for lying. the same relationship holds. Within the frame of reference of Christian doctrine, lying is a sin. Augustine gives it very precise meanings. But the analysis of lying as a social phenomenon lifts up something about the world that anyone can see, that society is corrupt, ensnared in "splendid vices." (See Outka, *Prospects*, 119ff) By giving something a name, it can be discerned in the social order without bringing to it all the theological baggage connected with its meaning in a traditional system of doctrine.

76. See Robert M. Adams, "Religious Ethics in a Pluralistic Society," in Outka and Reeder, *Prospects*, 93ff. What we lack is any common explanation or grounding of such moral principles that could give us greater confidence that what we hold in common is coherent, more possibility of fruitful inference and nuance in developing the shared moral content to cover new situations.

77. White, *Habermas*, 97.

78. Ibid., 97.

79. Michael Walzer, *Spheres of Justice* (New York: Basic Books, 1983). Walzer explores the thick fabric of assumptions about justice that obtains in each of a variety of spheres of life and arenas of concern, e.g. security and welfare, membership, money and commodities, social recognition, political power, and divine grace.

80. See Sander Griffioen, "The Metaphor of the Covenant in Habermas" in *Faith and Philosophy*, Vol. 8, No. 4, (October, 1991). 524ff. In *The Philosophical Discourse of Modernity* (page 325) Habermas compares the binding force of communicative reason with the covenant made by Yahweh with the people of Israel. The comparison comes in a passage defending communicative reason against charges of elitism. Griffioen writes, "Those who do not live by the light of reason are not set apart in an inferior form of life. Rather, their 'irrationality' is understood as 'unsuccessful communication' which as such remains linked to 'successful communication.'" In short "the norm of rationality is not divisive." The terms "covenant" (*Bund*) and "confederation" (*Bundgenossenschaft*) appear in this argumentative setting.

Habermas quotes Klaus Heinrich in such a way as to indicate that he has the biblical model in mind.

81. Habermas, *Moralbewusstsein und Kommunikatives Handeln* (Frankfurt: Suhrkamp, 1983), 100-103. See also Karl-Otto Apel, *Towards a Transformation of Philosophy* (London: Routeledge and Kegan Paul, 1980), ch. 7.

82. Ricoeur, *Symbolism of Evil*, 19.

83. Ibid., 19.

84. See William Werpehowski, "Ad Hoc Apologetics," *The Journal of Religion*, 66 (July 1986), 282ff.

85. Ibid., 287.

86. Ibid., 287.

87. Ibid., 292.

88. The two examples that follow are suggested by Werpehowski's article but heavily adapted in content and argumentative form to accompany my line of thought in this paper. Werpehowski, in turn, gives credit for the medical example to William May, *The Physician's Covenant: Images of the Healer in Medical Ethics* (Philadelphia: Westminster Press, 1983), and notes the relevance of Nicholas Lash, *A Matter of Hope: A Theologian's Reflection on the Thought of Karl Marx* (Notre Dame, IN: University of Notre Dame Press, 1982).

V

Householding

11

Remodeling the Household:
Ecclesiology and Ethics After Harare

My task at the World Council of Churches' Eighth Assembly (Harare, Zimbabwe, 1998) was to track "ecclesiology and ethics" issues through the meeting.[1] The result, it was thought, could help to frame the next stage of this discussion. I hope that will still happen. But time and distance have led me to reinterpret the original assignment. These pages turn out to be less a matter of specific issue-tracking and more an attempt to see the Assembly itself as a "household" in which ecclesial and moral concerns interacted and became concrete. I seek in conclusion to generate some insight for the road ahead.[2]

The "Household" First-Hand

If one came to Harare with mind tuned narrowly like an internet "search engine" to catch the words "ecclesiology and ethics" in conjunction, one scored rather few "hits." Yet a search for references of this kind proved to be largely beside the point. The point lay in the ecclesial and moral implications of the Assembly's discourses themselves. One did not need to talk *about* the household. This *was* the household, directly experienced. Those present who had been involved in the "ecclesiology and ethics" study were able to test what they had thought and done in the company of nearly 5000 people from virtually every corner of the earth. The Assembly served as a reality-check on five years of much smaller-scale deliberations. Writing the word "global" in an ecumenical document is one thing. Experiencing that reality through interactions with persons from so many places with so many visions and concrete agendas is quite another. Stereotypes are repeatedly broken, as they should be. The "third world" is not one thing. In fact it does not exist as such. What one felt was "difference" along every conceivable axis of opinion and interest. Yet there remained the real, yet surprisingly difficult-to-articulate, sense of living in one household of faith.

Certain insights rang true along Harare's often muddy pathways. Three points especially. First, that what counts is the wholeness and concreteness of the presence of the church in the world and therefore the importance of moral formation at the level of the family and the local congregation. Second, that the moral problems facing us in the 21st century are unprecedented in character, threatening the continuation of the human race itself and challenging the churches in ways for which they are largely unprepared. And third, that the church in all its forms is a generator and maintainer of "space" for reconciliation of the issues dividing humankind.[3] Seen in these terms "ecclesiology and ethics" issues were intrinsic to the subject-matter discussed at Harare and to the Assembly itself as an ecumenical space.

Indeed, in this context, the very formula "ecclesiology and ethics" may have been misleading. This terminology suggested that two known quantities were to be brought into closer relationship. Instead, "ecclesiology" and "ethics" functioned more as *inter*dependent perspectives for grasping the concrete presence of the People of God among the social realities of contemporary humankind. In many ways, the Theology of Life study formulated the central concern better: the real, lived articulation of the Body of Christ in the social world as a "household of life" in with and under the common life we share as human beings. One could consider "household" ecclesiologically, and thereby relate it to a complex institutional-theological past and present. Or one could consider it ethically, thereby asking what it should "say" in moral terms that such a community exists and acts in the world, and also *how* this saying is actually done. Questions such as these everywhere accompanied Harare's struggles with the multiple questions surrounding the life and witness of the churches at the close of the twentieth century.

Above all, much conversation at Harare directly or indirectly concerned the human impact of "globalization," both in the economic sphere and in the realm of communications. And hence much talk had to do, directly or indirectly, with tactics and strategies of resistance. I caught two notes which corresponded to the first two insights generated in the "ecclesiology and ethics" studies. The third note, that of the church as "space" for reconciliation, offers an opportunity for conceptual progress recently developed in a number of contexts.[4]

Cultural-Theological Particularities

First, one could not avoid the sense of a world church composed of multiple cultural particularities. Awareness of the pluralism of Christian faith-expressions is of course not new. Robert Schreiter treated this trend analytically and constructively fifteen years ago in *Constructing Local Theologies.*[5] In this work he wrote,

> Theological procedures...follow to a great extent the patterns of production of meaning within a given cultural context. What has counted for theology since the thirteenth century in Western Christianity has been dominated by a university model.... But other ways of engaging in theological reflection are available and are giving shape to how Christians understand themselves in their situations.[6]

Schreiter went on to analyze cultures and their theological components by means of a semiotic method that uncovered the significations and codes of meaning built into cultures and the theological discourses occurring within them.

At Harare it was clear that this localizing movement has now taken hold and gone further that Schreiter saw when he wrote.[7] Even among long-convinced ecumenists, there appeared to be less confidence that academic theologizing--Eastern or Western--could build bridges between cultural particularities in faith than had been the case just seven years ago when the question of acculturation was sharply raised by a keynote presentation at Canberra. Of course this is only a matter of personal intuition. But as the sway of uniform "liberation" formulas declines, the importance of "culture" grows. "Post-modern" insights proclaiming the incoherence of our forms of life and the inability of language to represent "reality" make steady inroads in our theological classrooms. It helped to recall that that "difference" also exists back home. Particular congregations, even within the same denomination or communion, are often now emerging as "cultures", or at least communities of entrenched habit, in their own right: unique in certain respects in their perceptions and articulations of the gospel.

Among the most important consequences of such theological developments are their implications for moral formation. The "ecclesiology and ethics" study placed great emphasis on primary formation in the life of faith as the work of the local church: that which primordially ties ethics to *ekklesia*. But such formation can no longer be standardized, new catechisms notwithstanding. And formation can go wrong. It can represent partial insights, or distorted vision. It can be "mal-formation." In a pluralistic Christian world, what do we do about this?

And the obvious question follows. How do myriad locally specific expressions of the church communicate with one another? How can they share standards of adequacy and faithfulness? Can there exist a common Christian theological and moral language today? *Is* there one gospel for the whole world? Yet these many expressions of faith do communicate with one another when by rights, that is by all the canons of post-modern theory, they should not be able to. Is it time to try to say why this is possible by constructing some sort of "theory of communicative action"[8] for the world church? In our present circumstances how could this be prevented from becoming an arbitrary, Euro-hegemonic project?

Hope rests in the fact that the more culturally specific a theological language is, the more it is likely to be grounded in what we make of our common earth. The very word "culture" arises from images of what we human beings do with "nature," as in agri-culture. At Harare I was bemused--while picking my way carefully across springy plank bridges (themselves rather good ecumenical metaphors) spanning trenches in the earth in which were to be laid fiber-optic cable for the University's new computer system--to think that communications can be close to the earth as well as conducted by satellite dishes. I am not quite sure where this metaphor leads. But it seems to be that culturally specific treatments of the gospel need to be able to communicate *directly*, through common earthy concerns, and not through westernizing translations inspired by the formulas of European anthropologists.

We do not have a theory to explain why, but the theoretically unexplained did happen at Harare. That is what we must meditate about. Perhaps the answer is that conversation needs to go on, not through the right sort of theory, but in the right kind of household. Harare sought to embody such a household--of mutual confidence and trust--as well as to begin to remodel the house that is the WCC to make it more viable and effective.

Global Theological Flows

But something else was also happening at the Assembly. The participants indicated by their various interventions that besides representing many "local theologies" they were also participating in what Schreiter has more recently called "global theological flows."[9] In the Padare[10] as much as anywhere, we saw how several discrete *theological* strategies of resistance to economic and communicative "globalization" are beginning to link themselves together internally across the globe. Schreiter writes,

> Global theological flows...are theological discourses that, while not uniform or systemic, represent a series of linked, mutually intelligible discourses that address the contradictions or failures of global systems. They are theological discourses, that is, they speak out of the realm of religious beliefs and practices. They are not uniform or systemic, because of their commitment to specific cultural and social settings. Yet they are intelligible to discourses in other cultural and social settings that are experiencing the same failure of global systems and who are raising the same kind of protest.[11]

Schreiter mentions liberationist, feminist, ecological and human-rights discourses. I would add a fifth: the discourse around democracy and civil society, and possibly a sixth, the discourse about the nature of localism or multi-culturalism itself! Each discourse, or problematic is in a sense "universal" but paradoxically exists only in a multitude of distinct cultural expressions. In each local expression the "flow" is at a different point in its development as a culture-linking theological problematic. In each of these cases one has a species of "universality" quite unlike the universality claimed by Enlightenment rationality, or even that claimed by European or North American academic theology. Despite highly diverse cultural forms these expressions understand one another when gathered around a particular moral concern. Here a series of conversations girdle the earth without sharing common theoretical structures.

Such "flows" consist of shared bundles of interrelated questions, hypotheses, models, methods and the like which constitute a field of knowledge and inquiry. At any given moment one may cross-section such a problematic to discover not one "state of the question" but many for those involved in the dialogue. Moreover, each of the flows mentioned by Schreiter has its own special characteristics. The liberation project has always taken different forms on different continents. Today it is rapidly changing to give more attention to culture and less to class warfare. Participation in the feminist discourse is highly uneven: as one might expect. More than the others, the ecological flow gathers around scientific findings, but is differentiated by political perspectives. The most global Christian involvement no doubt focuses on the issues of human rights.

In one sense, these flows sweep like high-level jetstreams of interconnected discourse among elites. But they are also counter-systemic and to a remarkable degree are grounded in myriad specific cultural expressions and analyses. People fly from everywhere to Cairo for the population summit, to Beijing for the women's summit, or to Rio for the earth summit. Yet their authenticity as interlocutors rests less in common ideology than in a grounding in specific situations.

One was struck by how much both Padare presentations and Assembly resolutions involved these global discourses, existing both within the churches and beyond them. One also noted the importance, here too, of having been engaged in these questions as they were manifested in the localities from which the discussants come. If delegates had their heads up in these global jet-streams they had their feet on the ground in the very special ways demanded by the life of congregations in particular times and places. Harare prescinded from attempts to achieve universal theological expression but succeeded in enabling mutual comprehension. Here, for all its faults (and the Padare must be arranged and administered differently next time) was the right kind of house, or encampment, for this to happen.

It is interesting, however, that these *different* global discourses tended not to intersect with one another. Presentations tended to focus in one arena or another: feminism, or ecology, or liberation, or human rights. The linking factor was resistance to "globalization" in the economic sense. Few participants sought seriously to link the different flows as such into a larger picture. The exception might be the occasional use of human rights talk as a bridge discourse. One *could* hear syntheses of global feminism with human rights, of economic liberation with human rights, and so on. But one the whole, while each of these global "flows" was and is "theological" in intent, they do not yet add up to anything approaching a single body of coherent theological insight.

Moreover, one has to note that not everybody sees "moral" issues in these terms. It would be interesting to ask what sorts of questions seem to lend themselves to potentially unifying flows of discourse, and which do not. The flows named are capable of being divisive as well as reconciling. Many who seek the unity of Christ's church feel largely left out of discussions of this kind. It is ironic that we speak of "catholicity" but have not generated a global theological flow of discourse about what it means to be church. [12] Perhaps that is because there is no secular flow of discourse corresponding to the ecclesiological question and helping to sustain it.

Another way to say this is that ecclesiology, the science of the "space" in which such global theological flows might meet, does not yet constitute a "global theological flow" in its own right. Nor is there any coherent theory of the human or of the human condition emerging here. All this speaks much of the state of affairs in which we find ourselves. Our theological initiatives and insights come from no central place. There is no single dominant theological style or conceptuality at work either between the diverse cultural expressions of each of the themes. Moreover no new over-all expression of the Christian faith *as such* appears to be growing out of these parallel problematics. No brief description can so justice to the complexity of what is going on.

Perhaps such observations suggest a new way to define the theological challenge facing Faith and Order and other centers of ecumenical theological work. How can global discursive spaces for the formulation of discrete moral issues be brought into the space of the church, both to enrich it and to suggest ways in which we can similarly understand the ecumenical task? Harare seemed content to bring all this together into many adjacent rooms (some of which could just as well have been ten thousand miles apart for all the communication that took place). How can we understand these rooms to belong within a common house?

A Ground Floor Strategy

The General Secretary's report at the opening of the Assembly made extensive use of "space" as ecumenical metaphor. Konrad Raiser spoke of the "free space" of the sabbath day that foreshadows the greater space of the Jubilee, the year of liberation and reconciliation. He went on to apply the "space" metaphor in several further ways: space where ecclesio-moral communion can come to fruition, space ample enough for diversity "and for open mutual confrontation of differing interests and convictions", space for the church to be a truly inclusive community, the earth as space provided by the Creator for all living things to live together in sustainable communities.

One thought immediately of the temporary space constituted by assemblies such as this one, and of the larger space denoted by the image of a "household of life." Both call for an adequate ecumenical *architecture*, as was evident from the report on "Common Understanding and Vision" combined with announced plans for remodeling the internal structures of the Council. What sorts of spaces, metaphorical and actual, are needed for local realities on the ground to be connected with "global theological flows" in ways faithful to Christian faith as it has been transmitted down the ages from the Apostles until now? How can the WCC conceive of and maintain spaces in which dialogue among Christian confessions and communions both promotes the wider human dialogue and learns from it?

In asking such "architectural" questions we were, probably unwittingly, echoing the thoughts of Michel Foucault, who spoke these words in an interview a quarter-century or more ago:

> A whole history remains to be written of *spaces*--which would at the same time be the history of *powers* (both these terms in the plural)--from the great strategies of geo-politics to the little tactics of the habitat, institutional architecture from the classroom to the design of hospitals, passing via economic and political institutions. That development must be extended, by no longer just saying that space determines a history which in turn reworks and sediments itself in it. Anchorage in a space is an econ-omico-political form which needs to be studied in detail.[13]

WCC Assemblies and the WCC itself are theologico-political forms which likewise need to be studied in detail. Beginnings have been made, but the inquiry must go further. We need to think of the geometry of ecumenical spaces, the places assigned to institutions and persons in such spaces. There is need to rethink the shape of the ecumenical household in the light of the "Forum" proposal and the dissatisfactions of the Orthodox. This is only beginning and will go on for years. We know that Foucault is right: institutional architecture reflects and perpetuates power. Space determines history "which in turn reworks and sediments itself in it."

One searches for the right architectural metaphor to energize this inquiry. Like most metaphors, the one now to be suggested will be misleading if pushed too far. But perhaps it is good for a start. In many parts of the world, including the one I come from, land for building houses is scarce. And laws--in the interest of light, air, and limiting environmental impact--also limit the amount of a lot that may be covered by the house's "footprint." So, to make space for growing families you remodel. But you dare not spread sideways, so you try to build higher. But what if the existing ground floor is not strong enough to support a second floor above (typical of wooden as opposed to cinder-block buildings)? Then you build a new ground floor, a new *rez de chausseé* ("at the level of the street"), *below* what you already have, lifting the former house eight or ten feet higher in the air, radically changing its aspect and its outlook while keeping it recognizably the same structure. And in doing this, you need a better foundation as well, and you dig deeper into the soil, looking for bedrock.

I think the plan of our ecumenical remodeling now needs to be rather like this. We need to remodel so that the ground floor becomes the primary ecumenical space: a space which sustains, as it were "above" it, the conversations of the theologians who reflect *to* the ground floor reality something about its own nature. At the same time, the household of faith needs to dig a deeper foundation into the soil of cultures, to listen with ears to the ground, to become more one with the earth. Something like this needs to go on in the action and thinking of our member churches as well to prepare them to support the possibility of being constituent participants in a "household of life" with high enough profile to be conversant with global intellectual trends and deep enough foundations to rest comfortably in the earth where they are planted.

New WCC projects concerning ethnicity and violence in various locations, conceived as continuing the "ecclesiology and ethics" inquiry in a fresh form, represent precisely such a "ground floor" strategy. They connect *both* to "upper floor" flows of human rights and other discourses, *and* to the soil of particular places, particular identities, particular conflicts. But can such projects bring us closer to being able to articulate the global discourse of the church a such? Can they contribute to what Schreiter calls "the new catholicity"? It is deeply ironic that the "global theological flow" we have not achieved or even begun to clarify is that which constitutes the household of Christian faith itself. Unless we are prepared to say that the household *consists in* its projects, involvements, relationships, alliances and so on with theological flows that are indeed global, the "ground floor" is not truly ecclesial in nature. Is there a way to state criteria for the inclusion of ground-floor space within the household of God: criteria which reflect understanding of the fact that this is a space in which global theological-moral insights and particular cultural realities interact?

A Dialogue of Criteriologies

What are the limits? Whose discourses belong in the house and why? Should the WCC mainly foster tightly controlled dialogues among traditional conceptions of the church, or should it be hospitable to all comers? To put it another way, which is the model for the future, Faith and Order dialogues and Assembly business sessions on the one hand, or the Padare on the other? Why not both-and? Must a choice be made? Both visions were present at Harare, although in the organization of the Assembly they seldom directly interacted. Let us look at each.[14]

The first-named perspective, despite all deconstructive and localizing tendencies, continues to exhibit high confidence in theological language and argument as such as able to grasp and convey, supply criteria *for*, the concreteness of the church's life. The resulting projects play out as tightly organized, "closely held" as is said in the realm of finance, dialogues among official representatives which seem to look for new hegemonic language in the European discourse tradition. The influential participants--and certainly the methods used--have been mostly European and North American. The perceived task is to draft formulas of convergence, to build "fragile bridges of words between worlds." Allowing ethical and contextual issues into the debate as proposed in the "ground floor" strategy, is seen by many--not all--as confusing and divisive. Some--not all--see such moves as threatening the achievement of several generations of Faith and Order work. This position exhibits resistance to the post-modern assumptions which often accompany ecclesiological communitarianism in Western countries. It distrusts attitudes which pry words loose from the realities to which they are supposed to refer. In short, this is a classic "upper floor" strategy: resolve the historic theological differences through studies and debates conducted by experts and the leadership of the churches will one day be willing to pull down the walls which still separate us at the Table of the Lord.

Those who hold the second view have far less confidence in conceptual analysis *per se* and high confidence in direct practices of interaction among those who operate in a variety of situations at the ground floor. They resist those who wish to supply, or withhold, legitimating language coming from Northern Hemisphere academic or ecclesiastical traditions. Holders of this position observe that in the Southern Hemisphere interest in Faith and Order projects and formulas is not high. Interest rather focuses on ground floor issues, and on the stance the church takes in relation to immediate issues in particular communal settings. In short, the question is what form of gospel-generated ethic is acted out not only by individuals but by what the church stands for in its immediate social setting. In its extreme form, this position distrusts all linguistic forms that attempt to universalize Christian experience or social engagement, preferring that persons representing the reality of such experience meet directly in a Padare or Sokoni-like setting. As Larry Rasmussen puts it,

> ...the most promising way forward is not that of finding the language of normative common ground as that might be offered by theologians and agreed to by heads of communions. This understanding of ecumenical formation is essentially doctrinal and jurisdictional. The most promising way is by arranging a common table, open to participation by the whole people of God, to see what emerges as living church when faith is freely shared on the burning issues we face.[15]

I would argue that the former position is too focused on criteriological issues of a conceptual type, or on hegemonically formulated issues of legitimacy. The latter position is in danger of tolerating any expression of the gospel, becoming too contextual, so open that we have little in common, or cannot actually articulate our common ground. Together, these distinct visions raise the question of how different contextual theologies or contextual ecclesiologies communicate with one another. If not through some northern European conceptuality, and not through open and unstructured gatherings either,[16] then how?

The "Resonance and Recognition" Model

It would be presumptuous to suppose that I can answer such questions. But it may be worthwhile to think again about the clue provided in "Costly Obedience" which Konrad Raiser lifted up as an "important suggestion." Paraphrasing the Johannesburg report. Raiser proposed that the oikoumene be understood as

> an "energy field" of mutual resonance and recognition generated by the Holy Spirit. "By choosing resonance and recognition as our metaphors we are able to turn to a biblical formula found in the Johannine literature... The sheep know the shepherd's voice (John 10:3, cf. Rev 3:20). Discipleship means hearing, being drawn, being formed, by the voice: not just its sound but also the content, the authentic note of a way of speaking by which we are shaped, attesting to an identifiable way of being in the world, yet a way of being having many different forms.... The focus of ecumenical recognition is that the other community has an acted commitment analogous to one's own, and one's own commitment is analogous to the other's. The analogy exists because of a shared recognition-pattern of moral practice in the Spirit. People...recognize that others "have the same spirit"... Such recognition is something holistic, never *merely* doctrinal or jurisdictional but also including both doctrinal and jurisdictional elements. It is recognition of a lived reality: a sense of moral communion. This is what *oikoumene* means.[17]

The majority opinion at Harare, for those sounded out on the matter, was that such images are not *sufficiently* criteriological: that we need something more precise. Yet it may be worthwhile to explore the implications of the "resonance and recognition" approach somewhat further.

Resonance and recognition clearly fulfill the requirements of a "ground floor" strategy. Resonance is felt and recognition granted by those engaged in many diverse, culturally specific, practices of ministry. The upper-floor project may well be to clarify what is involved if and when such things happen. I argue that such resonance and recognition linking many ground-floor projects and places of application are precisely what eventually create "global theological flows." Flows of this sort are aided and clarified by theoretical, upper floor reflection and conceptualization. Liberation, feminist, ecological and human-rights discourses are carried on by organic intellectuals (that is, thinkers with their feet well set in particular cultural settings) riding the global flows which connect their diverse situations of moral struggle.

The key insight is that the Holy Spirit generates a kind of resonant energy field among the many instances of Christ's presence in the world.[18] This identifiable resonance, for example, *connects* instances of evangelical hospitality (Matthew 25:31-46; Luke 24:28-43). Jesus comes to us in the persons of the poor, the outcast, the hungry. God's incarnate presence in history can be seen as articulated in the *ensemble* of the many perspectives in which the spiritual or moral resonance implicit in Christ's presence has been, and continues to be, known and appropriated by those who follow him. Each particular place of discipleship in each cultural setting generates a community distinguishable from, yet recognizable to, other such communities. The Holy Spirit instigates an energy field of resonance *among* these diverse responses to Jesus.

Such a notion, as we will see, calls for the invention of a method which seeks to grasp what happens when such recognition takes place, protecting us from recognizing the sorts of "false spirits" which, according to I John, have also gone out into the world. Suppose we were to think of upper-floor discourses--such as those which take place in Faith and Order--as not definitive or referential in their own right, but rather as designed to understand the nature of these ground-floor processes of recognition. Can we then see those efforts as attempts to articulate hermeneutical principles which can permit us to hear one another, and be heard in turn, across diverse situations and ecclesial cultures? Is it possible to think of a sort of *ecclesiological* hermeneutic of the *koinonia* we share when we find ourselves united on some moral issue, say the impact of global economic greed on the earth and all its inhabitants? Faith and Order work could then be understood as the shared attempt to articulate how the embedded discourses of actual practice on the *rez de chausseé* constitute an ecumenical space of spiritual resonance in which we find the possibility of mutual recognition.

What kind of hermeneutic might this be? Something like Wittgenstein's concept of "family resemblance" seems called for here: that elusive mental ability by which we can recognize diverse individuals, each with his or her unique appearance, as nonetheless belonging to the same family. Or perhaps we have here something very like Gadamer's metaphor of a "fusion of horizons" with its emphasis on concrete practice and the practical reasoning (Aristotle's *phronesis*) embedded in that practice. Or we could think of Paul Ricoeur's notion that social phenomena can be likened to "texts" ready to be read, which in turn connects with Schreiter's creative use of semiotics or sign-theory. The gathering of the people of God in the Spirit is by nature an *expressive* phenomenon. It can be interpreted as belonging within a household, a space, or a cybernetic network of similar expressions.

There is no Platonic idea or essence of ecclesiality to account for this. People know the distinctive "voice"[19] of Jesus Christ when they hear it or see peoples' response to it. People who know this voice can see that enormously diverse manifestations of ground-floor articulations of faith--as different from one another as a small Baptist congregation or a Latin American base community is from a gathering for papal high mass in St. Peter's or a celebration of the Liturgy of St. Chrysostom in the Patriarchal Cathedral in Moscow--belong together in the same household. There is no conceptually articulable ideal form existing "above" or beyond this world of particulars, no humanly achieved univocity connecting these distinctive instantiations of faith. There is only a recognition of common resonance that tells us in actual experience that these expressions of faith, however different, belong to the same household.

Such recognition of resonance in the faith is what makes a WCC Assembly more than a business meeting. It is what can make the projected Forum possible. Is this what contemporary work on "ecumenical hermeneutics" is aimed at? I think so, at least in part. What sort of hermeneutic is implied in our mutual recognition, the recognition of a certain coherence-in-diaspora, across wide differences?

Does it help the hermeneutical imagination to think of the resonance of *different* expressions of faith living within a space of the Spirit's working, in a determinate yet hospitable household of faith? If so, it becomes worthwhile to try to think out what is happening in this spiritually resonant space, within which all our studies are located.

One could begin with the metaphor of "space" in Konrad Raiser's Assembly address. What constitutes a "space" in the social or ecclesial senses of the term? "Spaces" do not exist in the abstract. They are constituted by the symbolic interactions which go on within them. What maintains the space is the active and communicative discourse which gives it its characteristic shape. Ever championing the Enlightenment, Jürgen Habermas tells us that "communicative action" can be understood by setting forth the logical presuppositions of "speech-acts" as such, and following the resulting chains of reasoning until "the better argument" wins. If, on the other hand, one believes that no universal logic of the Enlightenment type exists, the Habermasian argument fails and one is back to the question of hermeneutics, the science of *understanding*. I argue that the space of human discourse cannot be understood in content-neutral terms. Rather, a space of discourse exists when there is something to talk *about*. There must be a primordial Word having a determinate content which sets the conversation in motion. In Christian faith that Word is made flesh, and therefore becomes "voice" in the sense of an identifiable personal style of speech. The "voice" in question is above all recognizable in the literary form of narratives which give all within earshot something concrete actively to communicate about.

Most contemporary human beings live in a discursive space whose characteristic *logos* is the cost-benefit analysis. There is an alternative household. It is the one in which the Master's voice is heard down through the ages through the witness of those who were "with Jesus". The identifying voice-print of *that* witnessed content is the Kingdom-parable. If there were to be a "global theological flow" connecting the myriad culturally specific instances of faith communities in Christ it would need to consist of discourse about the meaning of God's reign.

Thinking about the resonance of "kingdom" language today could lead us to an eschatologically-oriented theological anthropology in which we articulate what we believe about the future of the human race. It could also lead us toward a new way of thinking about "catholicity" as a mark of the church.[20] Catholicity might be envisioned as a field of hermeneutically conceived communicative action among those living within the household of action-discourses in which the kingdom parables of Jesus can today be heard and reenacted. Our various communions, confessions and denominations each in effect present visions--seen through their respective theological lenses--of what the church's wholeness should consist of. They need to be helped to reflect how it is that they already meet on the ground floor of a larger household of life.

Notes

1. I am happy to acknowledge the help of several colleagues in compiling this essay: Martin Robra, Alan Falconer, Tom Best, and Paul Meyendorff among others. Their generosity saddles them with no responsibility for my opinions.

2. As explained in the Introduction to this volume, an inquiry into the relationship between "ecclesiology" and "ethics" was conducted by the WCC between 1993 and 1997. The writer participated in this study and was principal drafter for its final session in Johannesburg, South Africa, in June, 1996. The official results of the work were published in the volume *Ecclesiology and Ethics: Ecumenical Ethical Engagement, Moral Formation, and the Nature of the Churches*, Thomas F. Best and Martin Robra, eds. (Geneva: WCC Publications, 1997). A personal account and evaluation of the studies may be found in Lewis S. Mudge, *The Church as Moral Community* (New York: Continuum Publishing Co., and Geneva: WCC Publications, 1998).

3. Alan Falconer has called my attention to a number of important earlier sources for this metaphor of ecumenical "space," among them the Faith and Order Commission meeting at Louvain, 1971.

4. For example, a paper for the WCC Executive Committee by Alan Falconer and Martin Robra on the Nature and Ethos of the Harare Assembly, a shorter version of which appeared in the Padare Handbook.

5. Robert Schreiter, *Constructing Local Theologies* (Maryknoll, NY: Orbis Books, 1985).

6. Schreiter, *Local Theologies*, 4.

7. I am not referring to forms of theological particularity which *mean* to be incommensurable with others. (See the paper by Alan Falconer, "Models of Unity: the Wider Context," presented at the 1999 Meissen Conference.) These are the views--the fundamentalisms, pre-modern revivals and primitivisms--that simply resist *everything* about the modern world. Such views were little represented at Harare, if at all.

8. I am thinking of the book by this name by Jürgen Habermas, who argues

that the necessary structure of "speech acts" is universal--at least among persons educated as he is. This last is an important, if not fatal qualification. It implies an eschatology in which everyone on earth is finally brought into a realm of communicative reasoning modeled, with modifications, on that of the Enlightenment.

9. Schreiter, *The New Catholicity* (Maryknoll, NY: Orbis Books, 1997, 15ff.

10. The "Padare," a unique feature of the Harare Assembly, consisted of a series of open forums in which local and contextual experiences of ecclesial world-engagement were presented and discussed. A very wide range of themes surfaced. The word *padare* means a kind of village meeting to which anyone may bring concerns for public discussion.

11. Schreiter, *Catholicity*, 16.

12. I distinguish the needed global flow of ecclesial discourse from the important but different work of the WCC Commission on Faith and Order. The latter is a global dialogue on theological issues, including ecclesiology, which keep the churches of different confessions and communions as such divided from one another. The former, if achieved, would be a global flow of discourse among witnessing communities, often involving many communions and confessions in concert, striving in different particular contexts to be the church concretely in those places, wrestling always with the moral implications of being so.

13. Michel Foucault, "The Eye of Power," in *Power/Knowledge: Selected Interviews and Other Writings*, 1972-1977, ed. Colin Gordon (New York: Pantheon Books, 1980), 149.

14. I am aware, of course, that basic tensions in ecumenical discourse can be described in different ways with different outcomes: for example the classic distinction between "ecumenism in space" and "ecumenism in time," or the tension between local and universal. Much depends on the ethos within which the discourse in question occurs.

15. Larry Rasmussen, "The Right Direction But a Longer Journey," in Best and Robra, eds. *Ecclesiology and Ethics* (Geneva: WCC Publications, 1997), 107.

16. I am aware, of course, that the Sokoni event which Larry Rasmussen describes was in fact rather carefully structured, but in a different way from what probably would have happened in northern Europe!

17. "Report of the General Secretary", Harare Document PL 4-1, 7. I need to acknowledge having originally drafted the words (See Best and Robra, eds., *Ecclesiology*, 78) quoted by Konrad Raiser at Harare. Almost identical language appears by permission in my book *The Church as Moral Community*, 128f.

18. These ideas come from the work of Michael Welker. See his article, "The Holy Spirit," translated by John Hoffmeyer, *Theology Today* 45 (April 1989), 4-20. See also Welker's *God the Spirit* (Minneapolis: Fortress Press,

1994), 239ff.

19. We may think of the "voice" of Jesus in a textual rather than an acoustical way. We say that an author's works achieve a distinctive "voice" when style and content mark the writer's identity and personal force.

20. Similar formulations of the themes of theological anthropology and of catholicity are set forth in Schreiter, *Catholicity*. I acknowledge the stimulus of this source.

12

Moral Hospitality for Public Reasoners

An age obsessed with the "politics of difference"[1] needs to ask whether it can find grounds for formulating some new understanding of the shared discourse of the human race. In the West, we have witnessed the collapse of confidence in the universality of Enlightenment-style reasoning processes. A sensitivity to "difference" makes room for the flourishing of particular cultures and ways of life, yet simultaneously encourages a radical fragmentation of civic self-understanding. Religiously traditioned communities, churches for example, are now seeking to deepen their distinctive traditions of life. They should realize that they also have a vital interest in seeing human beings morally reconnected with one another through a larger, deeper practice of "public reason." Without wishing to bring back theocracy in any form, religious communities have a common calling to add further ranges of imaginative possibility--hopefully compatible with one another in *some* sense of "overlapping"[2]--to humanity's reasoning about life-together on this planet.

How might such religious contributions to public moral imagination now be conceived? This essay argues that households of faith might seek to draw in new ways upon ancient traditions of hospitality to the stranger. The focus now, however, could be on *moral* rather than merely material hospitality. Instead of seeking conversions, or imposing (often by political means) theologically derived moral convictions on skeptics, religious communities could in effect invite journalists, politicians, activists, intellectuals and others to move temporarily into spaces of discourse generated by their various traditions of faith, there to sample alternative forms of social imagination, alternative ways of seeing the world as action field.

Political thinking may be more open to such possibilities than we think. The social philosopher Georgia Warnke argues,[3] that political and social philosophies are at bottom hermeneutical in nature. However rational they may appear to be, they in fact rest upon imaginative constructs, stories, myths and the like. If this is true, one can imagine the potential power of religious traditions that can generate strategies of moral hospitality toward others, offering what are in effect invitations that expose public leaders, without proselytizing pressure, to these traditions as lived.

A New Philosophical Openness?

Indeed certain philosophers are now wondering--on their own terms of course--if there *are* religious traditions still around with sufficient force and coherence in the midst of the pluralistic maelstrom to provide needed infusions of wisdom. At a 1996 University of Santa Clara colloquy honoring John Rawls on the twenty-fifth anniversary of *A Theory of Justice*, six out of the seven speakers, in different ways spoke of their need for dialogue with religiously traditioned communities.[4] They were saying, in effect, that political philosophy should maintain its conceptual autonomy and secularity but that it should *also* seek sustenance from deeply traditioned and ongoing forms of life.

More recently the French deconstructionist Jacques Derrida has been doing much the same thing with the notion of "forgiveness." Derrida has clearly been mining the Hebrew and Christian Scriptures, as well as the Talmud, for sources of philosophical inspiration. John Caputo writes of Derrida that, still professing atheism, he "...follows with fascination the movements of what theology calls God, observing how theology speaks, and how it finds it necessary not to speak, under the solicitation of the wholly other."[5]

One wonders, in the larger scheme of things, what all this means. Are we approaching a great reversal, even a homecoming, in the philosophical world? Are we coming to the end of a centuries-long estrangement between religious traditions and their philosophical progeny? We know that at some watershed moment in the seventeenth century--perhaps with the publication of Hobbes's *Leviathan*, perhaps even earlier--visions of human society that had formerly functioned within religious frames of reference began to assert the autonomy we see so highly developed today. Like youthful offspring of not-always-wise and often quarreling parents, they decided to move out of ancestral households. If John Milbank is right, they continued to bear the marks of their origins as "theologies or anti-theologies in disguise,"[6] but they steered independent courses toward toleration, secularization, the marginalization of religious faith: all in the interest of social peace and well-being which had been gravely compromised by the seventeenth-century Wars of Religion.[7]

For obvious reasons I hesitate to call these enlightened offspring of pre-modern parents "prodigal sons." It might seem an indication of disrespect which I do not intend. Indeed, the biblical parable needs to be considerably re-written, especially at the end. Still it tells an important truth. Despite their best intentions, public reasoners seeking to re-express Christian values spent their religious patrimonies rather rapidly, discovering too late just how important specific religious doctrines, liturgies and communities had been in making former social arrangements function successfully.

Now, in the late twentieth century, there are signs that many of these offspring are disappointed by the shallowness and fragmentation of the beckoning secularities that had once seemed so attractive. Some, as we have seen, have now made clear that they would like at least to visit the homes of their parents in search of some almost forgotten wisdom. If they were to come for a visit they would also bring with them much knowledge and experience about worldly life gained during their years away: knowledge and experience which could transform and extend the older wisdom. These visitors would have much to teach those who had remained at home about how dimly remembered virtues had fared, or failed to register, in the larger world. They would also have much to teach about moral questions unimagined only a few decades ago: questions such as those generated by the rise of economic globalization and its exacerbation of environmental risks, or proposals extending the concept of human rights to future generations.

There could be no fixed formula for such encounters. They might have in common only the conviction that constructs such as "justice," "human rights," "amnesty" and the like need often unmentioned background assumptions, perhaps of a theological nature, simply to be authentically themselves. As Reinhold Niebuhr famously said in *Moral Man and Immoral Society*, "Any justice which is only justice soon degenerates into something less than justice. It must be saved by something that is more than justice."[8]

Hospitality in Social "Space"

What might churches and other religious communities do to prepare for such visits, both to impart wisdom and receive it? Is it ironic, or serendipitous, that just as the time certain public philosophers are acknowledging a need for some sort of reconnection with religious communities, many of those communities are turning inward in an effort to recover their ancient traditions of faith and practice? Are they avoiding the philosophical encounter, or preparing more adequately for it? "Post-liberal" theological positions place increasing emphasis on doctrine as regulative discourse for distinct faith communities and warn that believers may be led astray if they persist in trying only to prop up "the liberal project" in Western political discourse. Public participation by many religious groups is still limited to the defense of their institutional/political interests as they see them, rather than a desire to improve conditions of life for fellow citizens. If anything, such self-concern is exacerbated by the new particularism. Yet *without* such re-traditioning, such new attention to religious practice, religious communities have little to offer the public world even if they wish to be generous. One thinks of Jeffrey Stout's criticism of the distinguished ethicist James Gustafson.[9] To Stout, Gustafson sounds just like a good liberal, somewhere on the moderate left wing of the Democratic Party. Stout finds little of the theological "difference" he hopes for there.

I think there *is* a difference which Stout does not see, which lies in the way the underlying argument is constructed. I happen to share James Gustafson's "preference for the Reformed tradition,"[10] and intend the present argument to be a contemporary expression of it.[11] For Calvin, the same divine care attends both church and civil community. The civil magistrate pursues a distinctly Christian calling. He is a minister of God for our good. The implications of this position have been variously elaborated. A version of it worth contemporary consideration can be found in the so-called "Federal theology" (from the Latin *foedus*, or "covenant") in which the "covenant of grace" embracing the lives of believers reveals the further truth expressed in the notion of a "covenant of works" to which all human beings are responsible, whether or not they acknowledge it, in the civil realm.[12]

This conceptuality needs to be guarded against theocratic interpretations in which believers come to consider themselves a moral police force for the rest of society. Revised for a secularized, pluralistic world, it could offer a particularly fruitful way of conceiving of the relationship between the redeemed and believing community on the one hand and the civil community on the other. Believers and non-believers live together in a covenantal political order whose true nature is revealed in scripture and whose historical possibility is based on public service understood as religious vocation. The character of this order is such that it needs citizens who exhibit righteousness beyond the works of the law in order to fulfil what the law requires. Believers understand such righteousness to be the work of grace. The idea of righteous, yet theologically uncommitted, public behavior rests on the insight that the "covenant of works" notion sought to express: namely that *all* human life-together is covenantal in character, and that some persons are enabled by grace to live lives which contagiously manifest what such covenantal calling requires.

This position (or any other, whether Roman Catholic, Lutheran or "radical Reformation") of course needs profound readjustment to be of any use in a pluralistic, post-modern age. The translation to contemporary conditions I wish to make involves the idea that those finding themselves within the "covenant of grace" should seek to generate and maintain "spaces" in the midst of a predominantly secular society where members of that society can recognize their own secular virtues transfigured, reconnected to their sources as these sources themselves have been theologically reinterpreted in the light of their passage through secularity, their life beyond parental households. A public official who accepts moral hospitality in such a space--let us say a space of discourse--may therefore, without professing traditional faith, learn something important about his or her calling.

The notion of churches making "space" for things like this to happen has gained some currency without being adequately clarified.[13] The idea of social space is, of course, a metaphor, as is the notion that such space can have a distinctive "shape."[14] "Social space" of any kind becomes detectable in fact only when there is activity or discourse to "fill" it, to make it visible. One becomes aware of social space only when some tangible configuration of human interaction has flowed into it. The nature of the space determines what sorts of activity or discourse make sense within it at any given time. Michael Walzer's "spheres" of justice--the legal, the economic, the domestic, and so forth--are social spaces in the sense intended here.[15] Similarly, a social space is implied by the emplotment and characterizations of a given narrative. One is in the space of the narrative when one's actions and interactions make sense in terms of the narrative's characters and plot. One as it were continues the story. One can also discern when the social space for a given kind of activity is lacking: as, for example, the absence of cultural conditions for democratic processes in the former Soviet Union and parts of Eastern Europe. The nature, even the shape, of particular public spaces--spaces determining the possible shapes of public interaction--becomes apparent when one tries to conduct activities within them that either "fit" or do not.

Moral hospitality by religious institutions is, then, the conscious strategy of creating such spaces and using them for what William Werpehowski calls "*ad hoc* apologetics."[16] This becomes possible when religious or other distinctively traditioned communities generate and maintain spaces in the midst of society that make room for human interactions embodying emplotments or logics different from those obtaining elsewhere. Two obvious meanings of moral hospitality to such ends can be discerned at the outset. The first is literal enough: invitations for public reasoners to spend time in our ashram.[17] There is no reason why traditioned communities with sufficient "thickness" of shared practice should not offer hospitality to "nonbelievers" who feel they might gain something from the experience. Stanley Hauerwas maintains that the best kind of apologetics is this sort of "come and see." We should not present apologetic arguments, but simply ask an inquirer to kneel down with us and say the Lord's Prayer. In short, share if only temporarily, the faith-community's actual practice.

The second obvious sense of hospitable space is equally tangible: religious communities can make space for public reasoners and actors by helping create *political* conditions which give them room to act in certain ways. It is not hard to imagine courting "the Catholic vote" as soliciting a kind of moral hospitality for one's social programs. If a political will tending in a certain direction is present, if "the votes are there," it is going to be easier for public reasoners to follow along for their own reasons. But then the politicians in question should wonder how this moral space has been constituted, on what grounds and to what ends. At that point hospitality gains a deeper dimension.

Rethinking the Durkeimian Project

But I want to reach for deeper and more subtle understandings of hospitable space than these examples suggest. It is useful to begin by remembering the project proposed by Emile Durkheim well over a century ago. We must discover, the great sociologist wrote in his treatise on education,

> those moral forces that men, down to the present time, have conceived of only under the form of religious allegories. We must disengage them from their symbols, so to speak, and find a way to make the child feel their reality without recourse to any mythological intermediary.[18]

As we know, Durkheim substituted for the morally shaping force of "religion" the almost superhuman qualities he ascribed to "society," There may still be a temptation to borrow from, or refurbish, religious sources in this way, but we are much less confident that "society" as such can be the substitute agent for moral education. Secular society alone cannot generate the moral energy needed. We depart from Durkheim by insisting that the secular imprint of originally religious moral imagination can remain powerful only if bodies of believers remain in the society to renew and re-energize it. The shapes of religious imagination cannot be attached to some other power source such as the state, or popular culture, and remain the same, let alone continuingly influential. Moral hospitality of some sort is thus a continuing obligation of religious communities whose understandings have been secularized, lest they be distorted or attenuated beyond recognition.

How is such hospitality effectively extended? Not only by offering guest accommodations on one's turf, or by getting out the vote for some favored proposition. Hospitable spaces can be opened and maintained in the *midst* of a public world where much Durkheimian moral demythologizing has taken place. In such a world religiously traditioned communities can generate spaces for depth-discourse on civic issues: discourse that would not otherwise take place. This can be done in a variety of ways, depending on the circumstances. Certain reflective moves open the door. It is important not to be too schematic about these. In the "real world" they are often unspoken, intuitive, or elided. But, that said, I distinguish three such steps on the path to a notion of moral hospitality that can be offered in public space and in publicly available terms, yet simultaneously opening upon, offering a window into, the beliefs and practices of the hospitable households concerned.

First, follow the Durkheimian path back from secularity to sources. Identify those meanings, policies, possibilities, by-words in society at large, which have their origins in religious traditions. On Milbank's accounting these include practically everything about modern Western society: theological insights rearticulated in the register of a contingent construct called the secular. Be aware that, while in some cases secularization has meant a loss of focus or even evacuation of meaning, in other cases--in becoming secularized--these influences have often traveled routes which make them more sophisticated, ramified, and just plain interesting than they were before. Notions such as "justice" and "forgiveness" for example, have undergone fascinating transformations. Parents have much to learn from prodigal progeny.

Second, discern what can be learned *for* tradition from these elements that have disguised it in secular contexts. Reappropriate critically back *into* tradition certain aspects of what our traditions have become in their modern journeys. Distinguish between that we must disown and that from which we can learn. That for which churches make moral space by their actions and practices in society--even when society misunderstands--needs to be recognized as part of their own moral responsibility.[19] Religious communities need to take a special interest in understanding themselves, for better or for worse, at least partly in the light that for which they offer moral sanction by what they say and what they are. Recognize that secular forces have sometimes helped churches learn to be better churches by making out of original impulses what churches never could do on their own. Recognize that such adaptations of traditional elements into new contexts presents a creative challenge to the tradition's protectors and interpreters. Learn from Jacques Derrida, for example, the social potential of what we mean by forgiveness and where possible *connect* such new interpretations with original sources in a way that deepens the meaning of both.

Finally, act publicly in ways that generate spaces *in* society where people can encounter meanings and possibilities recognizable to them from secular learning yet transformed and deepened through carefully interpreted reconnection with scriptural and traditional sources. Such social space can at times be created by pronouncements, as for example the American Roman Catholic bishops were able to do in their pastoral letters by illumining issues of economic justice, and then of nuclear deterrence in the light of just war theory. These documents literally generated new spaces of social discourse in America: spaces in which argument could proceed in a publicly recognizable manner, yet one in which one could sense, and explore, the moral hospitality of the tradition of faith and practice lying behind them.

Once we understand how these complex interactions between original moral impulses intrinsic to traditions and their functional consequences in the public realm, it should be less difficult to think of ways to live so as to make spaces for public reasoners to rediscover such themes in religiously deepened forms. Generating and maintaining such spaces can be taken on as self-conscious strategy by religiously traditioned communities.

Are there other examples? Think of what we have seen in our own lifetimes. "Freedom riders" in the American South during the late fifties and early sixties opened moral space in the imagination for others to make analogous, if less courageous, moves. Churches in East Germany in the late eighties opened space for political boldness in leaders who knew that the communist regime could not last. Black churches in South Africa in the early nineties opened space for leaders of the ANC to imagine a peaceful outcome of their struggle rather than the widely predicted bloodbath.[20]

In the South African case, it has been emphasized by commentators that the Truth and Reconciliation Commission (one of the many varying examples, in different lands, of this mode of resolution of an atrocity-filled past) resulted from a hard fought *legal* (and (hence secular) compromise between prosecutions Nuremberg-style and a blanket legal erasure of the record of past events. But I maintain that the particular compromise reached would not have been possible unless the contestants were functioning in a religiously shaped cultural space which offered the notions of forgiveness and reconciliation as possibilities for the commitment of lives, spaces into which to move, spaces in which a secular but profound legal alternative could be constructed. A space of *forgiveness* in the Christian sense helped politicians build a space of *amnesty* in the legal sense. The fact that these are related ideas but not the same illustrates the opening to something further which amnesty-space was able to afford.[21]

Confessional Space and Public Space

In each of these examples there is an implicit conceptual transfer from confessional to public space. This needs elucidation, if only by mentioning seemingly parallel moves. David Burrell and Stanley Hauerwas have argued in an important article for the narrative basis of all moral reasoning, that is, for its being founded in specifically traditioned communities. "All our notions are narrative-dependent," they write, "including the notion of rationality" itself.[22] But by what *means* does religious narrative undergird moral reasoning carried on without reference to the religious narrative? And can the secular moral reasoning then subsist independently of the religious narrative? Burrell and Hauerwas do not answer these questions. Mark Johnson has argued to similar effect for the "moral imagination."[23]

There is something similar here to Paul Ricoeur's notion that the philosopher, without becoming a believer, can replicate in his or her own terms "the movements of the believing soul." The philosopher finds room, at least rhetorically, to move in a certain direction without adopting a new belief-system. I recognize too an affinity here with David Tracy's notion of the public power of religious narratives seen as "classics" that is, works which speak to the concerns of all human beings. I also believe Ronald Dworkin is making such a move in his book on abortion and euthanasia when he speaks of the "sanctity" of life.[24] Dworkin's point is to extract and secularize some common principle from within the very tenuous "overlap" of contending parties on these issues. The word "sanctity" is one small step away from "holiness."

A singular instance in which traditional moral content has been appropriated without commitment to "belief" is found in the most recent work of Jacques Derrida. The arch deconstructionist has been saying for some time that at least one notion is undeconstructible: that of "justice." Now Derrida is adding "forgiveness" to his list. At the recent (October, 1999) "Religion and Postmodernism" colloquy at Villanova University, Derrida dwelt for two hours and more on this theme, arguing that forgiveness reaches its true dimension only in the face of the unforgivable, e.g. the Holocaust, that only the victim can truly forgive and the victim is usually dead, that hence forgiveness is in human terms "impossible". But without forgiveness, human society cannot continue. We seem unable to forget. In the north of Ireland, in

Kosovo, in a hundred other places, politicians, in their own interests, make sure we remember over centuries. In the absence of the "singularity of the victim," God is the name of "the absolute singularity as such." "Forgiveness is the first and final use of the gift."[25]

Yet Derrida, who here so clearly "follows the movements of the believing soul" and if anything makes them more profound, remains a self-stated unbeliever. The Scriptural notion of forgiveness has here passed through an intensely secular experience, that is, an experience detached from explicit belief in God. But far from being weakened, the insight has been ramified in such a way as to place new demands on Scripture's institutional interpreters. The result, if faithfully pursued and realized, will be a permanently deepened *religious* understanding of forgiveness which Christian and Jewish communities can proceed to assimilate, and then enact in various forms of public space, thereby offering moral hospitality to non-believers for the deepening and further-ranging of an idea already at large in the secular world.

A similar transfer of "forgiveness" as a theme from religious to secular contexts has been the subject of a number of other recent writings, from which hermeneuts and theological ethicists can in turn learn.[26] The key point again is that one does not have to buy into the specific religious beliefs, e.g. atonement in the Christian sense, to be able to enter the *spaces* maintained by believing *practice* in order to replicate its content in non-believing terms. A signal example is the book *Forgiveness and Mercy* by Jeffrie G. Murphy and Jean Hampton,[27] in which these meanings are self-consciously transferred from their biblical settings into legal philosophy. Comparable arguments from a theological perspective are made in Donald Shriver's *An Ethic for Enemies* and Geiko Müller Fahrenholz's *The Art of Forgiveness*. It is clear that "belief" is not at issue in any of these cases, but a kind of creative and ramifying replication of the basic ideational content--within another set of commitments--is.[28]

By entering such spaces public reasoners do not become theologians or believers. They rather find their *own* spheres of reasoning enlarged, their *own* imaginative arenas for action extended. Derrida is far more interesting to us as a confirmed atheist than he would be as a convert! The question how "believing" practice differs from the same practice followed in the absence of "belief" is a profound one. It is not clear, indeed, that "belief" and "unbelief", as categories, furnish an adequate conceptualization of what is going on. Could the case be analogous to the relationship between "religious" and "secular" Jews? What does a claim to actual "belief," supposing we can specify what this means, *add* to a life shaped by all the accouterments of belief, a life manifesting all the consequences of belief, yet lived without subscription to the specific reality-affirmations of belief, e.g. theistic formulas? One can argue that the life described is inconceivable, or internally contradictory, and thus dissolve the question. Or, one can say with Stanley Hauerwas and others that Christian faith is *essentially* a matter of narratives and practices, to which "beliefs" have subsequently been added for regulative, polemic or defensive purposes.[29]

If one asks *how* narratives generate imaginative moral space even for those who do not regard such narratives as religiously revelatory we can only say they do so through communities of persons, either gathered or dispersed, that act out of faith in what their narratives project upon the world and thus demonstrate certain behavioral *possibilities*. In short, the answer must have an ecclesiological or communitarian dimension. The examples given suggest that religious communities can consciously strategize to help such conceptual transfers to occur. They can consciously constitute themselves as spaces of "moral hospitality."

A Coherent Conversation?

But pluralism reigns. There are countless religiously traditioned communities both abutting and living in the same public space. Are they not beckoning potential guests in a host of different directions? Can a society which opens itself to such invitations be other than incoherent?

It would at least help this situation if the major traditions would also learn to practice moral hospitality of the kind I have described toward one another. This is a suggestion which is heard today even in certain sectors of missiological discussion. It is also a suggestion offered on the final page of David Ford's collection of essays *The Modern Theologians*. Ford asks,

> ...how might Christian theologians appropriately celebrate
> the millennium? A simple yet rich answer is by being
> guests and hosts. A theology under the sign of hospitality
> is formed through its generous welcome to others--
> theologies, traditions, disciplines, and spheres of life. It has

the host's responsibility for homemaking, the hard work of preparation, and the vulnerability of courteously offering something while having little control over its reception. It also has the different responsibility of being a guest, trying to be sensitive to strange households, learning complex codes and risking new food and drink. Ideally, habitual hospitality gives rise to trust and friendship in which new exchanges can plumb the depths of similarity, difference, and suffering.[30]

I suggest that such inter-communal hospitality will best be achieved not only through direct comparisons of diverse moral traditions (i.e. "comparative ethics") but through common participation in a *public* space generated by an overlap of tradition-generated construals of the public world, as addressed to whatever particular problems may be at hand. The result, if the model offered in this paper is persuasive, would not depend on any supposed similarity of content among different traditions, or on "overlap" among certain discrete formulations, but rather a homology of lived translations of these traditions into neutral moral, i.e. "secular," form. The practice of mutual moral hospitality could keep these transformations of traditional contents in touch with the narratives standing behind them. Such mutually hospitable participation in the *ad hoc* construction of an ongoing public world could prepare the different spheres of life, religious, cultural, disciplinary and otherwise, of which Ford speaks, to respond to the willingness of today's public philosophers to ask questions about the communities of value their theories interpret into publicly accessible terms.

In such a scheme, of course, it would not be possible to determine in advance, from any given set of religious narratives or lived practices, what kind of commonly-held public philosophy, if any, would come to inform the resulting common moral space. Any proposed common philosophy would to be examined for its pragmatic implications, and then judged "fitting" or not.[31] The judgment would be whether it is fitting for "us," seeing who we are, to lend our social space to such a vision. If we hold as a religious group that our language helps decipher the way God is at work among <u>all</u> human beings, not just members of "our" group, then one of the qualifications for "fittingness" is going to be whether a given public policy also fits into the spaces provided by *other* moral imaginations and practices. In short, rather than depending on an autonomous, secular view of the human conversation, we ask whether the worldly expressions of our moral imaginations overlap with those of other groups to the extent that we can make public moral space together for what needs to be fittingly lashed together in bricolagic fashion to meet human needs.

But will this work without *any* prior common moral framework in which acts of hospitality can be offered and received? Implicit in this whole discussion has been the assumption that public reasoning processes in Western societies now exhibit little, if any, moral rationality of their own.

Alasdair MacIntyre[32] has told us, for example, that we live in many incommensurable moral worlds, while maintaining that these universes of discourse evince their own internal forms of coherence as "arguments" sustained over time. Tristram Engelhardt goes further.[33] Writing from a postmodern perspective, he sees Western society as a world of "moral strangers," individuals who find coherent moral discourse among themselves impossible. Moral communities do exist here and there, but none has the potential for integrating our fragmented public world. The modern liberal project in its various Kantian, utilitarian, or Rawlsian forms is thus itself a failure. Unlike MacIntyre, who hopes that an Aristotelian coherence may triumph over Nietzschian nihilism, Engelhardt concludes that Nietzsche accurately foresees our fate. Under such conditions, issues can only be resolved by "peaceable negotiations" of an *ad hoc* type, characterized by free and informed consent among individuals and rights of privacy in relation to the state. The result is a permissive sort of bioethics, a form of secular humanism, notably open to market mechanisms which offer a form of "pure procedural justice." Here is an utterly minimal framework for the practical cooperation of individuals whose lives are constructed around purely instrumental goals as they pursue "the goods and pleasures of this world."

Let us suppose that Engelhardt's account is at least descriptively accurate. Can morally traditioned communities, following a strategy of moral hospitality, address themselves usefully to such a world? I offer at least a hypothesis, building on the contributions of William O'Neill and William Galston. Notice in the first place that Engelhardt's vision depends on the *possibility* of "peaceable negotiation." There must exist, then, *some* tattered traditions of discourse in this fragmented, instrumentalist society which permits such peaceable negotiation to take place. It is useful to confront Engelhardt's picture with William O'Neill's reconstruction of a notion of discourse grounded in a conception of human rights embedded in community-sustaining language. In his article "Babel's Children: Reconstructing the Common Good,"[34] O'Neill works this out in somewhat Habermasian terms.[35] A common good is enacted in a discourse community in which "the practice of rational claim-making presumes the mutual respect of practically rational agents,"[36] in which human rights "derive their backing from the principle of mutual respect,"[37] and thus "serve as warrants in our 'reasoned speech',"[38] and in which there is a correlation between the "said" and the "shown" in the justification of rights.[39] O'Neill concludes, "Interpreted discursively, the common good signifies the regime of basic rights presupposed in reasoned speech within and across our narrative traditions."[40]

O'Neill's approach combines an appeal to universality with an openness to specificity that invites the participation of traditioned communities. Those who either defend or deny such practices of rational-claim making "appeal, implicitly to a universal audience for vindication."[41] But such "rights rhetoric does not so much suppress our native tongues in a grand metanarrative as ensure that all may speak.... The *universal* maxim of respect for the 'concrete other' bids us attend to its *particular* narrative embodiment."[42] Otherwise said, the traditions of particular communities are needed to clothe with specificity the abstract rhetoric of rights-language. The presence of such communities, in which practices assure some correlation between the "said" and the "shown," is therefore indispensable to the ongoing enactment of the public good as O'Neill understands it. One may *reason* about rights, but there *are* no rights historically deployed apart from communally lived narratives which embody them.

This viewpoint is at least in part compatible with William Galston's social vision. Galston wants liberals to abandon their addiction to a neutral public square open only to "peaceable negotiation" among "moral strangers." He argues that liberalism in its own right embodies specific conceptions of the good. A free society is sustained by specific virtues which, on the one hand, are inherent in the very idea of such a society, and, on the other hand, need articulation in and through particular moral traditions. While O'Neill and Galston identify the needed virtues differently, they agree on the need *both* for universalizable social maxims *and* for the specific embodiment of these maxims in particular traditions.

Galston, furthermore, offers a helpful alternative to my terminology contrasting "believing" and "unbelieving" adherence to traditionally transmitted moral virtues. He distinguishes between *intrinsic* and *functional* traditionalism. The former, I think, points to traditions lived out by their traditional adherents, i.e. "believers." The latter "rests its case on asserted links between certain moral principles and public virtues or institutions needed for the successful functioning of a liberal community."[43]

Mutually Hospitable Public Covenants?

Seen against such a conceptual background, the offering of moral hospitality would be a conscious strategy by traditioned communities to invite post-conventional moral reasoners to attend to the particular narrative and communal embodiments of virtues already recognized by them as needed for the sustenance of the liberal order. Moral hospitality in short would invite persons living overlapping *functional* versions of moral traditions to attend also to these traditions lived out in their *intrinsic* forms. Without the intrinsic, i.e. confessionally rooted, believing embodiment of moral virtues, their functional public simulacra are likely sooner or later to atrophy.

We live in a pragmatic, possibly even Rortyan, social space where many views jostle, where we lash our ruminations together by means of a sort of *bricolage*. I maintain that what makes sense in such a sociality is precisely what citizens of many persuasions in actual fact find "fitting." It is what comports with the overlapping possibilities of many forms of moral imagination or spaces of moral possibility. It is not that MacIntyre is wrong in holding that we live in many incommensurable moral worlds, and employ many different sorts of moral discourse. It is rather that out of those different moral universes we nonetheless create pragmatically overlapping spaces of moral imagination without assuming that we all reason the same way. Thus we can agree to a point what we will support in the commonly shared social world. We can agree, to some extent, to merge our public spaces of moral hospitality. So much the better if social policy does *not* claim to be based in some closed but supposedly universal system of secular reasoning which we are all asked to support.

So, why not covenants among the religious traditions to overcome today's version of the seventeenth-century conflicts that provided so much impetus for the secularization of the public world and the marginalization of faith? Why not covenants among religious and other bodies to resist the great global economic and communications systems that gobble up civil space? Why not contracts built on the principle of mutual hospitality among religious groups themselves and toward others? There needs to be something beyond simple, pragmatic, immediate-problem-centered *bricolage*. The very notion of moral hospitality implies that we understand one another up to a point. Without some basis for common understanding, the various "global morality" projects (e.g Hans Küng, Martha Nussbaum, Outka and Reeder) make no sense.

We need to generate a common space of human moral imagination beyond our particular symbol systems where there can be a content-rich, homologous synergism of our moral imprints. This synergism of hospitable spaces could offer scope for pragmatic efforts to ameliorate the condition of the human race. If these are the sorts of projects which take refuge and find support in the combined spaces of possibility generated by the narratives of the great world religions, then these religions will begin to be reinterpreted *through* the public movements for which they provide moral shelter. Religious communities, without compromise of their internally held theological and liturgical convictions, could in this way become focused on the practical issues with which human beings across the globe need to deal if they are to have a future.

Notes

1. Pursuit of the "politics of difference" is probably less shrill today than it was a few years back, but all the attendant concerns are still alive. If less immediately pressing within North America, such issues are, if anything, becoming more salient internationally. Samuel Huntington has recently argued that the present Russian attempt to subdue Chechnya is evidence for his "conflict of civilizations" thesis. Giant ethno-religious blocs are already struggling with one another along a number of obvious fault lines, with worse to come. The age of multicivilizational empires is therefore over. Obviously this is true for the former Soviet Union. Might it also become true for Europe and the United States? Are we all doomed eventually to disintegrate along religious and cultural lines?

2. I am of course thinking of John Rawls's idea of an "overlapping consensus" of "reasonable comprehensive doctrines" in support of a public

order based upon the principle of "justice as fairness," set forth in *A Theory of Justice* (Cambridge, MA: Harvard University Press, 1971).

3. See Georgia Warnke, *Justice and Interpretation* (Cambridge, MA.: MIT Press, 1993). Warnke observes that "many important political theorists no longer try to justify principles of justice or norms of action...by appealing to formal reason, to the character of human action, or to neutral procedures of rational choice.... Rather, these philosophers suggest that if a society wants to justify its social and political principles it can do so simply by showing their suitability for it, that is, by showing that these principles express the meaning of the society's goods and practices, history and traditions" (vii).

4. The six were Ronald Dworkin, Bernard Williams, Thomas Nagel, Michael Sandel, Amy Gutmann, and Rawls himself. The speaker who did not was, ironically, the one in whom theologians have shown the most interest: Jürgen Habermas.

5. John D. Caputo, *The Prayers and Tears of Jacques Derrida: Religion Without Religion* (Bloomington and Indianapolis, IN: Indiana University Press, 1997), 4.

6. John Milbank, *Theology and Social Theory* (Oxford: Blackwell Publishers, 1988), 3.

7. One must not forget how continuingly "religious" were the motives of many of these seeming secularizers, at least in England and America. Many sought to replicate a range of Christian values in the new vocabulary of independent, universal, reason. Carl Becker's famed book *The Heavenly City of the Eighteenth Century Philosophers* (New Haven: Yale University Press, 1921), 28-31, argues that such thinkers had far more in common with those of preceding Christian centuries than they did with the materialists and positivists who followed them. In fact they sought to continue the work of Christian civilization by other means. Reason was to replace revelation, but it was to perform the same function: inculcating moral behavior in a universe ruled by God. Becker's opinion is the more striking when it is remembered that he himself vehemently rejected all theological claims as useless and unintelligible.

8. Reinhold Niebuhr, *Moral Man and Immoral Society* (New York: Scribner's, 1932), 258.

9. Jeffrey Stout, *Ethics After Babel: The Languages of Morals and their Discontents* (Boston: Beacon Press, 1988), 163ff.

10. A chapter title in Gustafson's *Ethics in a Christian Context*.

11 What I offer here parallels, methodologically speaking, John Howard Yoder's apologia for the Mennonite, or "radical Reformation" vision of the church in his books *The Politics of Jesus* and *The Priestly Kingdom*.

12. One widely-held variant held that a "covenant of works" was posited separately from and antecedently to the "covenant of grace." According to this view, God made a covenant of works with Adam, the "federal head" of all humanity, enjoining obedience to a perpetually binding moral law identified

variously with the Ten Commandments or some version of the law of nature. After Adam fell from innocence in the Garden, salvation was no longer available through the first covenant, so God established the covenant of grace, in which Christ fulfills the law and atones for its breach, becoming the "Federal head" of believers. Thinkers in this vein taught nevertheless that all human beings remain under the original "covenant of works" as a matter of obligation. The original covenant, that is, continues to be the basis of the human community as such. Elect believers living within the "covenant of grace" likewise continue to confront the obligations of the "covenant of works." But they are now enabled to see it as a pattern for a devout life possible for them by their redeemed state. Believers are subject, as Calvin said, to a "third use of the law," whereby Torah not only restrains sin in the civic world, and not only convicts human beings of their inability to follow it perfectly, but also sets out the conduct expected of believers. Thus the "covenant of works" *continues* in the time of forgiveness and grace, and grace renders good citizenship a special obligation of redeemed sinners. The disciplined society that the Reformers, and later the Puritans, envisaged was rooted in obligations laid upon humankind, for which believers had special responsibility. Covenanting, in both in a special and in a general sense, became applicable *both* to congregational and to political life. Theological insight into the meanings of sin and grace thus added depth to the understanding of what upholding the law truly required: both outrage at what contravened it and mercy toward the sinner, both determination to root out evil and forgiveness to heal the wounds. The model it entailed deeply influenced political philosophy, notably that of John Locke, and led to the conviction that Christians should as a matter of faith work for responsible democratic government. The seventeenth-century European idea of social contract was a rationalization and secularization of this originally religious formulation. Its biblical origin and intention were still clearly visible, but the idea thereby became available to those for whom the notion of making a covenant with God was not easily accepted or understood. [My account follows, with significant departures and glosses, the article on this subject by Dewey D. Wallace, Jr. in the *Encyclopedia of the Reformed Faith*, ed. Donald K. McKim (Louisville, KY: Westminster/John Knox Press, 1992), 136f.]

13. In his Report to the Eighth Assembly of the World Council of Churches at Harare, Zimbabwe, in December, 1998, General Secretary Konrad Raiser made much of this notion of "moral hospitality" and of the sorts of social "space" required to provide it (quoting my own recent book, *The Church as Moral Community,* on this subject: see "Report of the General Secretary," Assembly Document PL 4-1).

14. See Peter Hodgson's development of the spacial metaphors of "figure" and "shape" in *God in History: Shapes of Freedom* (Nashville: Abingdon Press, 1989), 83ff.

15. Walzer, *Spheres of Justice* (New York: Basic Books, 1983).

16. William Werpehowski, "*Ad Hoc* Apologetics," *The Journal of Religion* 66 (July 1986): 282ff.

17. In a certain thin sense it is perhaps no accident that the gatherings of philosophers celebrating Rawls's *Theory of Justice* and wrestling with "religion and postmodernism" with Jacques Derrida occurred at the invitations and on the campuses of two Catholic universities: Santa Clara (a Jesuit institution) and Villanova (a community of the Augustinian Order) respectively.

18. Quoted in Alan Wolfe, *Whose Keeper? Social Science and Moral Obligation* (Berkeley: University of California Press, 1989), 221.

19. Not unexpectedly, perhaps, the most obvious current example is negative. John Fife (a former Moderator of the General Assembly of the Presbyterian Church, USA, and leader in the sanctuary movement) is reported to have said that "every time a gay teen-ager commits suicide that death is marked down against the Presbyterian Church, USA." Clearly the point is that religious bodies which call homosexual behavior "sin" and refuse ordination to sexually active gay and lesbian persons provide a kind of moral "cover" for anti-gay violence and personal despair, both of which easily become lethal. It is not that these bodies consciously seek such consequences. On the contrary. But, seeking internal moral purity, they unthinkingly generate cultural space for such things to happen.

20. See, on both East Germany and South Africa, John de Gruchy's *Christianity and Democracy* (Cambridge, UK: Cambridge University Press, 1991).

21. The difficulties and recriminations accompanying the recent release of the Commission's Report do nothing to diminish the power of this idea as a social possibility for South Africa and elsewhere.

22. Stanley Hauerwas with David B. Burrell, "From System to Story: An Alternative Pattern for Rationality in Ethics," in *Truthfulness and Tragedy: Further Investigations in Christian Ethics* (Notre Dame: University of Notre Dame Press, 1988) 21.

23. Mark Johnson, *Moral Imagination* (Chicago: University of Chicago Press, 1993).

24. Ronald Dworkin, *Life's Dominion: An Argument About Abortion, Euthanasia, and Individual Freedom* (New York: Alfred A, Knopf, 1993), 68ff.

25. Derrida's words are as transcribed in my notes on the occasion of his lecture at Villanova University, October 14, 1999.

26. See Geiko Müller-Fahrenholz, *The Art of Forgiveness* (Geneva, WCC Publications, 1997), and Donald W. Shriver, Jr., *An Ethic for Enemies* (New York: Oxford University Press, 1995).

27. Cambridge, UK: Cambridge University Press, 1988.

28. One can also recognize in such transactions something of an older

problematic: the entry of Marxism (a prodigal religious eschatology if there ever was one) into the moral space, the space of moral awareness created by the Christian "base communities" in Latin America. One can also see that the reverse happened too: religious sensibility moved into the secular moral space created by Marxism, finding there new opportunities for theological self-understanding. In either case theology learned something from the discoveries of its secular offspring. This is still not to say that there was a direct connection between traditional theological concepts and Marxist concepts. The neurological and circulatory systems remained separate, but a certain osmosis occurred through the membranes between the two.

29. Is it possible that in availing themselves of religious spaces of moral imagination in which they find practical support, secular political theorists and actors could find ways of their own to rearticulate their transcendental origins? I am not so sure. In fact I am not sure that it is either necessary or desirable. One can conceive how this might happen, perhaps with the aid of some contemporary form of Maurice Blondel's theory of the completion of the meaning of action. Blondel's idea was that the meaning of things we do is incomplete until we grasp all their antecedents, all their consequences, and all their conditions of possibility. Fitting public reasoning into spaces created by practiced faith-convictions could suggest that secular accounts of such actions are in principle incomplete: that the actions in question really imply religious convictions which the actors themselves are unable, for many plausible reasons, to put into words.

30. David F. Ford, ed., *The Modern Theologians* (Oxford, UK: Blackwell Publishers, 1997), 727.

31. I am thinking here, of course, of H. Richard Niebuhr's discussion in *The Responsible Self* of what seems "fitting" in the light of interpretations of both sources and situation. The notion of what "fits" into the possibilities of a given moral formation in a given social space seems close to what I have argued for in this paper.

32. See *After Virtue* (Notre Dame, IN: Notre Dame University Press, 1981).

33. Tristram Engelhardt, *Bioethics and Secular Humanism: The Search for a Common Morality*, as described by Arne Rasmusson, *The Church as Polis* (Notre Dame, IN: University of Notre Dame Press, 1995), 273ff.

34. *The Annual of the Society of Christian Ethics*, 1998, 161ff.

35. One may add that such enacting and protecting of human rights as they pertain to a discourse community will always require some sort of legal system. Indeed it has been said that in contemporary America the language of law is familiar in some degree to everyone. It is the great exception to the general fragmentation of our discourse. Most of us know the rules for suing one another! Not without reason has Ronald Dworkin been called America's most important *social* philosopher.

36. Ibid., 164.

37. Ibid., 166.
38. Ibid., 166.
39. Ibid., 167.
40. Ibid., 169.
41. Ibid., 169.
42. Ibid., 170.
43. Galston, *Liberal Purposes*, 280, as quoted in Rasmusson, *Church as Polis*, 279.

Index

Note: Terms that occur frequently throughout the book--such as God, Christ, Jesus, Jesus Christ, world and church--are not listed in the index.